"This is a supremely helpful analysis of Messianic Judaism and a host of biblical questions raised by that controversial movement. To what degree is it appropriate for Jewish believers in Jesus to preserve Jewish ceremonies and rabbinical traditions in their worship? Baruch Maoz is uniquely qualified to write on the subject, and he has done so with a charitable tone and point-by-point thoroughness that will benefit people on all sides of the controversy. I greatly appreciate his relentlessly biblical approach."

—**John MacArthur,** Pastor and Teacher, Grace Community Church, Sun Valley, California

"Jewish believers in Jesus have long been plagued with critical questions: How are we to live our lives? Are we to worship in churches with our Gentile brothers and sisters or are we to commit ourselves to Messianic Judaism? This book is must reading for anyone who cares about the Jewish people."

—**Stan Telchin,** Jewish Christian and Author of *Betrayed!*

"Finally, a clear, contemporary exposition on evangelizing the Jews. This long-needed book, written with mind and soul by one intimately acquainted with the subject, is packed with spiritual and practical instruction. It is a must read for all Christians and denominations involved in, or contemplating, Jewish evangelism."

—**Joel Beeke,** President, Puritan Reformed Theological Seminary, Grand Rapids

"This book is written with a passion. The author is convinced that a visible unity of Jews and Gentiles in Christ is a demonstration of the gospel's transforming power. He longs for the day when God will sum up everything in Christ—everything in heaven and earth (Eph. 1:10)—and calls upon his readers to live for that day."

—**Richard Gaffin,** Professor of Biblical and Systematic Theology, Emeritus, Westminster Seminary, Philadelphia

"An excellent treatise on Jewish evangelism from a reformed perspective as well as an effective and appropriate messianic movement."

—**Harry L. Reeder III,** Senior Pastor

COME,
LET US
RE✡SON
TOGETHER

THE UNITY OF JEWS
AND GENTILES IN THE CHURCH

THIRD EDITION

BARUCH MAOZ

P&R
PUBLISHING
P.O. BOX 817 • PHILLIPSBURG • NEW JERSEY 08865-0817

Third edition 2012 P&R Publishing
© 2003, 2008, 2012 by Baruch Maoz

First edition published in 2003 by Christian Focus Publications, Ltd., under the title
Judaism Is Not Jewish: A Friendly Critique of the Messianic Movement
Second edition published in 2009 by Audubon Press under the title *Come, Let Us Reason Together: The Unity of Jews and Gentiles in the Church*

Unless otherwise indicated, Scripture quotations are from the NEW AMERICAN STANDARD BIBLE®. Copyright © 1960, 1962, 1963, 1968, 1971, 1972, 1973, 1975, 1977, 1995 by The Lockman Foundation. Used by permission. Italics within Scripture quotations indicate emphasis added.

Scripture quotations marked (NIV) are from the HOLY BIBLE, NEW INTERNATIONAL VERSION®. NIV®. Copyright © 1973, 1978, 1984 by International Bible Society. Used by permission of Zondervan Publishing House. All rights reserved.

Scripture quotations marked (NKJV) are from The Holy Bible, New King James Version. Copyright © 1979, 1980, 1982, Thomas Nelson, Inc.

Scripture quotations marked (KJV) are from the King James Bible, Pure Cambridge Edition.

Italics within Scripture quotations indicate emphasis added.

ISBN: 978-1-59638-406-4 (pbk)
ISBN: 978-1-59638-558-0 (ePub)
ISBN: 978-1-59638-557-3 (Mobi)

Printed in the United States of America

Library of Congress Cataloging-in-Publication Data

Ma'oz, Barukh.
  Come, let us reason together : the unity of Jews and Gentiles in the church / Baruch Maoz. -- 3rd ed.
      p. cm.
  Includes bibliographical references (p.   ) and indexes.
  ISBN 978-1-59638-406-4 (pbk.)
  1. Jewish Christians. 2. Messianic Judaism. I. Title.
  BR158.M37 2012
  266.0088'296--dc23

                        2012024732

To the glory of God,

to the beloved members of Grace and Truth Christian Congregation,
whom I was privileged to serve for almost 34 years,

and to Paul Liberman,
a Messianic leader who disagrees with most of what I have said in
this book
and from whom I have learned a great deal

Contents

CONTENTS

Foreword

Trusting My Jewish Savior

Stan Telchin

SOME MONTHS AGO, I was asked to be a principal speaker at an International Conference on Jewish evangelism. It was only after I had agreed to do so that I was assigned my very challenging topic: "Trusting My Jewish Savior."

"Trusting my Jewish Savior"? That was a subject I'd never really thought about. Certainly, it was one I had never spoken about. But that was the assignment given and that was the assignment accepted.

I want to share with you some of the things I learned as I prepared that message. My purpose in doing so is threefold: First: I want you to learn some important truths about me. Second: I want to encourage you to consider these truths because they may apply to your life. Third, my overwhelming objective is to help you become even more effective in your outreach to Jewish people.

As I first thought about the subject "Trusting my Jewish Savior" I realized that, like you, I have a whole list of things to trust him for: my salvation, my life, my family, my work, my health, my relationships, my ministry, my finances. Later, as I continued to think about this assignment, I realized that there is yet another fundamental and extremely important matter for which I am trusting him. I am trusting him for my identity.

Think about that word "identity" for just a moment. If you had to define it, what would you say? Do this: take a pen or pencil and write down how you would define your identity. Here's how I used to define it: I am a first generation Jewish American. Please note the order of what I have just said. I am not an American Jew. I am a Jewish American.

Why the emphasis? Because as soon as I was able to understand, I was taught that I am a Jew before I am anything else. Continually in the late '20s and early '30s, as I grew up in a ghetto on the East Side of New York, I was reminded that I was a Jew! Anti-Semitism was a very real part of American life in those years. Indeed, if anyone asked me my nationality, I knew they weren't asking if I was an American; they wanted to find out if I was Jewish. I would boldly say, "I am a Jew!"

As I grew up, I did the things that most good Jewish boys did. I went to Talmud Torah; I became Bar Mitzvah at age 13. That's also the age I joined and became active in a Zionist youth group. I celebrated all of the Jewish holidays with my family. Later, after serving for three years during World War II, I attended George Washington University in Washington, DC, and was very involved with Hillel, the Jewish centre on campus. During my last two years in college, I was on the air with a weekly radio program called "The Jewish Life Hour."

Years later I took a job on the staff of the United Jewish Appeal, which led to a job with the State of Israel Bond Office. That, in turn, led to a job with a public relations firm that handled Jewish organizations—among whom were Brandeis University and Bnei Brit. In 1955 I went into business for myself, and about eighty-five percent of my clients were Jewish.

In time, we moved into a Golden Ghetto, joined the best synagogue in town, contributed generously to the United Jewish Appeal, belonged to a Jewish country club, gave money to Jewish causes, supported the Hebrew Home for the Aged, and so on. With all that service and giving, came honors. I was a trustee of this Jewish organization, a board member of several others, Man of the Year for still another. It seemed as if the more money I gave, the more honors I received. I understood all of that. But I also understood that I *am* a Jew, and "we Jews have to take care of our own."

What I want you to see is that I was totally immersed in the Jewish community and in Jewish life. No matter what else I was, my identity was being Jewish.

Those of you who have read my books *Betrayed* and *Abandoned* know of the crisis that came into our home early in 1975, when my daughter called from college to tell me that she believed that Jesus is our Messiah. You may remember my reaction. I felt betrayed. I felt that my daughter had just left "us," the Jewish people, and had joined "them," the Christians. The very last thing in the world that I wanted her to believe was that Jesus is the Jewish Messiah. "If a Jew believes in Jesus," I thought, "he loses his identity. He ceases to be a Jew and becomes a 'Christian.' Who would ever want to do that? Who would ever want to give up his identity as a Jew?" In order to win my daughter back, I set out to disprove the Messiahship of Jesus.

As I searched the Scriptures to prove who he was not, I discovered who he is! In spite of myself, I soon began to believe! No matter how hard I tried to tell myself that believing in Jesus was absolutely impossible for me, no matter how often I reminded myself about the Crusades, the Inquisition, the pogroms and the Holocaust, as well as of the hatred I had experienced as a child, still, I kept hearing inside of me, "Yes, but it's true! Jesus *is* the Messiah!" I would argue with myself, proclaiming, "My identity is at stake in this decision! In view of all that I have experienced during my lifetime—in view of all the things I know about how we Jews have suffered at the hands of Christians over the centuries—how can I possibly consider leaving *us* and becoming part of *them*?" The struggle went on for months.

During these months, I continued to search the Scriptures. The time came when I could no longer deny Jesus' identity. Then new concerns arose. How will my wife Ethel and my children react if I accept Jesus as Lord? How will the rest of my family react? How will my neighbors react? How will my clients react? How will the United Jewish Appeal react? How will the rabbis and members of my synagogue react? The overwhelming question I struggled with was this: if I accept Jesus as my Messiah and Lord, what will happen to my identity as a Jew?

Despite these unanswered questions, my study of Scripture produced in me an overwhelming conviction that Jesus is indeed our Messiah, and on July 3, 1975, I confessed him as Lord of my life. I did so while recognizing that the Jewish community would consider me a traitor. I did so while recognizing that many of my neighbors, clients, and friends would turn their backs on me. I did so while recognizing that the Jewish organizations for which I had worked would no longer welcome me.

For the first two years after my wife and I received Jesus as Lord of our lives, we attended a messianic congregation every Friday night. I worked hard to help that congregation. I thought it was a way for me to retain my identity as a Jew and be a believer at the same time.

I remember in those early years the serious conversations held with countless Jewish believers from all over the country about how we are to live our lives. We were asked some of the following questions: "How are we Jews to function in what is primarily a Gentile world?" "Do we remain separate from Gentile believers, or do we worship with them?" "If we are to worship with them, will we have to join churches?" "Won't this lead to assimilation?" "Mustn't assimilation be avoided at all costs?" "As an alternative, should we strive to create a synagogue for our worship?" "If so, which kind: Orthodox, Conservative, or Reformed?" "If we establish synagogues, what will happen to our Gentile brothers and sisters who want to worship with us? Won't this make them feel like second-class citizens?" "If that happens, won't we be violating Jesus' prayer that we be one?" "How will the non-believing Jewish community react to messianic synagogues?" "Will such synagogues attract other Jews or repel them?" Most importantly, "how are we to reconcile messianic synagogues with the Word of God?"

As we talked about these things, dire predictions were made. Again and again I heard people threaten, "If we don't keep our families in a messianic congregation, our grandchildren will not be Jewish." One extreme statement was, "If we don't keep the law, we could wind up least in the family of God." Round and round the discussions went for more than two years. Then came the pronouncements: We will identify ourselves as the Fourth Branch of Judaism: Messianic Judaism. We will establish messianic synagogues. We will speak of our leaders as rabbis. We will insist that we are not Christians, rather we are Messianic Jews!

Though I met wonderful people in the movement, who seemed fulfilled by its distinctives, I soon realized that most of them had not been raised as Jews or, indeed, were not Jewish at all. They were making a very serious mistake by equating the totality of Jewish life with synagogue life. As I realized these things, I also realized that I was losing my joy.

Why? There were many reasons that we need not discuss here. Suffice it to say that I was being encouraged to focus more on my "Jewishness" than on my new life as a follower of Messiah Jesus. That is when I felt the Lord guiding me to leave the movement. Afterward I thought, "Well, Telchin, now you have really done it. You took your feet out of the traditional Jewish community and put them into the Messianic Congregation. Now you have taken your feet out of the Messianic Congregation, so where will you put your feet now? How will you retain your identity as a Jew and as a believer?"

Sobering questions! The only answer I could come up with was that I had to set my feet on the Rock. I had to put my trust in the Word of God and in Jesus, my Messiah, Savior, and Lord. As I continued to study the Scriptures, weeks stretched into months and months into years. I came to understand a number of things that have brought me much peace. Let me share some of these with you.

I am a Jew. I was born a Jew. I have led a Jewish life, and I will die a Jew. No one made me a Jew—no rabbi, no teacher, no organization. My Jewishness was not conferred upon me by public opinion or by government edict. No one has the right or the power to take my Jewish identity from me, no matter how much they would like to do so. Even if it were possible for me to reject my Jewish identity and heritage, I would never do so. As a matter of fact, I am so comfortable and so secure in my Jewish identity that I am not threatened by the fears and anxieties of some who would question it.

Hear me: My Jewish identity is not based upon external forms or actions. My Jewish identity is not based upon whether or not I attend a synagogue. My Jewish identity is an inner reality. It is a God-given reality. Accordingly, I am not to become embroiled in the futile tasks of trying to verify or justify my Jewish identity to anyone. I don't have to prove my Jewishness—not to other Jewish believers, not to the Jewish community, not to the United Jewish Appeal, not to the State of Israel, and not to the Church.

Still more important, I learned that my Jewishness is not the real issue. I can't imagine anyone rushing into the arms of the Lord because of my Jewishness! It is my relationship with God that will provoke them to jealousy. If Jesus truly is my Savior and the Lord of my life, my identity needs to be in him.

As I continued to study the Scriptures, I found more and more confirmation of this truth. My study of the epistles brought me great peace. They focused my attention upon the Word's promises of God. They taught me to feast on the Word of God. They also told me to meditate on his Word. One portion of Scripture on which I meditated was the apostle Paul's statement in Romans 2:25. He wrote, "Circumcision has value if you observe the law, but if you break the law, you have become as though you had not been circumcised" (NIV). As I thought about that truth, I substituted the word "Jewish" for the word "circumcision" and applied it to myself. Being Jewish has value if I observe the law, but if I break the law, I have become as though I was not Jewish. I was truly stunned as I struggled with that truth.

As I read Galatians 1:10, I was challenged in another way. Paul wrote, "Am I now trying to win the approval of men, or of God?" (NIV). As I meditated on this verse, I realized with the apostle that if I am trying to please men, I will not be a faithful servant of the Messiah.

In his letter to the Ephesians, Paul said something else that was critically important to me: In 2:14–16, writing of the fears and concerns which existed among Jewish and Gentile believers of that time, Paul wrote:

> For he himself is our peace, who has made the two one and has destroyed the barrier, the dividing wall of hostility, by abolishing in his flesh the law with its commandments and regulations. His purpose was to create in himself one new man out of the two, thus making peace, and in this one body to reconcile both of them to God through the cross, by which he put to death their hostility. (NIV)

When Paul wrote these words, he was addressing a misunderstanding of the law. Today, for many Jewish believers, the issue is not the law at all. It is our flesh. Our concern is more about ourselves and the Jewish community than about God.

Paul stressed,

> There is one body and one Spirit . . . one Lord, one faith, one baptism; one God and Father of all, who is over all and through all and in all. (Eph. 4:4–6 NIV)

He challenged us not to be infants, tossed back and forth by waves and blown here and there by the teachings and concerns of men. Instead, he urged us to speak the truth in love and to grow up into him who is our head. In 2 Corinthians 5:16 Paul declared: "So from now on we regard no one from a worldly point of view" (NIV). Oh, how that verse impacted me. I was guilty of regarding almost all men from a worldly point of view. Then Paul explained that if anyone is in the Messiah he is a new creation; the old has gone—the new has come! "Old things have passed away; behold, all things have become new" (2 Cor. 5:17 NKJV).

We Jews and Gentiles who are in the Messiah are all new creations. We Jews and Gentiles who believe are equally new creations! In God's sight there is no difference between us. There is to be no difference in our sight. We were saved in the same way, we have the same mission to accomplish, we have the same responsibility while we are on earth, and we will all receive the same reward.

As a result of study and prayer, I came to understand that celebrating my Jewishness is not what God wants of me. Nowhere in his Word does he tell me to do this. But he does want me to be transformed into the image of his Son, who always did what his Father told him to do. I am to put off my old earthly concern for the approval of men as I rejoice in the approval of God. I am to put on the grace and peace that God himself has provided. Every day of my life, I am to follow after that peace which passes understanding. I am to continually seek the wisdom that comes from above. I am to avoid wrath and anger and striving as God's love nature becomes manifest in me. I don't have to dance to the drumbeats of custom or of tradition, of old hatreds or of fear.

My God reigns! In him I live and move and have my being. I am complete in him. There is nothing more to add, no -ic and no -ism! Nothing can be taken from me either. I am a child of the King. I am sealed in his love. He knows every hair on my head and every thought in my heart. He has forgiven me of all my hard-heartedness and sin. He has called me to be his ambassador. He has called me to proclaim his nature and his love. He wants me to walk in love and in unity. He wants me to live a life of integrity. He wants me to speak the truth in love. He wants me to walk in agreement with him and with others who are in agreement with him. He has shown me that I am not accountable or responsible for what other people think or do. I am only accountable for all that I think and do.

For fourteen years, he called me to be a pastor. For the past six years, I have served as an evangelist to the Jew first, but also to the Gentile.

He has equipped me to share the miracle of his love with all who have ears to hear. I rejoice over all of these things. I rejoice too, that when my earthly days are done, I will spend eternity with him and with all my brothers and sisters—Jews and Gentiles alike.

In view of these scriptural truths, in view of all that God has done in my life, how could I not let go of my fleshly cares, fears, and concerns about my identity as a Jew? How could my spirit not soar in appreciation of his grace? How could I not trust my Jewish Savior totally?

Now we come to the application of this message to your life. In all that I have said about myself, I have had you in mind. If you are a Jewish believer I'm sure that, at one time or another, you have wrestled with Jewish identity issues as I did. It may be that you still struggle with them. If that is where you are today, then God has guided me to prepare this message specifically for you.

My message also has value for you if you are not Jewish. You may be struggling with different kinds of identity issues or you may know people who are. Be encouraged: just as God waited years for me to apply the scriptural truths I have shared, so too he is waiting for each believer to apply the same truths to his or her life. Each of us must come to realize that we can trust our Jewish Savior totally in matters of our identity.

Preface

SAYING "THANK YOU" is a moral privilege. I owe thanks to many for helping me with this book. My first thanks go to the countless messianic Jews from whose views, challenges, and practices I have learned. Special thanks are due to those whose views I controvert and who, by their sincere enthusiasm, reminded me that God is to be served wholeheartedly. Some are mentioned in this book, but I would especially like to thank Paul Liberman, an ideological foe and a personal friend. It was a joy to work alongside him for the cause we both cherish. His warmth of personality, generous spirit, practical wisdom, and high standards of morality will always be with me. Thank you for allowing me to dedicate this book to you.

Thanks are more than due to my loving and patient family and to the congregation of Grace and Truth Christian Congregation in Rishon LeTsion, who have borne with me so graciously.

My prayer is that this book will contribute in some small way to the glory of God and to the salvation of my beloved people.

Introduction

Behold Your God

Israel in the Light of Biblical Prophecy

"Comfort, O comfort My people," says your God.
"Speak kindly to Jerusalem;
And call out to her, that her warfare has ended,
That her iniquity has been removed,
That she has received of the Lord's hand
Double for all her sins."

A voice is calling,
"Clear the way for the Lord in the wilderness;
Make smooth in the desert a highway for our God.
"Let every valley be lifted up,
And every mountain and hill be made low;
And let the rough ground become a plain,
And the rugged terrain a broad valley;
Then the glory of the Lord will be revealed,
And all flesh will see it together;
For the mouth of the Lord has spoken."
A voice says, "Call out."

Then he answered, "What shall I call out?"
All flesh is grass, and all its loveliness is like the flower of the field.
The grass withers, the flower fades,
When the breath of the LORD blows upon it;
Surely the people are grass.
The grass withers, the flower fades,
But the word of our God stands forever.

Get yourself up on a high mountain,
O Zion, bearer of good news,
Lift up your voice mightily,
O Jerusalem, bearer of good news;
Lift it up, Do not fear.
Say to the cities of Judah,
"Here is your God!"
Behold, the Lord GOD will come with might,
With His arm ruling for Him.
Behold, His reward is with Him
And His recompense before Him.
Like a shepherd He will tend His flock,
In His arm He will gather the lambs
And carry them in His bosom;
He will gently lead the nursing ewes. (Isa. 40: 1–11)

Isaiah devoted the greater part of the 39 preceding chapters to warning the people of impending doom because of their sin. From time to time, a shaft of promised blessing lightened the burden of his message, but, on the whole, it had been one of divine anger and of its awful consequences. In spite of God's kindness, Israel sinned consistently. Isaiah tells us that God is offended. Judgment has been decreed and, unless the people repent, nothing can avert it. Only a remnant will remain. The country will be destroyed, the people exiled, and the nations will witness the punishment of God's elect nation. God is a holy God who should never be taken lightly.

Then, transported by the Spirit of God to a later date, after judgment was consummated, Isaiah devotes the remainder of his message to comfort. It is our happy lot to study the opening statements of this Book of Consolations. As should always be the case, we will first explore its content and then apply that content to ourselves.

THE GRACE OF GOD

"Comfort, O Comfort My people," says your God. (v. 1)

Whom is the prophet addressing? No one in particular. Everyone in general. "Whoever catches the message that God would have his people comforted should spread the good news."[1]

"Speak kindly to Jerusalem; and call out to her that her warfare has ended, that her iniquity has been removed, that she has received of the LORD's hand double for all her sins" (v. 2). Addressing the people as if judgment had been accomplished and after they experienced the brunt of God's wrath, Isaiah is instructed to assure the people that their unfaithfulness cannot annul the faithfulness of God. In spite of their sin, they are still his people and he their God. He has not forsaken them nor become indifferent to their fate.

Israel, called to a life of obedience, was the object of grace. By grace God called them into existence. By grace he formed Moses, led the people out of Egypt, and gave them his law. The same grace continued when they rebelled against him in the wilderness. In the land, they sinned against him time and again, yet God sent prophets to warn them. Some of the prophets they stoned, others they ignored. None were heeded. The people had incurred God's righteous anger, but, by grace, he had not forsaken them. God is faithful though every man a liar. "'Comfort, O comfort My people,' says your God."

How is Israel to be comforted? The prophet is told: "Speak to her." Later on we read, "Call out!" The primary means the prophet was instructed to employ was speech. God's word brings life and hope. "Get yourself up on a high mountain, O Zion, bearer of good news, lift up your voice mightily, O Jerusalem, bearer of good news; lift it up, do not fear" (v. 9). The message of good news is to be declared to the people. The remainder of this passage deals with the content of the message.

What is the prophet to say? What could possibly comfort Israel in exile, when their land had been destroyed, their cities demolished, and

1. Herbert C. Leupold, *Exposition of Isaiah* (Grand Rapids, MI: Baker Books, 1978).

they exiled from their homes? "Speak kindly to Jerusalem; and call out to her, that her warfare has ended, that her iniquity has been removed, that she has received of the LORD's hand double for all her sins." The good news is this: the state of the people was the just reward of their sin, but sin is not allowed to determine the course of history. God rules, and he will save Israel.

The people rebelled against God. They transformed their society into a money-grabbing, heartless society in which the strong devoured the weak. They worshiped God as if all he had the right to expect was the blood of bulls and goats, religious rituals, and a habitual presence in his temple; so long as they maintained outward religiosity he should be satisfied.

God is not to be tampered with. The people's punishment would come. He would not rest until they bore the full weight of that punishment. Once their *warfare* (a term which indicates a predetermined measure of hardship) was ended, the God who punished them would also terminate their punishment. He will not be angry forever.

Suffering at the hand of God, Jerusalem will have had her sins removed. She will have "received of the LORD's hand double for all her sins." This is not the voice of legal justice, a formula for mathematical morality. No one in his right mind imagines that God would impose a punishment greater than Israel deserves. This is the voice of merciful love, now declaring, "I am more than satisfied. I require nothing more of you with regard to your sin." The term "remove" in the original indicates full payment of all that is due (Lev. 26:43). God's justice is real and exacting. None should think otherwise. His grace is no less real.

THE GLORY OF GOD

"A voice is calling, 'Clear the way for the LORD in the wilderness; make smooth in the desert a highway for our God'" (Isa. 40:3). God will return to his people. There is no indication of repentance or of worthiness on the part of the nation; Israel is passive. God alone is active here. His grace is sovereign, unilateral, unconditional. It is divine grace and therefore reflects all the attributes of his godhood.

God will return to his people. Nothing can stand in his way. Mountains will be brought low, valleys filled. Nothing can separate God's chosen people from his love. He will come in the power of his majestic grace. He will return to the people with the fullness of his love. "Clear the way for the LORD in the wilderness; make smooth in the desert a highway for our God." Every obstacle will be swept away. "Then the glory of the LORD will be revealed, and all flesh will see it together" (v. 5).

There are many ways God could choose to be glorified. He has chosen one—he will be glorified by the mercy he extends to sinful Israel. Having laid upon them the full burden of their punishment, he will love them freely. The gifts and the calling of God are irrevocable.

To what end has God determined to work this way in the history of Israel? Isaiah replies, "Then the glory of the LORD will be revealed, and all flesh will see it together." All God does is for his glory. Mankind will come to know him as a God whose holiness is not to be compromised or ignored. Sin will be punished. But God's grace is not to be forgotten. He delights to choose the "not many wise . . . not many noble" (1 Cor. 1:26). He delights to show his love to men in spite of their sin. God framed Israel's history to reveal himself to the world. That mission will be accomplished, "for the mouth of the LORD has spoken" (Isa. 40:5).

THE TRUSTWORTHINESS OF GOD

Once again, "a voice says, 'Call out.' Then he [the prophet] answered, 'What shall I call out?'" (Isa. 40:6). The answer comes: Call out that "all flesh is grass, and all its loveliness is like the flower of the field" (v. 6). The reference here is not to the frailty of human existence but to the weightlessness of human effort in contrast to God. "The grass withers, the flower fades, when the breath of the LORD blows upon it" (v. 7). Nothing can withstand God; no empire however great, no nation however determined. "Surely the people are grass" (v. 7).

God's purposes cannot be frustrated. His will shall be done. "The grass withers, the flower fades, but the word of our God stands forever" (v. 8). Isaiah does not call upon the people to trust in a hopeful intention on his part, or in his contingent goodwill. They are called upon to trust him whose word can never fail and who will accomplish his will come what may.

COMFORT FROM GOD

God is so mighty that his message of comfort is to be declared with a confidence worthy of him. "Get yourself up on a high mountain" where you are clearly seen and heard, "O Jerusalem, bearer of good news" (v. 9). Have you noticed? Jerusalem, the recipient of this message, is now to declare it. Is this an intimation of the remnant?

"Lift up your voice mightily . . . lift it up, do not fear" (v. 9).

> [These] words constitute a true picture of the manner in which the word of God is to be proclaimed to the world. The messenger is to be bold; he is to raise his voice that all may hear. The Church is not to keep this message to herself but is to present it to Judah's cities with a holy boldness. She is not to pose as a seeker after truth, unsure of her message, but to declare in clear, firm, and positive voice that her message is true. She must be vigorously and militantly evangelistic. Hesitation, timorousness, and trembling are out of place. There is no need to fear as though the word of God would not be fulfilled, or as though the message would prove to be untrue and embarrassment would result.[2]

What is to be proclaimed by Jerusalem and to whom? We are dealing with Israel and its history in the hand of God. Those addressed are described in verse nine of this passage as "the cities of Judah." Israel remains the object of Isaiah's message, although the message is now being borne by a group described as "Zion" and "Jerusalem."

The message is simple: "Say to the cities of Judah, 'Here is your God!'" (v. 9). Look at him! Take notice of him. Note what he has done in your history. He deserted you when you sinned as he said he would. Now he is returning in mercy as he promised. "Behold, the Lord GOD will come with might, with His arm ruling for Him," like a mighty king whom none can withstand. "Behold, His reward is with Him and His recompense before Him" (v. 10).

All will receive from his hand what they deserve. Opponents who do not believe the good news shall be destroyed from the presence of his glory. Those who believe shall experience his grace. "Like a

2. Edward J. Young, *The Book of Isaiah*, vol. 3 (Grand Rapids, MI: Wm. B. Eerdmans Publishing Co., 1972; repr. 2001), 37–38.

shepherd He will tend His flock." The picture is one of amazing tenderness. Mighty—yes. Overwhelming—well, yes. But overwhelming as only sovereign love can overwhelm. "Like a shepherd He will tend His flock, in His arm He will gather the lambs and carry them in His bosom; He will gently lead the nursing ewes" (v. 11).

Have you ever seen a shepherd bend down, swoop a lamb into his arm, and lovingly carry it to pasture? At first the lamb is terrified. It is suddenly swept off its feet, away from the familiar order of things and into the arms of a tall, strong creature that controls the herd. A short while later the lamb settles quietly in its benefactor's arms, enjoying his embrace and the warmth of his affection. Such will be the fate of Israel. God will swoop down with the irresistibility of his love and make them his own.

CONCLUSIONS

Such is the message of Isaiah 40:1–11. What has this to do with us? A great deal. We have "caught" the message. We know the grace of God in a way that is possible only in Christ. We have learned from the history of Israel. We have learned preeminently from that part of Israel's history that has to do with the coming of Messiah, his life, atoning death, and justifying resurrection.

We also know that God is not to be tampered with. His hatred of sin is awful, altogether just. His love is amazing and can never be suppressed. His power is beyond resistance. He brings down mountains and lifts valleys, if necessary, to fulfill his will. His will includes the salvation of Israel. Although they have sinned, they are, irrevocably, his people and he, irrevocably, is their God.

We have a message to proclaim and, as the old poem says, we "must not stay to play with shadows or pluck earthly flowers till [we our] work have done and rendered up account." The end of our endeavors is secure. "The glory of the LORD *will* be revealed, and all flesh *will* see it together." We refuse fear and temptation. We are determined to love God more than we love our lives. We shall work together for the glory of God in the salvation of Israel.

Our primary task is and ever shall be to *cry out*, call, proclaim. Preaching the good news is our ultimate duty. Social and economic aid is often called for. Political encouragement may sometimes be necessary. But our primary task is to lift up our voice mightily, addressing Jerusalem in the name of God.

We shall focus on nothing but the majesty of God's grace. "Behold your God" is the crux of it all. His mercy and faithful love are its corollaries. May we be faithful to our task. May we live, declare and, if need be, die in hope and expectation of the salvation of Israel.

Biblical Assumptions

IN THE FOLLOWING PAGES we will discuss the Messianic Movement. We will weigh the Movement's assumptions, claims, theory, and practices in the light of biblical truth. I engage in this discussion as a friend, acknowledging that many in the Messianic Movement are motivated by a longing to know God and serve him, to be more effective in addressing our nation with the gospel. These longings echo in my heart. Yet we disagree on the methods employed and the doctrinal bases to be laid. Since this discussion will be controversial, we must lay a number of agreed foundations.

Surely, all who fear God and believe that Jesus is the Savior of the world agree that everything done in the service of the gospel should be grounded in God's word (Lev. 11:44; 19; 20:2, 26) and directed at his glory (1 Cor. 10:31). The motive, the logic, the mode, and the goal of all we do should be the product of God's commanded will. Human reason, human needs, and human preferences should all be subservient to the divine "thus says the Lord" which commands our obedience and governs our every act. In matters of faith and obedience, nothing but God's word can bring light.

We are not free to do whatever we deem useful or effective in the service of God (1 Sam. 13:8–14; 15:2–3, 9, 13–23). We are not smart enough to identify what is useful or effective in ultimate terms, and "ultimate" is all that really matters. Appearances often deceive (1 Sam. 16:7). Short term advantages have often turned out to be long term mistakes. What we consider to be the best sometimes turn out to be the worst of all possibilities. We need the Scripture to guide us.

GOD'S WAY

God's work is to be done in God's way. There is no room for human ingenuity, except in the careful application of the word of God in a manner that is true to its meaning. Nor is there need to innovate—are we wiser than God? Have we a better perception of the challenges, pitfalls, and opportunities? We are but dust. Our Lord is the eternally wise one. Every act we undertake should be an act of worship, an expression of loving obedience rather than arrogant human wisdom. Obedience is a response to command, and God's commandments are to be found in Scripture.

GOD'S GLORY

The gospel is thought of nowadays as a means to meet human needs. Man needs forgiveness, salvation, comfort in life, a sense of worth, a loving community, and so on. The gospel is presented as the panacea for human ills, the solution of all man's problems. This is not the biblical perspective, where the focus is on glorifying God (Isa. 40:2; Eph. 1:6). Man comes afterward. I am confident that my readers agree.

That is the biblical perspective for our discussion of the pros and cons of Messianic Judaism. We need to think and speak clearly, but in honest love. We should not cloak our thoughts with Machiavellian ambiguity. We need to speak the truth in love and, for love's sake, speak the truth.

We must dare disagree with each other graciously, listen to each other kindly, argue our cases clearly, and have the courage to examine our respective positions and correct them if necessary. Barrett and Hengel speak of

> the importance in theology of saying exactly what you mean and not using compromise formulas that can be interpreted in more ways than one or attempting to let everyone have at least a bit of his own way. To become as a Jew to the Jews is good as a matter of social courtesy; as a way of salvation, such occasional obedience would be worse than no obedience at all.[1]

Do we agree on this as well?

1. C. K. Barrett and Martin Hengel, *Conflicts and Challenges in Early Christianity*, ed. Donald Hagner (Harrisburg, PA: Trinity Press International, 1999), 74.

GOD'S STANDARDS

In an effort to meet this biblical standard, we measure issues by the word of God. Other considerations might be admitted, but must never be allowed to determine our response to questions that arise. God has given us his word. The closer we adhere to that word, the less likely are we to stray. Most of my readers will agree that no consideration may impinge upon the authority of the word of God. We question that modern theory of missions that insists that the gospel is best promoted by a focus on perceived human needs. The assumptions underlying such a theory are sociological, not biblical. They prefer human needs, human wishes, human cultural practices, and human preferences to sacrificial obedience to God, seeking his glory and recognizing his right to rule over all.

Such an approach lacks the biblical undergirdings of faith in an almighty God who bends the hearts of men and women according to his will, in spite of their perceived needs and contrary to them.

> If anyone comes to me and does not hate his father and mother, his wife and children, his brothers and sisters—yes, even his own life—he cannot be my disciple. And anyone who does not carry his cross and follow me cannot be my disciple. (Luke 14:26–27 NIV)

It lacks a biblical recognition of the depth of sin and its power over man, and of the nature of the powerful, saving work of the Holy Spirit in persuading sinners, granting them faith and repentance through regeneration, and uniting them with the Savior in his death and resurrection. "No one can enter the kingdom of God unless he is born of water and the Spirit. Flesh gives birth to flesh, but the Spirit gives birth to spirit" (John 3:5–6 NIV).

If God can make the very stones cry out for Jesus, can't he break through every barrier that hinders the spread of the gospel? Is he not able to lay aside every objection and overcome man's sinful resistance toward the truth? After all, conversion is something God does for man (we are born "again" or "from above" [John 3:3 NIV], "not of natural descent, nor of human decision or a husband's will, but born of God" [John 1:13 NIV]).

Salvation is an act of God, not a human achievement (Ps. 3:8; Jonah 2:9). None but God can impart it, and we can do nothing to

render God's action more effective. The very best we can do is falter-
ingly obey. We should, therefore, preach God's gospel in God's way,
and trust him to do his divine work in spite of our weakness. Any
other kind of faith in Jesus is not the faith that saves or sanctifies.
Maybe that is why so many who profess to be saved today display little
evidence of being sanctified.

There is reason to fear that a significant proportion of Jews who
profess faith in Jesus do not perceive him to be all that the Bible teaches.
This might be astonishing to some, but I am honestly concerned that
there might be some among us—God forbid, many—who are persuaded
that their sins have been forgiven through Messiah, but who have never
repented, never cast themselves on the mercy of God who forgives sinners
by his undeserved grace and transforms them by his irresistible power.
They remain in their sins.

This is a terrifying thought!

In the hands of some evangelists, the gospel has become no more
than the best religious option. It is disconcertingly possible that some
who profess to believe in Jesus have been impacted by a gospel shaped
to meet man's perceived needs, a form of faith that has little to do with
a biblical fear of God—the foundation of true wisdom (Prov. 1:7). They
do not submit to God's will (Ex. 19:5; Deut. 13:4; 1 Sam. 15:22, John 14:15;
15:10, 14) and conduct no ongoing struggle against sin, which aims to
obscure the glory of God and remove him from his throne.

I do not like to argue with my brethren, but the above concern
leaves me little choice. I must enter the fray and challenge assumptions
that have become common among a growing number of those engaged
in the evangelization of the Jewish people.

I believe it is wrong on the part of my fellow Jewish believers in
Jesus to define Jewishness in terms of the Mosaic Law or of rabbinicism.
Rabbinic Judaism is not Jewish.

I believe that it is equally wrong to import into our worship and
practice customs that are the product of rabbinic religious culture. Rabbinic Judaism should be challenged rather than embraced. It is high time
that rabbinic usurpation of Jewish national identity be brought to an
end and that Jesus be crowned King of the Jews. Nothing less is my goal
and heart's cry. I invite you to join me in an effort to love God better and
serve him more faithfully.

WHO AM I?

One issue I wish to lay to rest at the beginning of this discussion is my attitude to things Jewish.

I am Jewish. I was born in the Jewish community of Boston, Massachusetts, to which my family immigrated after fleeing the pogroms in Russia. My maternal grandfather's name was Potashnick, and he was a well-known cantor in the Jewish community of my hometown.

My parents met and married in Boston, and my father worshiped in the conservative synagogue of the city of his choice until the day he died. After my parents were separated, my mother immigrated to Israel in 1953 with my younger brother and me. I was about ten years old. I grew up in Israel, served in the army, met the delight of my earthly life, and married her. (In fact, ours was the first Jewish Christian wedding held in modern Israel, attended by practically the whole evangelical community.) Our three daughters have served in the Israeli army, from which I was honorably released in 1985.

I love being Jewish. My family still greets the Sabbath each Friday night with a traditional Sabbath meal, and we celebrate all the biblical and traditional feasts with gusto. If you think this constitutes a contradiction to the thesis of this book, read on. I sincerely believe that being Jewish is a calling from God (1 Cor. 7:24), and I embrace it with gratitude. I also believe that the continued existence of an identifiable Jewish entity within the body of Messiah is a testimony to God's faithfulness, and that it will be a means in God hands for Israel's conversion (Isa. 29:13–24), for which I have longed, prayed, and labored for more than forty years.

As the above text from Isaiah says, Israel's conversion is linked to a time when the nation will take note of a body of people "in his midst," which is recognizably both Jewish and the work of God's hands. E. J. Young puts it this way: "among the physical children of Jacob there will be found his true children, who are the work of God's hands."[2] Then, says the Lord, "Those who are wayward in spirit will gain understanding; those who complain will accept instruction" (Isa. 29:24 NIV). I believe that the salvation of Israel

2. Edward J. Young, *The Book of Isaiah*, vol. 2 (Grand Rapids, MI: Wm. B. Eerdmans Publishing Co., 1969; repr. 2001), 332.

is a promised future act of God's grace toward his covenant people (Rom. 11:26–27), and that it will be a means of blessing to the world that Paul compares with "life from the dead" (Rom. 11:15 NIV).

I have no doubt as to the right, need, or legitimacy of a Jewish Christian entity within the body of Messiah and as an integral part of our nation. I have been privileged to serve a congregation of believers in Israel, which has long been in the forefront of evangelism, social responsibility, and the absorption of immigrants in the country. A high percentage of the congregation I serve is Jewish and, since so many of the people had been stripped of their national culture by the communist regime that ruled the USSR, we taught them the cultural practicalities of Jewishness. I do not deny the legitimacy of a distinctly Jewish-Christian entity. It is my intention to think with you about the *form* that many of my brethren have chosen to accord that entity, and with the biblical arguments they raise to defend that form.

I love being a child of God's grace even more than I love being Jewish. The thought that all my sins have been forgiven because the Son of God loved me and gave himself for me never ceases to thrill me. To think that, in spite of my failures, God will glorify himself in me, bring me into his presence, and transform me into the image of his Son is something that I find difficult to believe although the Bible gives me solid reason to do so, and the Spirit witnesses with my spirit that I am a child of God. There is nothing in the world more important to me than to please God, love him more purely, and carry out his will more faithfully. There are also few things in the world I desire more than that others—especially my beloved people, Israel—would love the God of our fathers, Father, Son, and Holy Spirit, and join us, seeking to love and serve him with all their hearts, souls, minds, and strength.

There is absolutely no conflict between the Jewish and the Christian aspects of my identity. I dare say this in spite of the shameful history of relations between the Jewish people and many who bore the name of my Savior. Anti-Semitism is as contrary to the teaching of the Bible as darkness is contrary to light. But, if the irrational ever occurred again (which is more than a possibility in this sin-crazed world) and I had to choose between Jewishness and my Savior, I would prefer Jesus to Jewishness any day. In choosing Jesus I would be choosing God himself. Only he can save. Only he is worthy of total devotion. Jewishness without the Savior is like heaven without God.

True Jewishness is wrapped up in Jesus. He fulfills the promises to our fathers, accomplishes the covenant God made with the patriarchs and the covenant he made with their sons. What now passes for Jewishness is not Jewish; it is a 2000-year aberration that demands rectification.

I agree with many of the motives behind the movement I criticize. But the Messianic Jewish Movement has erred in important areas of truth. The result of such errors is a misinformed spirituality that needs to be corrected by the word of God. I am convinced that the Messianic Movement has sparked a trend that leads increasingly away from biblical truth. The number of Messianic converts to rabbinic Judaism and the increasingly numerous expressions of discomfort with the doctrines of the Trinity and of the deity of Messiah are but the inevitable, logical conclusions of Messianic Jewish teachings.

DEFINITIONS

The term "Messianic Jew" is used in this book rather than the terms "Jewish" or "Hebrew Christian." Jewish and Hebrew Christians define themselves as Jews who believe in Jesus and who reject Judaism's claim to determine what is Jewish. They adhere in varying degrees to national customs formulated by Old Testament and rabbinic injunctions, but do so as a matter of national custom, not of religious obligation. They believe Judaism is a departure from biblical norms, a religion that requires a rejection of Jesus and of the faith he taught.

Hebrew and Jewish Christians believe that the unity of the body of Messiah should be expressed by mixed congregations of Jews and Gentiles living according to their respective customs at home and worshiping together in a manner that does not exalt one culture over another. They believe that Jewish people in the Messiah are free from the Mosaic Law, while they are also free to keep aspects of the law that do not obscure the gospel. I will argue here that Jewish *and* Gentile Christians are bound by the moral law of God. Jewish and Hebrew Christians acknowledge that the gospel should be couched in terms that are relevant to the people addressed, but insist that such contextualization should not affect the essence of the gospel.

Messianic Jews, on the other hand, call for implementing a platform of what is commonly described as "Messianic Judaism." In its most consistent forms, Messianic Judaism insists upon establishing messianic synagogues where congregants are instructed by "rabbis," traditional synagogue attire is encouraged, the Torah scroll is accorded prominence, and adherence to rabbinic custom is taught as a matter of religious duty.

We have no argument with those who insist on the continuance of Jewish identity in Christ. Nor have we an argument with those who view Jewish custom as the language of their lives and therefore the terms in which they express their faith in Christ, so long as that language is informed and modified by biblical injunctions.

The rationale of the Messianic Movement is, above all, its insistence upon the need for the existence of recognizably Jewish believers in Jesus, who adhere to Jewish religious practice as an expression of unity with our people. The goal is to create within the Jewish people an entity that is both recognizably Jewish and true to the gospel. Such an entity would be uniquely capable of presenting the gospel to our nation. To achieve this goal, the Messianic Movement seeks to create a distinct Jewish messianic entity within the church or, as some would prefer to put it, a messianic entity within Judaism, by way of messianic congregations.

In the first part of this book, we will examine the doctrinal grounds for that effort. In the second part, we will examine its practical consequences.

Some in the movement have argued that the adoption of a "Torah lifestyle" is the duty of all Jewish believers in Jesus. A smaller number insist that such a lifestyle is spiritually advantageous to Gentiles as well as to Jews. Originally, the Messianic Movement insisted upon the right and duty of Jews to believe in Jesus. Jews should believe in Jesus *as* Jews, that is to say, as members of the covenant people. All Messianic Jews, and Hebrew and Jewish Christians share this conviction. The difference between them lies in the methods used and in the underlying presuppositions that guide those methods.

Inevitably, this book deals with generalizations. There are always exceptions. I know of those and welcome them. Nevertheless, my generalizations are pertinent to the majority of those who adhere to the Messianic Movement and to the direction in which the views of the Movement inexorably lead. This may be demonstrated by a visit to an average messianic congregation anywhere in the world—except Israel. In Israel most congregations are, in fact, Jewish Christian although designated messianic. Rabbinic lore plays a minor role in their lives and, on the whole, is limited to the celebration of the Jewish feasts in a moderately traditional Jewish manner. The only religious significance attached to the feasts is the measure they portray the person and work of Jesus.

So, while Israeli congregations insist on being described as "messianic" when speaking in English, most of them are poles apart from the practices and assumptions that underlie those of messianic congregations in the Diaspora.

The Hebrew term "Meshichi" indicates all who, in English, would be described as evangelical Christians, including Plymouth Brethren, Lutherans, Baptists, Anglicans, Pentecostals, Charismatics, and others, Jewish or Gentile. Messianic Jews mistakenly insist that the Hebrew term should be translated "Messianist," or something of the kind. In terms of the semantic meaning of the Hebrew they are right, but in terms of the word's common meaning they are mistaken. Meshichi means, pure and simple, evangelical Christian. Notsri, on the other hand, means simply Christian—of any stripe.

The term "Messianic Movement" as used in this book does not relate to most Israeli congregations. However, there is a recent tendency among some congregations in the country to emphasize their Jewishness in terms of the American-born Messianic Movement. Where that is true, our conclusions are relevant.

PART 1

A Theological Assessment

1

Should We Preach the Gospel to the Jewish People?

THE JEWISH PEOPLE need to hear the gospel. It is embarrassing to have to insist on this. It is even more embarrassing to hear it questioned. The apostles repeatedly addressed the people of Israel with the gospel, calling them to turn from their sins (Acts 2:38; 3:19; 8:22) and from their unbiblical religiosity (Acts 3:13–14; 5:28–29; 7:42; 10:28), and to submit to the Messiah God sent for the nation according to his promises. Jews are sinners too. Like Gentiles, we need forgiveness because, like Gentiles, we will perish in our sins unless granted salvation by virtue of the sacrifice of Messiah.

> There is no difference, for all have sinned and fall short of the glory of God, and are justified freely by his grace through the redemption that came by Christ Jesus. (Rom. 3:22–24 NIV)

The apostles did not preach one gospel to the Jews and another to the Gentiles. They preached to those in Damascus, in Jerusalem and throughout Judea, the same gospel later preached to the Gentiles; namely, "that they should repent and turn to God" (Acts 26:20 NIV). This was the gospel, Paul told the Colossians, which "has been proclaimed to every creature under heaven" (Col. 1:23 NIV).

> As the Scripture says, "Anyone who trusts in him will never be put to shame." For there is no difference between Jew and Gentile—the same

Lord is Lord of all and richly blesses all who call on him, for, "Everyone who calls on the name of the Lord will be saved." (Rom. 10:11–13 NIV)

Do Jews need to turn to God? We most certainly do. Is Israel not the people who always served their Maker? We most certainly are not, as a survey of the Old Testament will show. Jews need Jesus because we are sinners as much as any. We need to be forgiven. Our sins need atoning. We need to be converted (the old word for "turned") from sin to God. We need a Savior. We cannot save ourselves, and no one else can do it for us. Jesus is the promised Savior.

Nothing less than the outline above is the gospel. Nothing less should be preached to Jews or to any sinners. *How* it is to be preached is another matter, but the one gospel addresses Jew and Gentile alike. There is no difference, for "all have sinned and fall short of the glory of God" (Rom. 3:23 NIV).

The gospel is not "Come to Jesus and be happy." It is not "accept Jesus" or "believe that he is the Messiah so you will find purpose in life." It is, pure and simple, repent, acknowledge your rebellion against God and your inability to make amends to a holy Maker. Despair of yourself and turn to him in shame and in longing, aware of your need. Cast yourself on his grace and beg him for forgiveness. Trust in his love but do not take it for granted. Rely on him because he promises to save all who call upon him sincerely.

Nor is the gospel a matter of "come to fulfill your Jewishness." Instead it is, recognize your sinfulness, both as a human being and as a child of the covenant God made with your forefathers (Eph. 2:3). Admit your inability to do anything about that sinfulness. Acknowledge the fact that you are lost, without God and without hope in the world, even as are others (Eph. 2:12), unless God shows you mercy in Christ.

Jews need that gospel. We need it as much as the Gentiles.

HOW SHOULD WE PREACH THE GOSPEL TO THE JEWISH PEOPLE?

Should the gospel be preached in a special way to Jews? To some extent, yes—on condition that the mode is not allowed to modify the content or become paramount to it.

The apostles accommodated the mode of their message to their hearers. Simon Peter did so in Jerusalem when he appealed to the covenant, the prophets, and the promises (Acts 3:12–26). Paul preached in Athens (Acts 17:16–34) in a way he did not preach in the synagogues of Southern Galatia (Acts 13:16–41), Asia, or Europe. He used terms that indicated the relevance of the gospel to his hearers and that could be understood by them. We should not preach the gospel to the Hutus in the same way we preach it to the Hungarians, or to modern Mr. Sophisticate in the way we preach it to the streetwise children of Brazil. But it must always be the same gospel, couched in different terms and approached from different angles.

There is need to contextualize the way we present the gospel. Paul always sought common ground between his message and his audience. Did the Athenians believe in an unknown God (Acts 17:23)? He would speak to them of that God. Did they acknowledge a providential relationship between life and the Maker of all? Paul appealed to that knowledge (Acts 17:24–25). Did his hearers identify with the history of Israel (Acts 13:16–41)? Paul, like Peter (Acts 2:16–36) and Stephen before him (Acts 7), would establish his witness on that common denominator.

The terms in which the apostles couched their message were readily understood by their hearers. These served as starting points. Once the gospel was believed, each culture was subjected to a gradual transformation in which some elements remained intact. The core of each culture was transformed. What remained had to do with externals: customs, foods, language, and the like. The apostles did not accommodate the content of their message to the context into which they spoke, only its form; they challenged the context into which they spoke, doing so in terms likely to be understood. He spoke, for example, to the Athenians without accommodating their idolatrous concepts or conceding the reality of the resurrection. On these points he challenged his hearers, whatever the consequences.

Where core values and conceptual frameworks conflict with the gospel (the use of visible images in worship, for example, the awe in which holy places were approached, the attribution of deity to material objects, the separation of Jews from Gentiles, or the religious validity of circumcision), they were blown to the wind, much like the sorcery books that were burned by the believers in Ephesus. The apostles did not stick out like a sore thumb in the cultures they addressed. Paul accommodated himself to his audience (1 Cor. 9:20), so long as doing so did not threaten the fabric of the gospel (Gal. 2:5).

We should preach to the Jews primarily from the Old Testament. We should appeal to them through the promises made to the fathers. We should present Jesus to the Jews as the fulfillment of Old Testament promise, hope, ritual, symbol, and history. But this must not imply that we must embrace Jewish religious custom and conceptual frameworks, or that we should fashion our worship in primarily Jewish cultural terms.

On the other hand, there is a difference between evangelism and congregational life, as there is between religious authority as represented by rabbinicism and cultural mores represented by Jewish consensual custom. Paul and the twelve did not embrace the cultures they visited. They did not identify with those cultures, rejected most of their core values, and did not develop a theology that justified them. They moved comfortably from one culture to another without hesitation (1 Cor. 9:19–23) precisely because they were not bound to any of them. They were Jews to the Jews, Gentiles to the Gentiles, as under the law to those who were under the law and as without law to those who had no knowledge of the Mosaic Law. They did not accord any of those cultures religious validity.

"Ah. But the Jews are special!" I can hear you say and, to some extent, I agree (after all, I'm Jewish too). But does this mean that the restraint described above is lifted? Does it mean that we preach a different gospel to the Jewish people? Absolutely not! The gospel—the same gospel—is "to the Jew first, and also to the Gentile" (Rom. 2:10 KJV). Peter preached to Cornelius (Acts 10), exactly what he preached to his fellow Jews in Jerusalem, and both groups were accepted on the same grounds (Acts 11:17–18). This must be clear, otherwise we will be liable to corrupt the gospel by modifications intended to further its cause.

A Jew to the Jews

One of the failings of the Messianic Movement can be seen in relation to their attitude to Jewish custom. Adherents of the movement frequently explain that their motive for adopting Jewish custom is evangelistic. But the arguments presented far exceed evangelistic considerations. For example, Messianic Jews argue that Jews in Messiah must, as a matter of faithfulness to God, remain Jews and that the means to do so is by adherence to rabbinic custom. What does that adherence require? Is it a matter of religious obligation, or are we merely exercising our freedom when we maintain the cultural symbols by which our people identify themselves? Paul vociferously opposed tendencies to impose any customs on religious grounds.

In modern times Jewish Christians worshiping in churches are under tremendous pressure to leave their churches and join the Messianic Movement. When they refuse to do so they are described as turncoats and traitors. Gentile Christians are encouraged to believe that joining a messianic congregation accords one spiritual advantage—at least, they are "closer to New Testament Christianity."

Barrett and Hengel write that the conflict between an emerging "normative [that is to say *rabbinic*] Judaism" and the Messianic Movement represented by the followers of Jesus, centered on "the relation between messianic redemption and the traditional validity of the temple and the Torah," with the latter two more or less comprising "the heart of the Jewish Faith. Faith (*emuna*) and obedience were no longer directed primarily to the law, which was delivered to Israel on Sinai, but to a messianic person . . . it is no longer Moses and the law that mediates between God and humanity, but the Messiah, Jesus, the bringer of the new covenant (cf. Jer. 31)."[1]

As aptly summarized by their editor in his concluding remarks, "the basic issue between Judaism and Christianity is Christ and Torah, indeed, Christ or Torah."[2] Barrett and Hengel remind us that the High Priest ordered the stoning of James, the brother of the Lord and, by all accounts, a Torah-observant leader.[3] He sought the execution of other Jewish Christians "as offenders of the law."[4] In other words, Judaism understood faith in Jesus to be a contradiction of continued obedience to the Torah, even when such a faith was accompanied by dutiful practice of the Torah. How, then, can modern Messianic Jews think otherwise?

1. C. K. Barrett and Martin Hengel, *Conflicts and Challenges in Early Christianity*, ed. Donald Hagner (Harrisburg, PA: Trinity Press International, 1999), 10–11.
2. Ibid., 82.
3. Ibid., 11.
4. Flavius Josephus, *The Antiquities of the Jews*, 20.9.1.

Their practice is contradicted by their faith in Jesus, and the rabbis are quicker to recognize this than others. Rabbinicism recognizes an inherent contradiction between practicing the Torah and faith in Jesus. The adherents of Messianic Judaism are blind to this contradiction. They are so focused on being recognized as Jewish that they fail to reflect sufficiently on the greatness and finality of the person and work of Jesus. But the rabbis are consistent with their faith and ours when they refuse to recognize Messianic Jews as practicing a legitimate form of Judaism, and find it difficult to believe the sincerity of Messianic Jews who affirm both a faith in Jesus as Savior and faith in the law as an expression of spiritual vitality.

If acceptance by the Jewish people is the major objective, Messianic Jews will have to increasingly erode their biblical convictions with regard to Jesus and his atoning sacrifice, until they ultimately turn their backs to him and embrace a wholly rabbinic Judaism.

It is a matter of grave concern to note that such tendencies are evident among some Messianic Jewish groups. Few messianic congregations ever hear a sermon on the Trinity. Mark Kinzer has recently called for a moratorium on preaching the gospel to Israel, intimating that sincere Jews may be assured of eternal life in spite of their rejection of Jesus. This erosion will become a landslide unless we have the courage to take a stand for our people and for our mistaken brethren. "The Son of God makes compromise impossible and he himself constitutes the alternative to compromise. One does not ask, 'Can we give a little here and gain a little there?' One asks, 'What does it mean to have Christ the Son of God as Lord and Redeemer?' When the question is so put, there is no doubt what the answer will be."[5] Jesus is our all in all. He is not required to "give" one whit. If at all, it is our Jewishness that must "give."

THE ARGUMENT FROM GALATIANS: RIGHTEOUS PEOPLE LIVE BY FAITH

Introduction

Paul wrote his letter to the Galatians addressing just such a predicament. Some were insisting that believers are obliged to the Mosaic Law.

---

5. Barrett and Hengel, *Conflicts and Challenges in Early Christianity*, 69.

Some scholars claim that the issue was not whether Jewish believers are free from the law, but whether Gentile Christians should be required to keep it, or whether obedience to the law was necessary for salvation. There are three ripostes to this claim.

Paul's position is based on universal principles related to the gospel itself, not with matters concerning Gentiles or Jews. Paul takes Peter and himself as illustrations of and evidence to his point of view—and Paul and Peter were undeniably Jewish.

The issue was not the way of salvation because the issue at stake was not how to be saved but how those who are saved by Christ should conduct themselves. His view of an ongoing Christian life is based on how one enters such a life. The group that arrived in Antioch from Jerusalem and taught the necessity of keeping the Mosaic Law addressed Christians (Acts 15:1) precisely because they were Christians. The question was how to be *completed* (Gal. 3:3), how the saved may enter fullness, not the grounds of salvation. The pro-circumcision party sought to convince the Galatians to accept the yoke of the Mosaic Law in consequence of their faith in Jesus. Whether they were Jewish or Gentile, Paul insisted that for them to accept the yoke of the law was to embrace "another gospel" (Gal. 1:6 KJV); to preach such a gospel was to incur the anger of God and to be in danger of condemnation (Gal. 1:6–9).

Historical Background

Paul refers to his "previous way of life in Judaism" (Gal. 1:13 NIV), to his former advancement "in Judaism" and to his former great zeal "for the traditions of my fathers" (v. 14 NIV). Note that he speaks of these in the past tense, juxtaposing his former commitments with present ones by use of the word *but* in verse 15: "But when God, who set me apart from birth and called me by his grace, was pleased to reveal his Son in me . . ." (vv. 15–16 NIV). Former commitments had come to an end when God chose "to reveal his Son" in Paul. From that moment on they belonged to his "previous way of life." Judaism was replaced by Jesus. Paul did not return to Jerusalem, to relearn the traditions in light of what he had discovered; he went to Arabia and visited Jerusalem only three years after he had come to a mature understanding of the faith of Jesus. There his message received apostolic approval (vv. 17–24).

Years later, when Peter, Barnabas, and Paul were in Antioch, the city was visited by a group apparently sent by James (Gal. 2:11). Their mandate is not stated, but they apparently exceeded it. Their presence intimidated Peter and Barnabas. Prior to the group's arrival, the two had open table fellowship with Gentile believers, an indication that they understood there was in Christ no difference between Jews and Gentiles. When the group arrived, the two withdrew and began to observe Jewish religious custom. Paul took them to task over this because, as he put it, "they walked not uprightly according to the truth of the gospel" (Gal. 2:14 KJV). In other words, drawing a distinction between Jews and Gentiles in Christ is tantamount to "walking" contrary to "the truth of the gospel"!

Paul embarrassed Peter and Barnabas by publicly stating that before the group arrived from Jerusalem, when they—or at least Peter—had led lives more consistent with the gospel, they lived like Gentiles (v. 14). Until the emissaries arrived from Jerusalem, Peter lived like a Gentile (so much for the argument that the apostles led a Jewish lifestyle!). Distinguishing himself from the Gentile believers when the group arrived was what Paul described as "hypocrisy" (v. 13 NIV).

Paul then turned to a theological argument. "We," meaning he, Peter, and Barnabas, "who are Jews by birth" (v. 15 NIV), no longer look to the law for justification. Instead, they "have put our faith in Messiah Jesus" (v. 16 NIV).[6] That is the foundation of his case concerning a believer's relationship to the law.

Rebuilding What We Have Destroyed

At this point some might exclaim, "That is just the point! Paul is not arguing against the keeping of the Mosaic Law as such, only against those who insist on doing so for justification." Not quite. Whatever the group from Jerusalem might have said to the Galatians, they did not challenge them about the way one is initially justified (saved), but about how believers should conduct themselves following their salvation. Remember that the Galatians had heard the gospel and were already Christians. The issue of justification, as the initial experience

6. Out of deference to my Messianic readers, I have consistently preferred to use the term "Messiah" rather than the non-Hebraic "Christ," even when quoting Scripture. Readers will, of course, know that most translations of the New Testament prefer the anglicized Greek "Christ."

of saving grace, could not have been in question because the Galatians were already justified.

The biblical view of salvation considers the new birth, faith, justification, and sanctification as aspects of a whole. One cannot be born again without being justified, and one cannot be justified without being sanctified (Rom. 8:28–30). Our sanctification is secured by the blood of Christ, but it becomes gradually evident as one grows in Messiah. The extent to which our sanctification is visible serves as a test of our justification. All the justified are "saints," "sanctified in Messiah Jesus" (1 Cor. 1:2).

Returning to Galatians 2:17–21, what does Paul say? In verse 18 he talks about rebuilding "what I destroyed" (NIV). What does he mean? What had Paul destroyed, and what does he now so firmly refuse to rebuild? He is simply saying that if he returned to keeping the law as a means for spiritual achievement (of whatever nature because no qualifying nature is designated) after having stopped doing so to be justified, he would be reestablishing the law. He had turned from the law to Messiah. He must not reestablish what he had previously set aside. He must not rely for sanctification on what had proven insufficient for justification.

Through the law Paul became dead to the law (Gal. 2:19) because the law had pronounced a death sentence on the apostle. He had been "crucified with Messiah" (v. 20 NIV). He "died to the law" in the death of Messiah and rose to a new life in which he now lived "by faith in the Son of God, who loved [him] and gave himself for [him]" (v. 19–20 NIV). To live otherwise, Paul starkly insists, is to "set aside the grace of God" (v. 21 NIV) because it implies—no less!—that Messiah's death was unnecessary! This is a horrible thought, unacceptable to any who love God. Paul taught that the glorious sacrifice of the Son of God was not only for our initial justification, but it secured a whole salvation, including sanctification and glorification in the presence of God for eternity. To reestablish the Mosaic Law as a means to spiritual advantage through keeping the law is no less than to "set aside the grace of God" (v. 21 NIV).

Paul's opening words in chapter three are strong. Convinced that such a view of the Mosaic Law constitutes "another gospel" that threatens the glory of Messiah as well as the salvation of believers, he calls the Galatians "foolish" for thinking in such terms, and claims they have been "bewitched" (Gal. 3:1 NIV). What kind of inconsistency is this, he asks, demanding they respond. "Did you receive the Spirit by observing the law?" (v. 2). Obviously not. "Or by believing what you heard?" (v. 2). Obviously yes. Well, then, "Are you so foolish? After beginning with the Spirit, are you now trying to attain your goal by human effort?" (v. 3). Why should you think that you could be sanctified by any means other than that by which you were forgiven? Why should you think that justification is granted on the basis of faith, but that sanctification—the necessary product of salvation—is achieved by the keeping of the law? "Does God give you his Spirit and work miracles among you because you observe the law, or because you believe what you heard?" (v. 5). The answer is clear.

Abraham

Abraham illustrates Paul's point. Abraham "believed God, and it was reckoned to him as righteousness" (Gal. 3:6). So law-keepers are not considered Abraham's sons, but "those who believe" (vv. 7, 9 NIV), while those who rely on the law are under a curse because they cannot "abide by all things written in the Book of the law" (v. 10). Perfect obedience is beyond reach (v. 11).

Messiah came to deliver us from the curse that the law imposes because no one can perform "all things written in the Book of the law." He did so by becoming a curse for us. Righteous people live by faith, not by keeping the law (v. 11). Indeed, there is a fundamental contradiction between law-keeping and believing (v. 12). Faith, not works, is the essence of true spirituality. Of course, such a faith inevitably expresses itself in works, but those works are never viewed as according spiritual advantage. They are the product of the Spirit's work in our hearts.

Faith, not the law, is necessary. Abraham was not required to keep a law—any law—but to have faith. The Mosaic Law, which was "introduced 430 years later, does not set aside the covenant previously established," because to do so would be tantamount to doing away with the promise (v. 17 NIV). The Mosaic Law is not essential to godliness; faith is. That is why the inheritance depends on faith and not on the law (v. 18). The law does not oppose the promises of God, but it cannot accord its adherents a part in those promises. Scripture declares all men to be prisoners of sin, incapable of obtaining the promise through law-keeping, so that "the promise by faith in Jesus the Messiah might be given to those who believe" (v. 22) rather than those who exert themselves.

The Mosaic Law kept us "in custody"; we were "shut up to the faith which was later to be revealed" (v. 23), but "now that faith has come, we" (Jewish Christians like Paul, Peter, and Barnabas are explicitly included in Paul's "we" and "us") "are no longer under the supervision of the law" (v. 25 NIV). Paul, the Jew, is making this argument. All who have faith in Jesus are the sons of God apart from keeping the Mosaic Law. There is in this regard no difference between Jew and Gentile because in Christ "there is neither Jew nor Greek [Gentile], slave nor free, male nor female, for you are all one" (v. 28 NIV). Jews and Gentiles do not differ in their duties to God. One might prefer grilled meat to gefilte fish, and kleizmer music to Karl Offenbach; one might prefer to live in Israel and another in Italy, but with regard to their duties before God there is no difference, and none should be introduced if we wish to walk according to the truth of the gospel.

The Tutor

Paul illustrates his point from the traditions of the Greek-impacted culture of Galatia, according to which children had no rights until they came of age. In terms of civic privileges, they were equal to slaves (Gal. 4:1) and subject to tutors until the time set by their fathers. "So also, when we were children," (Paul again includes Peter, Barnabas, and himself) "we were in slavery. . . . But when the time had fully come, God sent his Son . . . that we might receive the full rights of sons" (vv. 3–5 NIV), and the gift of the Holy Spirit (vv. 6–7), who assures us of our sonship and of our relationship with God. So then, Paul asks the Galatians, how is it "that you are turning back to those weak and miserable principles? Do you wish to be enslaved by them all over again? You are observing special days and months and seasons and years!" (vv. 9–10 NIV). Paul describes the laws as "weak and miserable principles"—not quite the way some might prefer to describe them.

"I plead with you, brothers," says Paul. You can ignore the evidence and assume he is writing to a purely Gentile audience if you wish, but take note of what he says. Seeking to persuade his listeners to leave off keeping the Mosaic Law he says, "I plead with you, brothers, become like me, for I became like you" (v. 12 NIV). In other words, learn from my example how to view the law.

In their effort to prove that Paul kept the law, Messianic Jews tend to forget the full text of 1 Cor. 9:20–21. Let's look at that text for a moment;

it will help us understand the letter to the Galatians. Paul chose to adopt Jewish custom when it served a gospel purpose among his fellow Jews. But, like Peter, he also freely lived as without law, that is to say, as not under the Torah. Since most of his labors for the gospel were in Gentile contexts, it is fair to say that, for most of the time, he lived "like a Gentile" (Gal. 2:14 NIV). First Corinthians 9:20 cannot be construed as biblical justification for the Messianic Movement's efforts to create Messianic Judaism.

Become Like Me

That is what Paul means when he says to the Galatians: "I plead with you, brothers, become like me" (Gal. 4:12 NIV). Although free from the law, in certain situations I am willing to abide by its requirements. I do not do so as a matter of religious duty but of evangelistic expedience. Paul then expresses his deep concern for the Galatians because they were being persuaded to keep the law as a religious duty. "My dear children, for whom I am again in the pains of childbirth until Christ is formed in you, how I wish I could be with you now and change my tone, because I am perplexed about you!" (vv. 19–20 NIV). Paul is calling on the Galatians to learn from his example and recognize that they are free from obligation to the Mosaic Law. The very thought that they might not recognize this evokes his concern. He speaks to them lovingly, earnestly, pleading for the good of their souls.

An Illustration from Abraham's Two Sons

Paul then turns to another biblical illustration. Abraham had two sons, one of which was the child of promise, his legitimate heir and the gift of God's grace. The other was illegitimate, born to a female slave, the product of his wife's faithless manipulations and of his own lack of faith. Both were sons of Abraham. Could they not learn to live together and share the promise? "What does the scripture say? 'Get rid of the slave woman and her son, for the slave woman's son will never share in the inheritance with the free woman's son'" (Gal. 4:30 NIV). There is no room for faith and grace to live in harmony with law and law-keeping: "Get rid of the slave woman and her son. . . . It is for freedom that Christ set us free. Stand firm, then, and do not let yourselves be burdened again by a yoke of slavery" (Gal. 4:30–5:1 NIV).

This is a serious matter, insists the apostle. It threatens the very heart of the gospel because the introduction of a works principle will inevitably corrupt one's understanding of grace—regardless if the issue is salvation obtained, maintained, or enhanced. Such corruption might be a slow, imperceptible process, but it inevitably occurs. Where works of any kind are deemed contributory to one's standing with God, works always—but always!—displace grace. "Mark my words! I, Paul, tell you that if you let yourselves be circumcised, Messiah will be of no value to you at all" (Gal. 5:2 NIV).

Brethren, hear Paul's warning. It is the very voice of God.

Paul repeats it in verse 3, "Again I declare to every man who lets himself be circumcised that he is [thereby] obligated to obey the whole law" (NIV). One cannot accept the law piecemeal. Take it or leave it, but don't think you can use it for sanctification and not for justification, that you can keep kosher and celebrate the feasts as a religious duty while excusing yourself on other issues such as mixed cloths, the wearing of fringes, and the practice of ritual purity. There is an unbreakable link between all such uses of the Mosaic Law, just as there is between all aspects of the law.

Faith and Grace

That is why Paul goes on to say, "You who are trying to be justified by law have been alienated from Messiah; you have fallen away from grace" (Gal. 5:4 NIV)! Why should Paul make such a stark, seemingly unkind statement? Why should he talk to believers about justification? These people belonged to the church in Galatia. They had already been justified. He describes them in chapter 4:6–8 as those who now have the rights of sons. "God sent the Spirit of his Son into our hearts, the Spirit who calls out, 'Abba, Father'" (Gal. 4:6 NIV). Formerly they did not know God, but now they know him, rather, are known by him. Yet, in spite of all this, Paul writes to them about justification!

That is just the point, as I tried to show earlier. The willingness evidenced by some in Galatia to accept the yoke of the Mosaic Law indicated that they had been "alienated," "fallen away from grace" (Gal. 5:4 NIV). Instead of trusting God for sanctifying grace, they were trying to achieve it by keeping the law. In their efforts to achieve a greater spirituality through keeping the Mosaic Law, the Galatians had undergone the corruptive process I claim is inevitable. Let me repeat: One can't accept the law piecemeal. Take it or leave it, but don't think you can use it for sanctification and not for justification, that you can keep kosher and celebrate the feasts as a religious duty while excusing yourself on other issues such as mixed cloths, the wearing of fringes, and the practice of ritual purity. There is an unbreakable link between all such uses of the Mosaic Law, just as there is between all aspects of the law.

The Galatians' views of grace and of the gospel had been corrupted by their attribution of spiritual advantage to keeping the law.

In contrast with those who seek spiritual growth by keeping the Mosaic Law, says Paul, "by faith we eagerly await through the Spirit the righteousness for which we hope" (v. 5 NIV). Paul speaks of his ultimate sanctification and that of his fellow believers ("we") in terms of a "righteousness" (another word for *justification*), which they "await through the Spirit." Why "await"? Well, how else are they to obtain it? Ultimate justification is a matter for the future because it includes our ultimate salvation, when we enter the presence of God and are sanctified by being transformed into his glorious image. That waiting was eager, active, confident: the Galatians had been justified, they were being justified, and they will undoubtedly yet be fully justified in the Last Day. What will be is now present, but the present is only a hint of the glory that is to be.

Paul goes on in verses 6–15 to warn the Galatians (be they Jewish or Gentile). They had begun to run well. Who had interrupted their race and kept them from obeying the truth (v. 7)? He is referring to those who insisted the Galatians were obliged to keep the Mosaic Law. By so doing they were obstructing the Galatians' race in the running-track of truth. In verse 10 Paul says that such a view of the law throws the believer into confusion. In verse 11 he makes it clear that no one can claim he taught the Gentiles to be circumcised (he would hardly need to teach that to Jews, they were all circumcised anyhow).

The Real Offense

A believer's attitude to the Mosaic Law is no small issue. Paul had indicated that how one views the law affects how one understands and experiences the gospel. Now he warns that "a little yeast works through the whole batch of dough" (v. 9 NIV)—a minor error has inevitably extensive consequences. He enlarges on this in verses 11–12. Paul first insists that he did not teach anyone to be circumcised. He did not call upon Gentiles to become Jewish. Had he done so he would not have been persecuted by his fellow Jews, because the "offense of the cross" would have been removed—after all, he would be calling Gentiles to convert to Judaism!

That is important. Paul is telling us that long before the church adopted an anti-Semitic stance—before the Crusades, forced conversions, and the Holocaust, the message of the gospel was an offense to the Jewish people. The real offense of the gospel in the eyes of a Jewish person has nothing to do with Christianity's moral failure in relation to the Jewish people. It has to do with the gospel itself, with what the gospel must always remain. Paul refused to remove the offense of the gospel by preaching it in a way that would satisfy Jews because to do so would involve an alteration of the essence of the gospel.

Why?

Because the real offense of the gospel is its insistence that man can do nothing to save himself or earn a standing with God; that he is wholly dependent on God for every aspect of his salvation, including sanctification. That is what the defenders of the Mosaic Law did not understand. The gospel is the opposite of Judaism; it is what Jews and Gentiles do not like. Having begun preaching forgiveness by grace through the regenerating work of the Spirit, the proponents of the Mosaic Law were now teaching advancement in spiritual matters by law-keeping. Such a view subverted the gospel because it attributed something to man. Paul was vehement in his opposition to it: "As for those agitators, I wish they would go the whole way and emasculate themselves!" (v. 12 NIV).

Law in the Christian Life

To say that believers are no longer subject to the Mosaic Law is not to say that they are free to live as they please. The essence of the law—its moral aspects—remains intact and finds fulfillment in the process of salvation by grace through faith rather than in sanctification by works. As the ancients put it, the moral aspects of the law now serve as an authoritative guide for Christian living, while the whole remains a revelation of God and teaches us about him. The freedom purchased for us by the blood of Messiah inevitably leads to "faith working through love" (Gal. 5:6). "The entire law is summed up in a single command: 'Love your neighbor as yourself'" (v. 14 NIV). So life by the Spirit does not lead to gratifying the flesh but to a life of "love, joy, peace, patience, kindness, goodness, faithfulness, gentleness and self-control" (vv. 22–23 NIV).

A life led by the Spirit rather than by the Mosaic Law will lead to the gradual crucifixion of the sinful nature, its passions and desires (vv. 24–25). That is what it means to belong to Messiah (v. 24). Those who are led by the Spirit are not under law (v. 18), yet fulfill the righteousness of the law by the power of the Spirit (compare Rom 8:1–3). On the other hand, those who live by the flesh in an effort to keep the law will be subject to all the sinful motivations described in verses 19–21. They "will not inherit the kingdom of God" (v. 21 NIV).

Following practical guidance at the beginning of chapter 6, Paul returns to his subject:

> Do not be deceived, God is not mocked; for whatever a man sows, this he will also reap. For the one who sows to his own flesh will from the flesh reap corruption, but the one who sows to the Spirit will from the Spirit reap eternal life. (Gal. 6:7–8)

Paul is again contrasting efforts to keep the Mosaic Law with faith expressing itself through love and relying on the merits of Messiah.

Barrett summarizes the issues as follows: "Paul is arguing not merely that Gentiles are not to be obliged to observe the rules of purity; it is wrong for Jews, who also are justified by faith and not by works, to insist that such rules should be observed in order that they may be able to join in a meal."[7] In other words, Paul is discussing the nature of Christian fellowship, the unity of Christians' obligation to God and to one another, and the freedom of all who own the name of Jesus as Messiah and Savior from the Torah and from rabbinic dictates. Paul preached a "radical gospel of radically unconditional grace."[8] That is the gospel we should believe. That gospel is the ground of relations between man and God, and between one man to another, regardless of national, social, or religious background.

Paul's statements in his letter to the Galatians are clear. We should heed the message.

---

7. Barrett and Hengel, *Conflicts and Challenges in Early Christianity*, 64.
8. Ibid., 72.

YES, BUT HOW ABOUT THE EVANGELISTIC OPPORTUNITY?

Where Our Focus Should Be

We should be engaged in preaching the gospel to the Jewish people, rather than in seeking their acceptance by insisting we are Jewish in spite of our faith in Jesus. I am aware that present-day Jews object to the gospel on the grounds that their Jewishness excuses them from the gospel's claims. I also recognize that the gospel is perceived to be a threat to our continued national identity, and that this constitutes a real obstacle for Jews. But we must not allow ourselves to be deflected from the duty to preach the gospel. God is able to turn the hardest of hearts and rob the most obstinate of the ploys man might use to protect himself from the claims of the gospel. Our focus should be the same as the Bible's: the authority of the word of God, the horror and bondage of sin; man's inability to please God; his need of an atoning sacrifice; the saving work of the Messiah; the transforming power of the Holy Spirit and the life forgiven people should lead and are enabled to lead for the glory of God.

Instead of busying ourselves with Jewishness, we should glory in the marvelous body of Messiah in which Jews and Gentiles are equal—in the hope of eternal life in the presence of God and in the sustaining grace of a God who will not fail his weak and erring children. Those are the issues with which the Bible is occupied. The most effective way to evangelize is to maintain a biblical emphasis, to focus on the core of the biblical message. God saves, not our persuasive arguments.

It is time to get out of our trenches and go on the offensive. We need not defend our Jewishness; we need to proclaim Jesus, the True Jew. When we regain the confidence of our biblical convictions and begin to live courageously as disciples of Jesus, we will be more likely to command the respect of our people than by subjecting ourselves to the obedience of a false religion engendered by the Pharisees. Evangelism is best served by a clear message, not by one obscured by the trappings of a Christ-denying Judaism.

The Power of Jesus

Jesus said, "I will build my church, and the gates of Hades will not overpower it" (Matt. 16:18). The picture is wonderfully vivid: the hordes of Hades have fled for refuge to the darkness of the pit and barred the gates. They are now shivering, supporting those gates with their shoulders and hoping for the best because the army of King Jesus has arrived and is battering at the gates with the mighty word of the gospel. Will the gates hold? Will Satan's host be secure? Will even one of those appointed to salvation, taken captive by Satan to do his will, remain in the hands of the enemy?

We need not wait until the end of the commercials. The climax of history is spelled out in Scripture. Hell's gates will collapse under the blows of God-centered evangelism. Hell will be vanquished. Not one of those given to the Son by the Father will be lost. All will be introduced into the presence of God with exceeding joy to obtain eternal life.

> I have sworn by Myself,
> The word has gone forth from My mouth in righteousness
> And will not turn back,
> That to Me every knee will bow, every tongue will swear allegiance.
> They will say of Me, "Only in the LORD are righteousness and strength."
>   (Isa. 45:23–24)

Hallelujah!

The Scriptures are full of such statements. Modern day evangelical pessimism has no basis in Scripture. The message of the Bible is optimistic. The book of Revelation assures us that Jehovah will make everything new, that he will dwell with men. The slain lamb is the mighty "Lion of the tribe of Judah" (Rev. 5:5 NIV), and he shall reign. The redeemed will be "his people, and God himself will be . . . their God" (Rev. 21:3 NIV). He will "wipe away every tear from their eyes . . . there will no longer be any mourning, or crying, or pain," for the old order of things will have passed away and God will make all things new (Rev. 21:4–5). The redeemed of the Lord will number ten thousand thousands, and their song of worship will be like the sound of mighty thunder, rolling over eternity to the praise and glory of him who reigns in mercy and love, whose wonder and beauty more than fills the universe.

God is sure to conquer and will do so by the gospel, without our silly improvements. He made the world by no more than a word. He spoke and it was done. God the Son upholds the universe by a mere word (Heb. 1:3). Nature functions at his command:

He sends forth His command to the earth;
His word runs very swiftly.
He gives snow like wool;
He scatters the frost like ashes.
He casts forth His ice as fragments;
Who can stand before His cold?
He sends forth His word and melts them;
He causes His wind to blow and the waters to flow. (Ps. 147:15–18)

Praise the LORD from the earth,
Sea monsters and all deeps;
Fire and hail, snow and clouds;
Stormy wind, fulfilling His word;
Mountains and all hills;
Fruit trees and all cedars;
Beasts and all cattle;
Creeping things and winged fowl;
Kings of the earth and all peoples;
Princes and all judges of the earth;
Both young men and virgins;
Old men and children. (Ps. 148:7–12)

God also saves by his word:

Fools, because of their rebellious way,
And because of their iniquities, were afflicted.
Their soul abhorred all kinds of food,
And they drew near to the gates of death.
Then they cried out to the LORD in their trouble;
He saved them out of their distresses.
He sent His word and healed them,
And delivered them from their destructions.
Let them give thanks to the LORD for His lovingkindness,
And for His wonders to the sons of men!
Let them also offer sacrifices of thanksgiving,
And tell of His works with joyful singing. (Ps. 107:17–22)

Jesus stood before a grave in the heat of a Middle Eastern spring and commanded a body, dead four days, "Lazarus, come out!" At the sound of the Savior's word, the corpse stirred, rose from the dead, and came out. Such is the message we preach. Its words are mighty to demolish strongholds, arguments, and every pretension that sets itself up against the knowledge of God, taking captive every thought and making it obedient to Christ (2 Cor. 10:4–5). God is active in his word, which is the sharp, terrible, irresistible sword of the Spirit. The gospel is a message that has a life of its own because it is God's word (Heb. 4:12), it is "the power of God for salvation" (Rom. 1:16).

God will triumph in the world through the preaching of the gospel. That is the means by which he lays hold of men and women, Jews and Gentiles, young and old, releases them from bondage to Satan, unites them and transforms them into a redeemed and sanctified people. The kingdoms of this world will become the kingdom of God and of his Christ (Rev. 11:15). He shall reign and every knee shall bow before him to the glory of God the Father. All will own him as Lord. This will happen through the blessing of God on the preaching of the gospel. Preaching—faithful preaching—is so crucial.

It is God who converts the sinner, not we. That is why Paul avoided displays of professional eloquence and human wisdom. He preferred "a demonstration of the Spirit's power" (1 Cor. 2:4 NIV), so that conversions were not the spurious products of human effort but the enduring fruit of God's work in the hearts and minds of his hearers (v. 5). That is the logic behind Paul's thanking God for the Thessalonians' conversion and for the spiritual and moral consequences that inevitably followed (1 Thess. 1:2–3), rather than praising them for the wisdom they displayed in making the right religious choice. It is on those grounds that Paul could say to the Thessalonian Christians,

> But we should always give thanks to God for you, brethren beloved by the Lord, because God has chosen you from the beginning for salvation through sanctification by the Spirit and faith in the truth. It was for this He called you through our gospel, that you may gain the glory of our Lord Jesus Christ. (2 Thess. 2:13–14)

The Power of the Spirit

Peter reiterates this very conviction when he speaks of his readers as having been "born again to a living hope through the resurrection of

Jesus Christ from the dead" (1 Peter 1:3). How was this achieved? Peter replies: "You have been born again not of seed which is perishable but imperishable, that is, through the living and enduring word of God. . . . And this is the word which was preached to you" (vv. 23, 25). God changes individuals, communities, and nations through the preaching of his word. The Spirit uses the word of God to vanquish Satan's opposition, free his captives, and give life to the dead.

Once converted, we discover the power of the Spirit through the word in the everyday of our lives. We are made spiritually and morally wiser by the word (Ps. 119:7), encouraged by it and made joyful (v. 14). By the word we are kept from sin (vv. 1, 4), enlightened (v. 130), and strengthened (v. 28). God works according to his word and through it in the lives of those who belong to him, warning them against sin (vv. 9–10), teaching them the path of righteousness (v. 30), and evoking in them a desire for heavenly things (v. 97).

In this way God sets the redeemed sinner on the path to eternal glory. He preserves sinners in that path, secures their safe arrival, and succors them along the way by his word. Salvation is a divine work, executed by means of the Spirit's blessing on the word of God, applied to human hearts.

Jesus taught his disciples that his words must reside in them (John 15:7, 10). How is that done if not, among other means, by coming under the sound of the gospel as it is preached in church? The Spirit works by the word and through it. He cleanses stumbling Christians by the washing of the water through the word (Eph. 5:26), and they, in turn, sanctify themselves by obeying the truth proclaimed (1 Peter 1:22).

God will overcome every opposition Satan can throw in his way, and he does so through preaching. He captures sinners and brings them to himself through preaching. The book of Revelation portrays Christ as overcoming Satan by his word (Rev. 19:17–21—note the sword in the mouth of the Lord). Faithful, believing, Spirit-filled preaching of the word of God is the means by which God prepares us for eternity. We are given foretastes of heaven as we contemplate the truths of God's word and have lain out before us the wonders of the world to come. The word of the Lord teaches us to pray, informs, instills and stirs our hope, drives us to further action on behalf of the kingdom, and assures us of God's blessing as we labor for him. We Jewish Christians need the gospel to move us to trust in and live by the power of God.

DO JEWS REMAIN JEWS ONCE THEY ARE CONVERTED?

Of course we do. Why should we not? Because Jesus is the promised Messiah, there is no reason we should cease to be Jews in consequence of faith in him. Believing in Jesus is a very Jewish thing. Rabbinic Judaism is not Jewish. That is why we refuse to bend the knee to rabbinic dictum, as our people have done for 2,000 years. History will prove that they were wrong and that Jesus is the Messiah of Israel.

The apostles assumed that the faith they proclaimed was Jewish. So much so that they were surprised by the growing number of Gentiles who embraced it, and they were at a loss for what to do with them. Discussion was even held whether or not Gentiles should embrace Judaism and join the nation of Israel (Acts 10–11); after all, they believed in the God of Israel and were redeemed by the Son of Israel's hope.

None of the Jewish religious leaders of the day questioned the right of the Jewish disciples to be considered Jewish. That came later, when the rabbis took over the nation's self identity and posited themselves as the sole arbiters of Jewishness. The conflict over whether or not Jesus is the promised Messiah was, until then, an internal Jewish affair (Acts 18:15, 23:6–9).

The apostles addressed the people as Jews: "Men of Judea and all you who live in Jerusalem" (Acts 2:14); "Men of Israel" (Acts 3:12; 13:16). The apostles argued the case of the gospel from the Hebrew Scriptures (Acts 2; 3:18–26; 7; 13:16–41). But the message was always the same: "Therefore repent and return, so that your sins may be wiped away" (Acts 3:19); "Let it be known to you, brethren, that through him forgiveness of sins is proclaimed" (Acts 13:38). The gospel is not a negation of Jewishness but an affirmation of it, just as it is not a negation but an affirmation of Gentile identity and of God's love to both Jew and Gentile. Jews need not cease to be Jews to follow Messiah (1 Cor. 7:18). Neither should Gentiles be expected to embrace Jewish culture in consequence of their faith in him (v. 18). We were bought with a price and should not become the slaves of men (v. 23).

Each should remain in the condition in which he was called (vv. 20, 24). If there is doubt as to what the apostle meant, he spells it out: was "any man called being circumcised? Let him not become uncircumcised. Is any called in uncircumcision? Let him not be circumcised. Circumcision is nothing and uncircumcision is nothing" (vv. 18–19 KJV). In other words, whether we are Jewish or Gentile, that is what God has called us to be, and that is what we should remain. Jews in Messiah remain Jews, and Gentiles in Messiah remain Gentiles. Both believe the gospel and are saved. Both enjoy forgiveness of sin and are baptized by the Spirit "into one body," whether they be Jews or Greeks, slaves or free, and all are "made to drink of one Spirit" (1 Cor. 12:13).

Christians and Nothing Else?

Sometimes people tell us that we Jewish believers in Messiah are "Christians and nothing else." This is patently untrue. We are all also human beings, men or women, married, single or widowed, educated or unlearned, rich or poor, Swiss or American, Jews or Gentiles. Our conversion should bring to fruition every aspect of what God has made us to be, serving as a channel for our loving obedience in every department of life.

The issue is not *what* we are but *how to express* what we are in the context of worship and obedience. There, our being married or single, poor or rich, Jewish or Gentile should make no essential difference, even if it requires, for example, worship in a different language or relating to a spouse, so long as these do not affect the substance of our obedience.

IS IT IMPORTANT FOR JEWS IN MESSIAH TO REMAIN JEWS?

It most definitely is, although we have no right to condemn any who opt out of the nation. The loss of any is painful, but we have no right to force people to remain Jewish. On the other hand, we should reject the opinion of those who deny the right of Jews to remain such in Messiah, or who prefer that option for purported biblical reasons.

Embarrassing Historical Facts

For almost two millennia, the church has insisted that Jews who believe in Jesus are no longer Jewish. The fourth century Confession of

Faith issued by the church of Constantinople required Jewish converts to declare: "I do here and now renounce every rite and observance of the Jewish religion, detesting all its most solemn ceremonies and tenets of faith that in former days I kept and held." In other public statements, Jewish converts were required to affirm, "I altogether . . . shun all intercourse with other Jews and (will) have the circle of my friends only among honest Christians," "Nor (will I) associate with the cursed Jews who remain unbaptised."[9]

They were called upon to promise that they would never return "to the vomit of my former error, or associate with the wicked Jews. In every respect I will lead the Christian life and associate with Christians." As far as the family members are concerned, "we will not, on any pretext, either ourselves or our descendants choose wives from among our own race, but in the case of both sexes we will always link ourselves with Christians." Such language bespeaks an antagonism from which the church still needs to be cleansed.

One of the few issues on which church and the synagogue have agreed for two millennia has to do with this issue. Jews who professed conversion were expected by both the church and the synagogue to disavow their national customs and sever themselves from their people. Some Jewish converts were required to prove the sincerity of their faith by eating pork in public, while rabbinic edicts ensured that Jewish believers in Jesus could not remain effective members of the community. As a result, some Jewish converts evidenced loyalty to their new religion by becoming enemies of their people. A shameful chapter in the history of Jewish-Christian relations was thus written and now awaits an honest historian's research.[10]

It is reasonable for the rabbis to insist that Jewish Christians are no longer to be considered Jewish. But why should the church agree? To claim that loyalty to Jesus implies a rejection of Jewish identity is to imply that Jesus is not the promised Messiah of Israel. If he is not Israel's Messiah, he is no Messiah at all, for no other Messiah is spoken of in either the Old or New Testaments.

9. Stefano Assemani, *Acta Sanctorum Martyrum Orientalium at Occidentalium*, vol. 1 (Rome, 1748), 105.

10. David A. Rausch, *Messianic Judaism: Its History, Theology and Polity* (Lewiston, NY: The Edwin Mellen Press, 1982), 16–17; James Parkes, *The Conflict of the Church and the Synagogue* (Philadelphia: The Jewish Publication Society of America, 1964), 394–400.

Jewishness and Being Christian

There are no biblical grounds to require Jews to reject their national identity. That is why Rausch was right to quote Fanny Peltz, a Jewish Christian, who stated that "in accepting Jesus, I was not giving up anything Jewish!"[11] But, please note, we are speaking here of Jewishness as a *national* identity. When we speak of a *religious* identity, we are Christians. Judaism is not biblical while true Christianity is.

The rabbis claim that a change of religion necessarily leads to a loss of national identity. The majority of our people have bought in to that theory, but it is wrong. It even contradicts Jewish halacha (religious dictum), which states, אַף עַל פִּי שֶׁחָטָא, יִשְׂרָאֵל הוּא (although he has sinned, he still belongs to Israel).

History has rendered the cause of Messiah a great disservice. The anti-Semitism to which the church succumbed imposed on converts a denial of their Jewishness. I need not elaborate. Anyone interested in the question of Jewish Christian identity is abundantly aware of the shameful history, the blot of which still has not been erased. Christian anti-Semites—a logical contradiction in terms—persecuted the Jews while seeking to obliterate every trace of Jewishness in their own faith and practice. Remnants of anti-Jewish sentiment are still to be found in Christian pulpits and commentaries.

ROMANS 1:16: TO THE JEW FIRST, BUT ALSO TO THE GREEK

Paul insisted that the gospel is "to the Jew first," and only then (*also*, to use his term) for non-Jews (Rom. 1:16). Paul was not discussing chronological order but the essence of the gospel. He was saying that the gospel has a primary claim on the Jewish people, and that the Gentiles have been "added." Many assume that the faith of Jesus is a Gentile faith, and that Jews who adhere to it are somewhat unusual. Paul insisted that the Jews are *first* in terms of the gospel, and that it is the Gentiles who are *also*.

God's Power to Save

In Romans 1:16 Paul describes the gospel as God's power to save. It is in the essential nature of the gospel to save in a way that differs greatly

---

11. Rausch, *Messianic Judaism*, 87.

from other purported ways to salvation. Other religions leave salvation in man's hands: he must make up for his sins, he must pray, he must make pilgrimages, he must placate God through sacrifice.

Not so the gospel. The gospel divides between the redeemed and the lost because the gospel is not a way by which man saves himself, but "the power of God for salvation." It is God who saves. No wonder Paul was unashamed of such a message! If God saves, then the saved are saved fully, powerfully, effectively. They are saved by the power of God.

Everyone

The gospel saves "everyone who believes." The gospel treats all mankind equally. It declares that all without distinction (Jews and Gentiles) have sinned and fallen short of God's glory; all (Jews and Gentiles) need to be saved; and God saves all (Jews and Gentiles) without distinction. According to the gospel, all men are equal.

Faith

Paul has still another important statement to make about the essential nature of the gospel: not only is it God's power to save, and to save everyone, but it saves everyone "who believes." The gospel does not allow man to be passive. Faith is a gift of God (Eph. 2:8–9) that drives men to work, moves them to change, modifies their priorities, and drives them to strive for goals they would never otherwise adopt. Faith and faithfulness are indistinguishable in both Hebrew and Greek, and they should be in our lives.

To The Jew First

Paul goes on to describe the nature of the gospel by saying that it is "to the Jew first." This, too, has to do with the nature of the gospel because the message of God's kindness did not appear out of the blue. It is the fulfillment of Old Testament promise, the accomplishment of all the Old Testament stands for.

What does "to the Jew first" mean? It means that the gospel most obviously, most directly, and most intentionally relates to the Jewish people, and only then to the rest of the world. It is to Jews *first* and to

Gentiles *also*. As Peter put it in Acts 3:18–20, 25–26 while addressing a Jewish audience,

> The things which God announced beforehand by the mouth of all the prophets ... He has thus fulfilled. Therefore repent ... that he may send Jesus, the Messiah *appointed for you*. ... It is you who are the sons of the prophets and of the covenant which God made with your fathers. ... *For you first*, God raised up His Servant and sent Him to bless you by turning every one of you from your wicked ways.

The point is this: the Mosaic Covenant has been replaced by the New Covenant promised in Jeremiah 31. But the Abrahamic covenant has not been replaced; it forms the basis for the coming of Messiah and his blessing to the world (Gal. 3). Jesus came in fulfillment of that covenant in order to redeem the elect within the nation (Rom. 9:6–13; 11:1–5) and those among the Gentiles whom the Father appointed for salvation.

The gifts and the callings of God are irrevocable. God will yet work within the Jewish nation so that "all Israel will be saved; just as it is written, 'The Deliverer will come from Zion, He will remove ungodliness from Jacob'" (Rom. 11:26). There is no need for a lengthy discussion about the meaning of "all Israel." It is enough for us to say that "all Israel" is not the whole Jewish nation but that remnant within the nation God has appointed to salvation.

We may conclude, then, that the existence of a visible, identifiably Jewish body of Christians within the body of Messiah is not in conflict with the gospel. A denial of the right of such an existence is tantamount to a denial of the Old Testament basis for the New Testament Faith. The continued existence of an identifiable body of Jewish Christians within the nation of Israel is a testimony to both the church and the nation that God remains true to his covenant, even when Israel failed. This is a vivid expression of the wonder of God's grace: even "if we believe not," he will remain faithful, for "he cannot deny himself" (2 Tim. 2:13 KJV).

A Jew to the Jews. There is at least one other reason why it is important for Jewish Christians to remain an integral part of their nation. The Jewish people must hear the gospel and see it lived out before them. This can be done most effectively by fellow Jews who live and speak in the cultural language of the people and who are able to address the nation from within. We Jewish Christians are no strangers to our people. We share the same joys and sorrows, hope the same hopes, and bear the same scars. We feel the anguish of the Holocaust. We are partners in the struggle against assimilation and the loss of Jewish identity.

God has not forsaken Israel, nor will he. He loves our people by grace, and we love our people because they are ours and we theirs, no matter what they do or how they treat us. We labor for their welfare and pray for their ultimate good, which we know can only be found in the Messiah.

HOW CAN JEWS IN MESSIAH REMAIN JEWS WITHOUT DENYING THE GOSPEL?

That is a crucial question, often arising for fear that the way Jewish Christians express their Jewish identity may conflict with the gospel.

National Culture

The only means for Jews in Messiah to identifiably belong to their nation are those employed by other nations for the same purpose. Jewish Christians adhere to the cultural norms adopted by the majority of their people so long as these do not contradict the gospel. Those norms constitute the national consensus which defines, expresses, and maintains the nation's identity. On the other hand, it is the duty of Jewish Christians, as it is of Christians from any nation, to challenge any part of the national consensus that conflicts with the gospel. Jewish Christians are recognizably Jewish by their national custom. We belong to the Jewish people by more than an accident of birth. We are Jews by choice, by heartfelt identification with our people in all aspects of life—with the notable exception of their rejection of Jesus.

That rejection creates a tension between our national and our spiritual identities, which cannot be resolved by our adopting a rabbinic way of life or returning to the yoke of the Torah. It will be resolved only when our people turn to God, repent, and believe all that the Hebrew Bible and the New Testament say of Jesus. We are assured by the promises of God that such a day will yet come, and, though it tarries, we wait for it with confident expectation. Someday Israel will cast away the part of its national custom that contradicts the gospel and constitutes a rejection of Jesus—who they will then adore.

Jeff Wasserman writes, "When, at the age of twenty, I became a believer in Jesus as Messiah, I strained to find reference points in Christianity that were in any way familiar to me."[12] If he had been made familiar in childhood with the truly Jewish themes of God, sin, grace, covenant, sacrifice, Messiah, forgiveness, and so on, he would have found many of the major "reference points in Christianity" to be exactly what he sought. But Jeff was looking for something else. He was looking for externals, rituals and customs. That is where he and many Messianic Jews have erred. What is really important cannot be found in national religious custom but in the faith that the Bible inculcates.

Why should Jeff be surprised not to find familiar reference points between his new faith and the customs in which he was brought up? Judaism, as developed over the last 2000 years, is a denial of the gospel, a rejection of Christ. Jeff's disappointment was misplaced when he says, "it was with a sense of mourning that I abandoned my Jewish heritage . . . and set aside all that I had been in order to apprehend what I had become in Christ."[13] He made the right choice, if a choice had to be made. Compared to Jesus, Jewishness is worthless. But no such choice is required. It is not inherent in either Jewishness or in the faith of Messiah.

It is amazing to note what Jeff means by "elements of . . . Gentile background."[14] In a footnote he speaks of "somberness in worship, magic-style incantations in Jesus' name, a pantheon of divine beings that included a very powerful devil, and an influential Mary."[15] One wonders what kind of church Jeff had wandered into! Most of the features that offended Jeff would offend every biblical Christian. As to sobriety, is that a distinctly Gentile attitude of worship?

Jeff goes on to describe what he believes is characteristically Jewish worship: "joyful celebration of God's presence and favor, and a strong consciousness of the need for human repentance in the face of the one and only God."[16] This is so idealized a version of Jewish worship that

12. Jeffrey S. Wasserman, *Messianic Jewish Congregations: Who Sold This Business to the Gentiles?* (Lanham, MD: University Press of America, 2000), 1.
13. Ibid., 2.
14. Ibid.
15. Ibid., 9.
16. Ibid.

the average Jew would hardly recognize in it a normative synagogue service. Jewish services are generally characterized by little reverence. Latecomers rush through their prayers, while others follow suit so they can talk with a business partner or client. It is not uncommon for the rabbi to call repeatedly for silence. There is generally little sense of joyful celebration and no need for repentance. God is absent from the thoughts of the worshipers.

Truth be told, the purported tension that exists between our national and spiritual identities is nothing compared to that under which our people presently labor. Present-day Jewish identity is the product of a sinful fluke of history during which our people rejected him who is the goal and culmination of everything truly Jewish, while those who professed to be our co-religionists harassed and persecuted their own people for their honest faith in him.

The tension our people live under is the result of a calling to which they subscribe yet refuse to obey, a duty which is the ultimate product of their Jewishness. It is not without reason that the pressing question "who is a Jew?" keeps rising in Israel. The Jewish people will never know the God of their fathers until they come to know Messiah, Jesus of Nazareth, God who came to live and die among men for their salvation. Only then will the issue of their identity be resolved.

Cultural Mores

Since the destruction of the temple in 70 AD, the synagogue has served as the national community center, while rabbinic custom was the glue that kept the nation together. It is now generally assumed that Jews are Jewish by virtue of their adherence—theoretical or otherwise—to biblical and rabbinic traditions.

All nations express their identity by cultural conventions. Religious concepts helped to formulate a substantial part of these Jewish conventions before they lost their significance. When they contradict biblical norms, they are forbidden to disciples of Messiah. For example, Paul allowed the eating of meat sold in the marketplace (1 Cor. 10:25) although he knew such meat came from pagan altars. Eating the meat, in and of itself, carried no religious significance. As soon as religious significance was attached to consumption, Paul forbade it (1 Cor. 10:28). In other words, the act was allowed or forbidden by the absence or presence of religious significance. The issue was not the act but the significance attached to it.

In the same way, Paul had no difficulty maintaining Jewish custom so long as doing so was not a matter of religious obligation. He "became" (amazingly, that is the term used in 1 Cor. 9:20 NIV) as a Jew to his fellow Jews, while insisting upon his liberty to become "as a Gentile" to the Gentiles. Paul did not consider himself obliged to practice the Judaism of his day. Peter, too, lived like a Gentile (Gal. 2:14), and when he did not, he acted hypocritically (v. 13), contrary to the truth of the gospel (v. 14). Again, the issue was not the act but the motive.

Paul consistently refused to accept Jewish custom when it impinged upon the gospel by taking on religious significance. He did not hesitate to enter into controversy with Peter when he considered the gospel to be at stake (Gal. 2). He led many Jews out of the synagogue but never led Gentiles into it. There is no biblical evidence that would cause us to think that Paul's converts attended synagogue for any length of time, or that they established their own once they left. The congregations Paul founded were not called synagogues. He coined a new term for them—churches. James used the term "synagogue" to describe a community of believers in Jesus. But he was probably addressing a Jewish Christian congregation that labored under the same misconception that guided the messengers to Galatia (Acts 15:1, 5; Gal. 2:4, 12–13). Its members therefore probably insisted on the religious necessity of maintaining national traditions.

There is no doubt that the gospel can be put at risk by some Jewish conventions, particularly those that retain religious overtones. For instance, fasting and giving are not, in themselves, unacceptable. But fasting on the Day of Atonement for the forgiveness of sins is a denial of the sufficiency of Christ. Giving to the church to obtain merit in the eyes of God is a contradiction of grace. We need to distinguish between cultural conventions and religious obligations. Circumcision and other traditions established by the law are not of themselves contrary to the gospel. But if we are circumcised, convert to Judaism, or keep what is described today as a Torah lifestyle because we believe ourselves obliged to do so or in any way spiritually advantaged, we are denying the sufficiency of the work of Messiah.

In matters of morality and religion, none but God has the right to bind a believer's conscience. Here God has exclusive authority, and he exercises that authority through his word. In matters of national identity, Jews are as free to be Jewish as are the Swedes to be Swedish and the Hottentots to be Hottentot. There is no spiritual advantage in eating pork or in abstaining from doing so. But neither Swedes nor Hottentots are free to adhere to national customs that contradict the gospel.

There are two major sources for the formulation of Jewish cultural norms: (1) the Old Testament, especially the Mosaic Covenant, and (2) the traditions of the rabbis. Let us examine these separately.

2

The Mosaic Covenant

DAN JUSTER TELLS US that the Messianic Jewish Movement is "a movement among Jewish and non-Jewish followers of Jesus of Nazareth who believe that it is proper and desirable for Jewish followers of Jesus to recognize and identify with their Jewishness."[1] In spite of Juster's proviso, "This Jewish lifestyle is to be maintained only as it is consistent with the whole of biblical teaching,"[2] Messianic Jews who subscribe to this view regularly transgress biblical teaching, and Dan himself goes further in his demand for Jewish religious observance than his proviso might allow us to expect. The reason is partly that Dan and those who agree with him actually use the terms "proper" and "desirable" to infer obligation. Who does the desiring? If God desires us "to recognize and identify" with Jewishness, then his desire is our delight—and duty.

Michael Schiffman affirms that believers may keep the law "as a part of a godly life-style."[3] This clearly implies duty because all the followers of Messiah are to be godly. Indeed, Jeff Wasserman reports, "more than half of the [messianic] congregational leaders who responded to my survey asserted the mandatory nature of Torah observance for Messianic Jews."[4]

Jeff confirms: "Half of the congregations surveyed asserted that not only was observance of elements of the Mosaic Law permissible

---

1. Dan Juster, *Jewish Roots: A Foundation of Biblical Theology for Messianic Judaism* (Rockville, MD: Davar Publishing, 1992), vii.
2. Ibid.
3. Michael Schiffman, *The Return of the Remnant: The Rebirth of Messianic Judaism* (Lederer Messianic Publishers: Baltimore, 1992, 1996), 69.
4. Jeffrey S. Wasserman, *Messianic Jewish Congregations: Who Sold This Business to the Gentiles?* (Lanham, MD: University Press of America, 2000), 62.

and recommended for Messianic Jews, but up to 23% thought it mandatory. Advocates [of the Messianic Movement] cite effective discipleship as the outcome of Torah observance."[5] He comments, "For these Messianic Jews, Torah observance becomes the essential element in discipleship."[6] On the same page he affirms, "30% of those surveyed recommend Torah observance for Gentiles."[7] In other words, a significant part of Messianic Judaism insists that Torah observance is a religious obligation. A recent example may be found in Mark Kinzer's recent book, *Post-missionary Messianic Judaism: Redefining Christian Engagement with the Jewish People*.

What is more, the Messianic Movement is far more than "a movement among Jewish and non-Jewish followers of Jesus of Nazareth who believe that it is proper and desirable for Jewish followers of Jesus to recognise and identify with their Jewishness."[8] It is also a movement of Jewish and non-Jewish followers of Jesus who believe that it is proper and desirable—if not necessary—for Gentiles to identify with Jewishness.

PHILIPPIANS: FOCUSING ON JESUS

One of the errors of the Messianic Movement is that it has placed Jewishness at the center—where Jesus should be. He alone deserves to be the focus of our devotion. He alone has the right to our hearts. A congregation that focuses on Jewishness (or anything else but Jesus) has misplaced its focus.

Paul's Jewishness

Paul has important things to say in this regard in his letter to the Philippians, chapter three. He had more to boast of with regard to Jewishness than most of us can claim for ourselves: he was a Jew, circumcised on the eighth day; from the royal tribe of Benjamin; a *Hebrew of the Hebrews*. As far as keeping the law, he was a member of the strictest sect of Judaism. He was taught by one of the most revered

5. Ibid., 96–97.
6. Ibid., 98.
7. Ibid.
8. Juster, *Jewish Roots*, vii.

rabbis in the history of Israel, Rabban Gamliel the Great. Paul was so zealous for God that he persecuted believers in Jesus with relish and determination. As to righteousness by law-keeping, he was considered "blameless." But he considered these a disadvantage in comparison to Messiah (Phil. 3:7).

Upon his conversion, instead of busying himself with being Jewish, Paul was taken up with "the surpassing value of knowing Messiah Jesus" his Lord (Phil. 3:8). As a result, he described his Jewishness as no more than "rubbish" (the actual Greek word is not used in polite company— v. 8 again). He no longer sought a righteousness "derived from the Law, but that which is through faith in Messiah, the righteousness which comes from God on the basis of faith" (v. 9). Paul contrasts faith with keeping the law. As he repeatedly states in this passage, he turned away from the law and put his faith in Messiah. Consequently, rather than being taken up with Jewish things, his attention was directed at Jesus. He describes his motivating desire: "that I may know Him and the power of His resurrection and the fellowship of His sufferings, being conformed to His death; in order that I may attain to the resurrection from the dead" (vv. 10–11).

Paul describes his view of Jesus in exciting terms. He paints a picture taken from the chariot races the Romans loved so much. Like a chari- oteer nearing the end of the race, neck-to-neck with others, Paul tells us that he is stretching forward with all his might toward the crossing line. To reduce any friction that might slow his pace, he becomes one with the panting beast pulling his chariot, its pounding gallop, and the chariot's screeching, groaning wheels. He stretches forward "for the prize of the upward call of God in Messiah Jesus" (v. 14), driven by the thought that God has laid hold of him (v. 12). The Messianic Movement's focus on Jewishness, the law, and rabbinic tradition has dispossessed Jesus, removing him from his rightful place in the center. The Movement's focus is thoroughly unbiblical.

Like Paul, we should be wholly taken up with Jesus. We should be enamored with who he is, what he taught, what he did on earth; how he vanquished Satan by his death and concluded the victory by his resur- rection and his ascension; and with his present glory, the wonder of his return, and his ultimate, eternal vindication when he will hand the King- dom to the Father. We should be in love with Jesus, not with Jewishness.

Jesus and the Torah

The Mosaic Covenant is, of course, the primary influence that shaped Jewish national culture. It is also a focal point in Judaism. As interpreted by the rabbis, it is the very essence of Judaism. According to Judaism, God may only be approached through the Torah, and the Torah may only be approached through the rabbis. That is what Judaism is all about. Richard Longenecker quotes W. E. Davies.

> Judaism came to place more and more emphasis on the Torah, that is, the demand uttered on Sinai, which was itself a gift, the figure of Moses being a colossus because he mediated the Torah. The Church, as it looked back to the new Exodus wrought in Christ, first remembered not the demand but the person of Jesus Christ, through whom the new Exodus was wrought, and who thus came to have for the Church the significance of Torah. That is why, ultimately, the tradition of Judaism culminates in the Mishnah, a code of *halachot* [binding rules], and in Christianity in the Gospels, where all is subservient to Jesus as Lord.[9]

Ariel and Devorah Berkowitz offer their own view of Judaism: "we want to introduce you to a wonderful, loving, giving, gracious and beneficent friend."[10] One would hope that they are referring to Messiah, whom God sent to free us from what Peter described as "a yoke which neither our fathers nor we have been able to bear" (Acts 15:10). But Ariel and Devorah's invitation is of an altogether different nature: "we want to introduce you to a wonderful, loving, giving, gracious and beneficent friend—the Torah." Even my good friend, Paul Liberman, errs in this matter. He says, "If a Gentile really wants to be like his Messiah, he should become"—holier, kinder, pure in heart? No—"he should become more interested in biblical Judaism."[11]

The early church considered Jesus to have taken the place of the Torah. A growing number of adherents of the Messianic Movement today think that the Torah should have the place that belongs to

---

9. Richard N. Longenecker, *The Christology of Early Jewish Christianity* (Grand Rapids: Baker, 1970), 41.

10. Ariel and Devorah Berkowitz, *Torah Rediscovered* (Littleton, CO: First Fruits of Zion, 1996), xvii.

11. Paul Liberman, *The Fig Tree Blossoms: Messianic Judaism Emerges* (Harrison, AR: Fountain Press, 1977), 49.

Jesus. Martin Luther was wise and biblical when he said in a sermon on John 2:23–24:

> I am to adhere to Messiah alone; he has taught me neither too much nor too little. He has taught me to know God the Father, has revealed himself to me, and has also acquainted me with the Holy Spirit. He has also instructed me how to live and how to die, and has told me what to hope for. What more do I want? And if anyone wishes to teach me anything new, I must say to him: "I will not believe it, dear preacher, dear St. Ambrose, dear St. Augustine." For anything that goes beyond and above the man who is called Christ is not genuine. It is still flesh and blood, and Christ has warned us against relying on that. He himself did not trust himself to any man.[12]

The New Testament teaches that all may approach God through Messiah. There is no need for mediation by rabbi, priest, or pope. "There is one God and one mediator between God and men, the man Christ Jesus" (1 Tim. 2:5 NIV). Jesus replaces the Torah. That is why early Jewish Christians spoke of Jesus as the *Nomos* (Greek for "law," see *The Shepherd of Hermas*, 8.3.2, and Danielou, *The Theology of Jewish Christianity*, 163 ff.). In a famous first century dialogue between a Jew named Trypho and Justin Martyr, Justin speaks of Jesus as "another covenant," "a new law," and "God's covenant." Clement of Rome learned from the early Jewish Christians to speak of Jesus as the "law and the Word," as "another law," "the eternal and final law." Clement of Alexandria tells us that the new law "is the Son of God."

HEBREWS: JESUS IS FAR BETTER

Jesus and Moses compared

The writer to the Hebrews reminds us that the Mosaic Law, wonderful in itself, was but a *shadow* of what was to come (Col. 2:17, Heb. 8:5; 10:1). In its place we now have a great, utterly sinless High Priest (Heb. 4:14–5:10; 7:23–28). We should "hold fast our confession" of his accomplished redemption and not return to the elementary principles

---

12. *Luther's Works*, vol. XXII, Sermons on John 1–4 (Concordia Publishing House, 1957), 254–61.

that led us to him (Heb. 4:14; 10:23). Jesus is greater than Aaron (Heb. 5:6), greater than Moses (Heb. 3:3, 5–6), greater than Abraham, greater than all the angels of heaven put together (Heb. 1:4). "To which of the angels did he ever say, 'You are My Son, today I have begotten You'?" (Heb. 1:5). Does God not command with regard to Messiah, "Let all the angels of God worship Him" (Heb. 1:6)? God subjected the world to come to Jesus, not to any of the angels (Heb. 2:5–8). When our people and others rebelled against him, God said to him, "Sit at My right hand until I make Your enemies a footstool for Your feet" (Heb. 1:13).

We ought to be very careful lest we drift away from the truths Jesus proclaimed (Heb. 2:1). If the Torah, delivered to our forefathers through intermediaries, was not to be altered and every transgression was duly punished, "how will we escape if we neglect so great a salvation" Messiah purchased by his blood (Heb. 2:3)? The good news of this salvation was first declared by our Lord, and then confirmed to us by his disciples who personally heard him and saw him act. God himself bore witness to the gospel with signs and wonders and by gifts of the Holy Spirit distributed according to his will (Heb. 1:4–3:19).

God spoke of Moses as a faithful servant; but he called Jesus his Son (Heb. 3:1–6). Moses was appointed by God to oversee his house (v. 5), but Jesus was appointed over Moses (v. 6). God brought our fathers into the land by the hand of Joshua, but he told them that the land was not their ultimate possession (Heb. 4:8). There was and is more to divine blessing than material, political, economic, or social gratification. Divine blessing includes the "eternal rest" that comes from the knowledge that our sins are forgiven, the broken power of sin, the image of God being restored in us, and the favor of God given eternally to us—all this may be had in only Jesus (vv. 1–11).

So, "let us leave the elementary teachings about Christ and go on to maturity" (Heb. 6:1 NIV). Let's take care lest anything we do regarding our Jewishness conflict with the message of the Savior. Otherwise, we might end up, like Esau, in the place of no return (vv. 1–9).

The majority of my fellow Jewish believers in Jesus wish for nothing more than to be faithful to God in Messiah (Heb. 6:9–12). I acknowledge their zeal, their devotion, their sacrifice, and their sincere love for God, and I envy them for these. That is why I have written this book: I am convinced that many fine people have been drawn into a path they had no intention of following, and that once the implications of their theory are seen, they will reject the errors in their thinking and stand up for Messiah and his truth. Are you one of these?

Jesus' Priesthood

Abraham, as it were, paid tithes through Melchizedek to the Lord Messiah, whose priesthood accomplishes far more than the priesthood of Aaron ever could (Heb. 7:1–10). The temple in which Jesus serves supersedes the tabernacle and the temple in which our fathers worshiped (Heb. 9:11, 24). Unlike the sacrifices offered in the temple, his sacrifice is "able to save completely those who come to God through him" (Heb. 7:25 NIV). Unlike the Aaronic priesthood established at Sinai, Jesus' priesthood lasts forever (Heb. 7:17, 21, 24), and he is compassionate, powerful, and untainted by sin or human weakness (v. 26).

Of course, in earthly terms he could not be a priest at all—he came from the royal seed of David, not from the priestly family of Aaron (Heb. 7:11). But his is a "new priesthood," implying the removal of the Torah to make way for the newer, "better covenant" (Heb. 7:11–8:7). "For if that first covenant," made with our fathers at Sinai, "had been faultless, there would have been no occasion sought for a second" (Heb. 8:7). But God found fault with our people as well as with the covenant (v. 8). He promised (in Jer. 31 and throughout Ezekiel, for example) a new covenant, unlike the one with our fathers when he led them out of Egypt.

Our fathers did not continue in that covenant because, like all humans, they were sinful (Jer. 31:32; Heb. 8:10) and because there was nothing in that covenant to ensure they could continue. God promised and has given in Messiah a different covenant with the power to ensure its continuance: he transformed us by the power of his Spirit (Jer. 31:33–34; Heb. 8:10–12). He made the covenant part of our innermost beings and wrote it on our hearts. We have been born again! The knowledge of God through Messiah is powerful, transforming. By promising this *new* covenant, God rendered the first obsolete (Heb. 8:7–13). Indeed, when the letter to the Hebrews was written, the former covenant was already "becoming obsolete," "ready to disappear" (v. 13) because the inexorable process of history was leading to the destruction of the temple and an end of the temple ritual.

The first covenant had its own procedures: the presence of God was hidden in darkness behind a heavy curtain, beyond a room which only priests could enter, in a court to which only priests and Levites had access. The people stood outside and could barely see the court. The High Priest was allowed access into that presence one day a year, alone, "never without blood, which he offered for himself and for the sins the people had committed in ignorance" (Heb. 9:7 NIV). "The Holy Spirit is signifying this, that the way into the holy place has not yet been disclosed" (v. 8). The continual need to offer sacrifices taught the people that those gifts and sacrifices could never perfectly cleanse the consciences of those who worshiped under the old administration (v. 9). Instead, they promoted a hope nourished by rituals, dietary regulations, washings, and the like, all of which were imposed *until* the time of reformation (vv. 1–10).

The work of Messiah is fuller, better than anything the Torah could provide because Jesus brought with him all the "good things to come" that the Torah promised but could not deliver (v. 11). These are a greater and more perfect tabernacle, a better sacrifice, and an eternal redemption that included the cleansing of sinners' troubled consciences (vv. 11–14). Jesus is "the mediator of a new covenant" (v. 15).

We and our forefathers transgressed the Torah and broke covenant with God (Heb. 8:9). How, then, could we "receive the promise of the eternal inheritance" (Heb. 9:15)? Covenants are, in this respect, like a will. A death must occur before anyone can inherit. Messiah died to ensure we partake of the promise. He now appears in the presence of God for us (v. 24). Next time he comes, it will be to accord salvation in the fuller, fullest sense to those who eagerly await him (vv. 15–27).

As we have said, the law was a "shadow" (Heb. 10:1). As such, it cannot perfect those who approach God on its terms. Jesus is the perfect sacrifice, offered once and for all, by which "we have been sanctified" (v. 10). He offered himself in our place once, and then "sat down," his work completed. By this one sacrifice he accomplished what the Torah could never accomplish: "he has perfected for all time those who are sanctified" (v. 14). It is worth noting that Hebrews uses the term "sanctification" for what Paul would describe as salvation. This supports what we said when reviewing Galatians. Salvation is more than forgiveness of sins; it is a transformation God works in and for us. Jesus, not the Torah, secures both forgiveness and sanctification. He saves utterly, effectively.

Evidence of the finished work of Messiah may be found in the nature of the promise given in the new covenant. Jeremiah speaks of an internalization of the law of God, that is to say of a fundamental change in the bent of our nature, so that we choose to glorify God (Jer. 31:33–34, cf. Heb. 10:15–18). Has that happened to you? Do you now desire as never before to live for God and his will? If so, God has done in you what he promised to do in the hearts of Israelites. You are redeemed, forgiven, a partaker of the eternal inheritance. I hope you are grateful and that you will love God with all your heart, soul, mind, and strength.

Let's not let go of what we have received. Let's keep on keeping on! God is faithful and we should be too. Let's take great care not to trample underfoot the blood by which we were bought. Remember that God is a terrible avenger. Do not draw away from your confidence in Messiah. Focus on him alone. You do not have to prove to anyone that you are Jewish, and you must not compromise the gospel in an effort to do so. You and I need to persist so that, having done the will of God, we will receive the promise (Heb. 10:19–39).

Faith

Faith is not merely rejoicing in what we have; it is being faithful because of what lies in the future. Look at the list of great heroes of the faith: Noah, Abraham, Joseph, Moses, and all the others—did they trust because of what they had? Of course not! They suffered, waiting in confidence while paying a price for their faith (Heb. 11). With such onlookers, "let us run with endurance the race that is set before us, fixing our eyes on Jesus" (Heb. 12:1-2), rather than on the Torah or on Jewishness. Remember what he endured for you—and remember that you have not paid the ultimate price in your struggle against sin. Jesus did that for you.

Do the rabbis claim that you are no longer Jewish? So what? Does that make them right? Do your family members say you have become some kind of "Jesus freak"? Is that too high a price to pay for what you have in Messiah? Your suffering is a mercy from God, shaping you to partake of his holiness. We should not shirk rejection, but bear it, demonstrating by our attitude the nonnegotiable nature of the message we proclaim (Heb. 12:1-17). It is not popular nowadays to insist on truth, but we should "buy truth, and do not sell it" (Prov. 23:23). It is truly nonnegotiable. It is not the means by which we buy popularity but by which God glorifies himself and transforms people, societies, and nations into the image of his Son.

The implications of your choice are extensive. The giving of the Torah was accompanied with terrifying manifestations in order to emphasize the dire consequences of disobedience. In coming to Messiah we have not come to a smoking mountain, to the sounds of trumpet blast, and to awesome physical displays. We have come to something far more substantial.

> You have come to Mount Zion and to the city of the living God, the heavenly Jerusalem, and to myriads of angels, to the general assembly and church of the firstborn who are enrolled in heaven, and to God, the Judge of all, and to the spirits of the righteous made perfect, and to Jesus, the mediator of a new covenant, and to the sprinkled blood, which speaks better than the blood of Abel. (Heb. 12:22–24)

Make very sure, then, that your focus on Jewishness does not lead you to refuse the message. Having received so much from God, let's express our gratitude. If need be, let's go with Jesus "outside the camp," forgoing national recognition, "bearing His reproach" because our hearts are not fixed on what we have here and now. Like Abraham, we seek "the city which is to come," whose builder and designer is God (Heb. 13:13–14).

The Weakness of the Torah

We need to recognize the Torah for what it is. There are important limits to what it can do. The Torah was "added" (Gal. 3:19) "until . . ." (Heb. 9:10). Its commandments are weak and beggarly because they can only bind the conscience, not cleanse it (Heb. 9:1–20; Gal. 4:9). The law is not weak and beggarly in itself; the cause of its weakness is in our sinful hearts (Rom. 8:3), but it is a real weakness, all the more evident in light of Messiah's work. Let me explain.

A thousand candles are a great light, but what are they in comparison to the light of the world? When I was serving in the army, we would sometimes use large projectors to expose suspicious movements at night. The strength of projectors is measured in "candles" (lumens), and the strength of ours was equal to 10,000,000 candles. But when the sun was up, we could not tell if the projector was on or off. That is what it is like when the Torah is held up to the light of Jesus. The law is good, spiritual, and worthy, but Jesus outshines the Torah.

The Torah cannot save or comfort. It cannot assure sin-sick hearts of God's good will. It cannot cleanse the conscience, secure salvation, or create holiness. It cannot give the Spirit. Jesus can do all that and a great deal more. Only he can. When Paul spoke of the Mosaic Covenant as a "ministry of death" (2 Cor. 3:7), he was not referring to the Torah's nature but to what it does because of our sinful weakness. That weakness drives us to disobey the Torah or transform it into a means of salvation or some spiritual advantage which, we claim, "draws us closer to God."[13]

That is what Judaism has taught, and that is the growing tendency in the Messianic Movement. Ariel Berkowitz writes, "all who are currently learning to apply the Torah to their lives are experiencing deep-seated and profound spiritual growth and by teaching you to keep the Torah [they are] ushering you into new depths of intimacy with your God."[14] Such a view of the law runs contrary to Scripture and to the testimony of our conscience.

The law was given to expose our inability, and lead us to despair of ourselves and cry out to God. Spiritual benefits are given by grace, not achieved by law-keeping. Let us "cast out the bondwoman and her son, for the son of the bondwoman shall not be an heir with the son of the free woman" (Gal. 4:30).

Both And

Why? Why can't we Jewish believers in Messiah adhere to both the Torah and the New Covenant? Because there is an essential conflict between becoming of age and submitting to a childhood tutor. There is an essential conflict between being in Christ by grace through faith and relying on law-keeping to gain or retain anything from God. That is the implication of Paul's point in 2 Corinthians 3, where he contrasts the Torah with the Spirit (remember Galatians?) and indicates that the Torah was divine truth "engraved on stones" (2 Cor. 3:7), never more than that. It cannot do what the Spirit does. The Spirit "gives life" (v. 6; see Rom. 8:1–4), but the law leads to death.

13. Shoshanah Feher, *Passing Over Easter: Constructing the Boundaries of Messianic Judaism* (Walnut Creek: AltaMira Press, 1998), 111.
14. Berkowitz, *Torah Rediscovered*, xvi–xvii.

In 2 Cor. 3 Paul insists that Moses hid his face so that the people would not gaze at the fading glory of God that shone on his face (2 Cor. 3:7). The ministry of the Spirit, on the other hand, is ongoing, able to save, able to transform individuals into the moral image of their creator. It is therefore "more with glory. . . . For if the ministry of condemnation has glory, much more does the ministry of righteousness abound in glory" (vv. 8–9). The reason is that the Spirit provides a righteousness which Torah can only demand.

> Indeed, what had glory [the Torah], in this case has no glory because of the glory that surpasses it. For if that which fades away was with glory, much more that which remains is in glory. (vv. 10–11)

Much the same kind of argument is made by Jeremiah in the thirty-first chapter of his book, verses 31–34. There he says that, unlike the earlier Covenant of Sinai, the New Covenant will be incapable of being broken because God will inscribe it on the hearts of his people. In this way he will make the people his, and himself theirs. All in whose hearts he works will know him, beginning with the least (Jer. 31:32–34). The grounds are spelled out: "I will forgive their iniquity, and their sin I will remember no more" (v. 34). Forgiveness is the grounds of sanctification, not its consequence.

Those who have tasted of the grace of God in the gospel will immediately recognize their experience in this description. The saving work of the Holy Spirit is here described, applying the atonement obtained by the death of Messiah and working out all the ingredients of salvation: the joy of sins forgiven; a love for God and his truth; a heartfelt desire to do his will regardless of the cost; an intimacy in prayer never known before. The Torah can provide none of these, so why return to shadows, images, and promises when reality has arrived, when the images and hope inculcated by those images have been fulfilled?

The Mosaic covenantal arrangements went no further than the symbolic rituals in the temple, all of which pointed forward to the substance that is in Jesus. The rituals were the intriguing "shadow" that could not make perfect (Heb. 10:1), and of which Messiah is the glorious reality (Heb. 8:5; 10:1). A "greater than the temple is here" (Matt. 12:6). The rituals were not the reality. They could not convey that reality but kept our forefathers in perpetual tension, awaiting what was to come. Only Jesus can satisfy the longings created, meet the needs indicated, and accomplish the reality promised by the older Testament.

Jesus is our all in all. In him we have a better hope (Heb. 7:19), a better covenant (Heb. 7:22), a better High Priest, a better ministry (Heb. 8:6), a better sacrifice (Heb. 9:23), and a better resurrection (Heb. 11:35). How, then, can Ariel Berkowitz claim that the Torah is capable of "hitting the mark of man's needs, including his need to know who God is"?[15] Only Jesus can hit the mark of man's need. Only in the light of the cross can we understand the awesomeness of God's righteousness (Rom. 3:21ff).

LIVING THE JEWISH WAY

Ole Kvarme is right when he insists that "to be a Jew is to live as a Jew."[16] His words echo the central message of the Messianic Movement, as well as of my own heart. But to live consistently as a Jew is not to deny or obscure the perfection of Messiah's work. It does not mean that we worship as Jews do today or that we submit to rabbinic authority. We must worship as Christians while retaining our national identity in the normal walk of life. If that is not acceptable to the rabbis, so be it. If our people reject us for doing so, that is not too high a price to pay. We owe Jesus more than we owe our beloved people.

Ole goes on to spell out what he understands by the phrase "living as a Jew," quoting an unnamed Israeli professor:

> To be a Jew is to accept Jewish history. . . . The historical consciousness is a distinct element of Jewish identity, and the historical experience of the people has helped to shape its culture, customs and Faith. To accept Jewish history is not only to rejoice in the victories of David and the Maccabees but, more than anything else, to carry the burden of centuries of suffering and the pain of the Holocaust.[17]

15. Ibid., 7–8.

16. Ole Christian Kvarme, in *Israel and Yeshua*, ed. Torleif Elgvin (Jerusalem: Caspari Center for Biblical and Jewish Studies, 1993), 16.

17. Ibid.

National Customs

We agree, and since the Jewish people are very much alive, being Jewish is not only bearing the burden of the past, but that of the present and the future. This no man can take from us. As Jewish Christians, we retain the historical consciousness shared by our people and "carry the burden of centuries of suffering and the pain of the Holocaust."

We also share with our people a present "historical experience" that renders us sensitive to outbursts of anti-Semitism around the world, to the fate of the State of Israel, and to the welfare of our people throughout the world. We share Jewish national customs and existential realities. But we reject what has become the Jewish religion because that religion denies Jesus' deity and glory, thereby denying his ability to save.

Freedom

To the extent that the present consensus of national Jewish custom is influenced by the Mosaic Covenant (in national festivals for example—and not all of these are biblical), we naturally adhere to that consensus. But we are not free to do so as a matter of religious obligation because that would be to act as if Messiah had never come, or as if his coming made no difference. Religious subservience to the Mosaic Covenant is tantamount to a denial of Messiah (Gal. 2:18–21; 5:3–4) because it assumes that the keeping of the Mosaic Covenant is part of the righteousness that should typify our obedience. It was "for freedom that Messiah has set us free" (Gal. 5:1 NIV). We must keep standing in that freedom as a testimony to the finished work of Messiah.

One of the problems with behaving as if we are subject to the law is the message our behavior conveys. Do we exemplify the truth that the law finds its fulfillment in Jesus and that because we benefit from that fulfillment we are no longer subservient to the law? Or does our lifestyle imply the opposite? Are we redeemed by the grace of God or not?

The issue at stake is the completeness of the work of Messiah and his sufficiency in a believer's life. By his sacrifice (Rom. 8:1–4) Jesus procured an entire salvation. He has secured it in us by the gift of his Spirit (Heb. 7:25, 10:14). That salvation includes our sanctification and growth in grace. Jesus is able to save fully (Acts 13:39; Rom. 8:3; Gal. 2:15–21; Heb. 9–10). Having begun in the Spirit, dare we think that we can achieve spiritual advancement by the flesh through the keeping of the Torah (Gal. 3:3)? Of course not! Nothing may be added to what Messiah has done. Believers obtain nothing through any means but the blood and Spirit of Messiah.

DID PAUL KEEP THE LAW?

What Is Salvation?

In his letter to the Galatians, Paul challenged *any* kind of Torah-keeping (see 2:18–21; 3:3, 5–6, 10, 23–25, 27; 4:1–11, 21–31; 5:1, 6–12, 16–19), for whatever gain or profit. Many interpreters wrongly limit the meaning of the term "righteousness" to what theologians like to call "justification," that is to say, the initial forgiveness of sins and the attribution of Messiah's righteousness to a believer which introduces the individual to salvation.

We saw that is not what Paul meant in Galatians, nor is it always what other New Testament writers meant when they wrote. Righteousness encompasses the whole of the Christian life. It is forgiveness, sanctification, godliness and spirituality, joy, moral conquest, and a hope that can never be disappointed.

Salvation is the ongoing development of righteousness and its increasing expression—"from glory to glory" (2 Cor. 3:18). It is the ongoing work of the Spirit, applying the finished work of Messiah. None who lead an unrighteous life may legitimately claim to be Christian; they are lost souls in need of Messiah. (See, for example, Acts 10:35; Rom. 1:17; 2:26; 5:17, 21; 6:13; 8:4; 2 Cor. 5:21; Eph. 4:24; 5:9; Phil. 1:11; 1 Tim. 6:11; 2 Tim. 2:22; Heb. 12:11; James 3:18. All such passages make a simple but important point: sanctification is the inevitable result of justification.) Moral transformation is a necessary ingredient of salvation.

Some of my Messianic friends claim that Paul remained zealous for the Torah, as did thousands of Jews in Jerusalem who believed in Jesus (Acts 21:18–23). This is incorrect. If Paul had kept the law as a matter of religious duty, he would not have been free to be "to those who are without law, as without law" (1 Cor. 9:21). He could not have insisted that the observance of days, holy days, months, weeks, and years (i.e. the Jewish feasts) is a matter for the flesh and belongs to the now-defunct "elementary principles of the world" (Col. 2:20). He could not say that he considered his Jewishness to be worthless in comparison with knowing Christ (Phil. 3:7–8). Nor could he say that those who insist upon the Jewish ritual and feasts are "not holding fast to the head" (Col. 2:19, compare Gal. 1:6–9; 5:7–12).

Messianic Views of the Torah

While writing this book, I was challenged by Paul Liberman. He insisted that "no recognized Messianic Jewish leader teaches that keeping the Torah is a duty before God, or that it conveys any kind of spiritual advantage." I wish that were true. I have already given evidence to the contrary. Here is more:

Dan Juster is a well-known and respected leader in the Jewish Messianic community. Speaking of the Mosaic Law he tells us (in *Jewish Roots*) that

> God chose Israel to be a nation of priests, a national mediator between God and the nations of the world. She was to bring the nations to God and God to the nations. How? By being a nation under God, under his rule or covenant, so that life would be blessed, just and healthy. And he has never changed this purpose.[18]

> [Only] the sacrificial dimensions of the law have been replaced by Yeshua's sacrifice.[19]

> Since Torah is essential to Judaism, a Messianic Jew must gain an accurate understanding of Torah.[20]

> Paul also maintained the validity of the law as uniquely related to Israel's continued religious national identity and special witness as a people.[21]

The confusion between national and religious identity is a significant factor in Dan's thinking, and is prevalent in the Messianic Movement. The Torah is thought of as constituting "God's external standards

18. Juster, *Jewish Roots*, 9.
19. Ibid., 39.
20. Ibid., 14.
21. Ibid., 90.

of righteousness,"[22] among which standards Dan includes the mainte-
nance of a strictly kosher kitchen, wearing fringes,[23] and celebrating the
biblical feasts.[24]

Ariel Berkowitz goes further. He states, "In the same way that Yeshua
is your life, the words of Torah are your life."[25] "As you live the Torah,
Messiah himself will stand up in you and through you for all to see."[26]
So, it is not by believing in and obeying Jesus that the righteousness of
the law is fulfilled in us (Rom. 8:3–4). As we keep the law, we partake of
Jesus who may thus be seen in us! "The words of the Torah are now our
life. When we practice Torah . . . we are also participating in our new
life—the life of God."[27] "The Torah community, created by obedience to
the Torah, is the place where life reigns instead of death. It is the place
of safety . . . the place of blessing and life."[28]

David Stern makes similar assertions. He insists, "the Torah is in
force and is to be observed."[29] In his *Jewish New Testament* he translates
Hebrews 7:12 as "there must of necessity be a transformation of Torah."[30]
He explains, "A transformation of Torah does not imply its abolition,"
only that it is "adjusted."[31] David further argues that the dietary laws are
in force and that "nothing in Galatians 2:11–14 can be construed to imply
that the Jewish dietary law shall not be observed."[32] Indeed, "when the
Jewish people become obedient and cease to break the covenant, God
will fulfill his promise to bless them as a nation."[33]

This is a disconcerting statement, which can be taken to imply
that faith in Jesus is not necessary to Israel, and that the nation can
find salvation by keeping the law. Israel's blessing is made subject to
law-keeping rather than to faith in Jesus. Conversion is not called for,

22. Ibid., 52.
23. Ibid., 56.
24. Ibid., 57.
25. Berkowitz, *Torah Rediscovered*, 145.
26. Ibid., 146.
27. Ibid., 39.
28. Ibid., 28.
29. David H. Stern, *Messianic Jewish Manifesto* (Jerusalem: Jewish New Testament Publications, 1988), 102.
30. David H. Stern, *Jewish New Testament* (Clarksville, MD: Messianic Jewish Resources International, 1989), Heb. 7:12.
31. Ibid.
32. Stern, *Messianic Jewish Manifesto*, 160.
33. Ibid., 100.

only an observance of the Torah. Then "God will fulfill his promise to bless [Israel] as a nation." By way of contrast, the writer to the Hebrews says the following:

> On the one hand, there is a setting aside of a former commandment because of its weakness and uselessness (for the Law made nothing perfect), and on the other hand there is a bringing in of a better hope, through which we draw near to God.... Jesus has become the guarantee of a better covenant. (Heb. 7:18–19, 22)

I know David well enough to know that he has said more than he intended, but such lack of caution discloses the tendency of the Messianic Movement away from Jesus toward a form of law-keeping that is contrary to the gospel. Dan Juster concludes, the law is "irrevocable."[34] "It is now by his Spirit that we are guided to do God's will" (that is to say, to keep the Torah) and "in this we are transformed step by step into the likeness of Messiah."[35]

Grace or Works

Such statements substitute Jesus' obedience to God and his finished work on the cross with our obedience to the Mosaic Law. Doing so attributes to human effort what the Bible attributes exclusively to the grace of God, supplanting the gospel of grace with a doctrine of human works. Of course, none among the above quoted authors intend to modify the gospel. They are honest, godly men. I know many of them personally and hold them in high esteem. But the direction to which their statements inexorably lead impacts the gospel in a way that renders it unrecognizable.

Either Paul was zealous for the Torah or he was not. Either the Torah filled his vision, or Messiah did. Either we obtain a full, complete, and perfect salvation from Jesus, or Jesus gets us onto the right road and the rest is up to us. One view is the gospel; the other is not. Which is which, dear reader?

Paul and the writer to the Hebrews insisted that the ceremonies of the Torah should not be observed as a means of salvation or as the way to spiritual progress. Paul was prepared to observe such ceremonies, but he refused to bind his conscience by them. Torah keeping forms no part

---

34. Juster, *Jewish Roots*, 29.
35. Ibid.

of our religion. The rabbinic assumption that Jewish national identity and religious duty are one is correct only in the sense that Jews are under obligation to believe in Jesus because he is the promised Messiah. Rabbinic Judaism is not Jewish. It constitutes a denial of the lordship of Jesus. Its fundamental concepts are contrary to biblical teaching.

Assuming that the people of Israel are still bound by the Mosaic Covenant, messianic congregations then claim that aspects of that covenant are no longer binding. This is nothing less than selective obedience, and selective obedience is no obedience at all. The Bible teaches that transgression of any commandment is tantamount to breaking them all (James 2:10). Either we are bound by the covenant or we are not. One of my correspondents insisted that those "who have faith in the promises of God, in the salvation through Jesus . . . know that there are many circumstances in which it is pleasing to God that we go beyond the boundaries established by the Torah (kosher meat laws, for example), if it will benefit the fellowship with our Gentile brothers/sisters, just as Peter and Paul did." We have no right to exercise judgment as to when duty should be suspended; God's law is not an elastic boundary which men may move when they deem suitable. Perceiving God's commandments in such a way threatens the fabric of our obedience and transforms our law-keeping into a relativistic sham.

Messianic congregations, every single one of them, fail to obey the covenant fully. They consciously and knowingly modify its commandments. None teach that gardens must lie fallow every seven years, none refuse interest on loans, and none forgive debts every seven years.

Spirituality and the Law

As we have seen, some messianic teachers insist that they find "joy"—even "life"—by obeying the law of the covenant. Apparently their experience differs from that of the apostles, who described the covenant as "a yoke which neither our fathers nor we have been able to bear" (Acts 15:10) and who insisted that Messiah had done what covenant keeping can never do (Rom. 8:1–4; Heb. 9:8–12; 10:1–18).

Covenant keeping can bring joy only when one toys at keeping the commandments. If we pick and choose, Torah-keeping becomes an interesting diversion. But when it is kept with the religious devotion that any commandment of God deserves, it becomes what it was intended to be—an exposure of our sinful inability, rendering us painfully conscious of the curse we deserve for our failures. That is what Paul meant when he spoke of the inability of the law to impart life or secure from condemnation (Rom. 8:3). That is how the law drives us to Messiah. We need him to do what we cannot do ourselves.

Those who love the Lord rejoice in him. There is nothing spiritual in a sullen, morose attitude. There is joy in having our sins forgiven because the Lord refuses to impute to us the iniquity of our sins (Ps. 32:1–2). There is joy in contemplating the Lord and his glory, reveling in his mercy, thrilling in the wonder of his love. What can be more joyful than to know and love God, who first loved us?

But those who love Jehovah may not introduce into his service duties he has not commanded, however much they may be cherished by the Jewish people. The introduction of fire, which the Lord had not commanded, and an unwarranted but well-meaning touch of the ark, brought death (Lev. 10:1–2, 2 Sam. 6:6–11). We must not worship God in terms of the Mosaic Covenant because we must not worship him as if the Messiah never came, never died, never rose, and never freed us from the ceremonial stipulations of the covenant Jehovah made with our people through Moses. We must not worship God except as he commanded because to do otherwise is to transgress his commandment. We must worship in truth, not just with sincere exuberance. Jesus has made all the difference, and our worship must reflect that difference.

Dividing the Body

One messianic ministry teaches Gentiles to keep Torah and claims a biblical basis for doing so. The editor of *Bikurei Tziyon*, published by First Fruits of Zion, writes:

> Gentiles drew closer to the God of Israel before the days of Messiah, (e.g. Ruth, Rahab) and eventually united completely with Israel in submitting to Torah. FFOZ [First Fruits of Zion] teaches that believers from the nations have that same privilege today—"one Torah shall be to him that is home born (Israeli), and unto the stranger that sojourns among you . . ." (Ex. 12:39, Num. 15:14).
>
> The prophet Isaiah also mentions those "that join themselves to the LORD . . . to be his servants, every one that keeps the Sabbath from polluting it, and takes hold of my covenant" (Isa. 56:6). Yeshua's words

cannot be clearer when he said "Whosoever shall do and teach them (the Torah), the same shall be called great in the kingdom" (Matt. 5:19). His instruction to his talmidim [disciples] was exactly this, that they should teach the nations to observe all these things (Matt. 28:20).

This is the message of the kingdom of God to those who were "born without God and without hope," to "take hold of his covenant." . . . Examples of ordinances of Torah that don't apply to those in the nations are to do with the Land of Israel . . . which even Jews outside of Israel can't observe. . . . Or those for kohanim [priests] . . . which even Jews who are not kohanim can't observe.[36]

A long-standing member of a messianic congregation wrote to Dr. Rich Nichol:

I am married to a Jewish believer and we have been attending services together for the past 20 years. Although I have been a part of the congregation for so many years I have never really felt like a member. If it were an Orthodox Jewish congregation I could convert and be accepted as a Jew. I know there are others who feel the same way. If God has called us to be a part of the body, why should we be separate?

Signed,
Feeling Excluded.

Dr. Nichol's response is indicative of the exclusivism common among adherents of the movement:

Your experience is not uncommon and actually touches on one of the most complex challenges facing Messianic Judaism. . . . In Scripture the basic human categories are Jew and Gentile. Contrary to popular opinion among many believers, these categories were not erased with the coming of the Messiah.

Nichol goes on to say that

If Jewishness is still important to God . . . then our Messianic Jewish congregations must seek to have a majority of Jews present. We must

36. "Readers' Views and Comments," *Bikurei Tziyon* 64 (May/June 2000), 9.

protect the "boundaries" so that over the long haul, the congregations will maintain their Jewish character. . . . If significant numbers of Gentiles buy in, how can the Messianic Jewish congregation ensure its Jewish makeup and character among future generations? And how can the larger Jewish community take Messianic Judaism seriously if significant numbers of non-Jews dominate the membership rolls? . . .

Such questions form a subtext in your congregation's interactions, which may lie behind your sense of low-grade rejection. . . . Messianic Jews, the remnant of Israel must protect themselves from dilution through the incursion of large numbers of Gentile believers who may or may not have as deep and abiding a commitment as your own.[37]

Dr. Nichol further states that because the New Testament does not adequately address the issue of Jewishness among Jewish believers we are "left holding the bag of an unresolved theological tension that touches the very nature of our Messianic Judaism."[38] Apart from the tacit admission that the New Testament does not provide sufficient grounds for Dr. Nichol's Messianic Judaism, and apart from charging the New Testament with inadequacy, the solution proposed is nothing less that astounding: he recommends that his correspondent convert to Messianic Judaism although, he warns, such converts are often not accepted on "an emotional/relational level"![39] In other words, even after converting to Messianic Judaism, Gentiles are likely to encounter rejection among Messianics. In conclusion Nichol urges his correspondent to "try to view your participation in a Messianic Jewish synagogue as a kind of sacrifice for the sake of the Jewish people. . . . You may be suffering a bit, but it may be very redemptive suffering."[40]

The unbiblical exaltation of Jewish religious identity in a congregation not only blurs the difference between cultural mores and biblical norms, it results in the attribution of religious authority to a tradition antagonistic to the gospel. No less grievously, it divides the body of Messiah.

We should use cultural terms that render our message intelligible to those we address. But we must never obscure the gospel. We must

---

37. Richard C. Nichol, "Ask the Rabbi," *Messianic Jewish Life* 72, no. 3 (July–September 1999), 27–28.
38. Ibid.
39. Ibid.
40. Ibid.

also respect the cultures we address by declining to attribute meanings that are not germane to their conventions. The imposition of Christian meaning onto cultural and religious symbols is not an act of respect; it is a distortion of those symbols. It cannot convey sincerity, moral courage, or confidence in the power of God's word. Evangelism is an act of worship, and our worship must always focus on him who is life eternal.

Semantics

This brings us to the issue of semantics. There is a tendency in the Messianic Jewish Movement to insist on a new, supposedly Jewish, terminology. Jesus is to be called Yeshua, the Old and New Testaments are to be described respectively as the Tanach and the Brit Chadasha, while the words "Christ," "Christian," and "church" are substituted with Hebrew terminology. It is amusing to witness the convoluted efforts that result. Messianic literature will carry reports such as the following: "On Sabbath (Saturday) our Kehila (congregation) met in order to worship Yeshua (Jesus)."

There is more to the change in terminology than meets the eye. Messianic terminology is semantics of disassociation: Christians are "converted" but Messianic Jews are "completed." Gentile evangelicals are "Christians," while Jews who believe in Jesus are "Messianic." When Messianic Jews say, "I am not a Christian,"[41] they are reconstructing the middle wall of partition, destroyed when Messiah died for Jew and Gentile. If we are fellow believers, then we are all either Christian or Messianic. The only difference between us is our respective nationalities. We share the same faith and should have the courage to admit it openly.

Moishe Rosen tells the story of a Jewish lady who heard about Yeshua and was fascinated with the beauty of his personality, the perfection of his teaching, and the wonder of his sacrificial death. "Of course I believe in him," she declared. So she became an attendee of a messianic congregation—until she discovered that Yeshua is Jesus—then she was seen no more. We must sound the gospel loud and clear, at any cost. We must insist on the essential ingredients of our faith, such as the doctrine of the Trinity, the deity of Messiah, the corruption of human nature, the

41. See Feher, *Passing Over Easter*, 80, among others.

sinfulness of mankind, the lordship of God, man's inability to please God, and the humanity and virgin birth, work, and teachings of Messiah. Less than that is less than honest, less than biblical.

Rabinowitz, a Jewish Christian pioneer in the late nineteenth century in Kishneff, worked hard to form a non-Christian body of Jewish believers in Jesus. His efforts collapsed following his death in 1899. The congregation scattered and the property he accumulated fell into the hands of his unbelieving family. Instead of focusing on Jesus, Rabinowitz focused on Jewish identity. He affirmed the deity of Jesus but avoided speaking of it in clear terms. He rejected the term "Trinity," asking, "Why should the Christian Church burden Israel? . . . We do not find anywhere in the Holy Scripture that the belief in 'The Persons' is to form a necessary part of our confession."[42] This is disconcertingly reminiscent of growing sections in the Messianic Movement. There is room to wonder to what extent Rabinowitz's adherents were truly converted.

The semantics of today become the theology of tomorrow. And unless we are careful to frame our teaching according to the word of God, our theology is liable to become false. Our main goal must be to remain true to the word of God, rather than to find acceptance by our people.

The term "Messianic" is preferred by some because it enables Jewish believers to distance themselves from the ills and evils of history. There is no denying that the Christian church persecuted the Jews in the name of the gospel and often represented the faith in ways that did little to commend it to them. However, one should not seek to disassociate oneself from those failings by disassociating from the church itself. We all have shameful pasts for which atonement is needed. We should certainly not use divergent terminologies when addressing different audiences. It is wrong for Jewish believers in Jesus to deny our Christian faith in the presence of fellow Jews, but affirm it when seeking the support and understanding of non-Jewish Christians. Honesty involves the courage to be consistent.

Some of us are in danger of obscuring the gospel by avoiding clearly biblical terminology. Jews (and Gentiles) do not need to be completed; they

42. Kai Kjaer-Hansen, *Joseph Rabinowitz and the Messianic Movement* (Edinburgh: Handsel Press, 1995), 92–93.

need to be converted. Their mindset, the tendency of their hearts, the direction of their life must be radically altered. If some among us have not been converted, they need to be.

Why has repentance all but disappeared from the language of the Messianic Movement? The gospel is a message about God's holiness and man's sinfulness, about God's grace to sinful man and about Jesus, the Savior God sent to save his people from their sins by dying in their place. Salvation is salvation from sin—forgiveness and forsaking sin. It has to do with man being freed from sin's power. Faith and repentance are necessary for salvation. If we do not preach repentance, we cannot claim to have preached the gospel.

THE PURPOSE OF THE MOSAIC COVENANT

The Purpose of the Law

The Mosaic Covenant served to distinguish Israel from the nations and their practices (such as cooking a calf in its mother's milk). No system of kashrut can be found in the Bible, only a forbidding of certain foods. There is no prohibition to eat milk with meat; that is what Abraham served the angels on their way to Sodom. The covenantal stipulations served as a tutor serves a child, until he is of age (Gal. 3:24). It preserved our national identity for a purpose, until Messiah instituted a new covenant (Jer. 31:31). God's covenant with Israel, commonly described as the Torah, was never meant to be a means by which individuals could justify themselves before God, obtain spiritual advantage, or retain their status before him. On the contrary, it taught Israel her total inability to meet God's exacting standards (Rom. 3:20).

Jesus is the goal of the Torah (Rom. 10:4). The Torah evokes a desperate search for someone to do for us what we cannot do for ourselves (Rom. 8:1–4). The Torah also teaches that salvation is all of one piece. It is impossible to claim a right standing with God unless one is *sanctified*—made holy—and the Torah teaches that none can be holy apart from God's grace. Now that Messiah has come we are "no longer under a tutor" (Gal. 3:25) and, in the context of church life, there is no room to maintain differences between Jews and Gentiles (Gal. 3:25–29, Eph. 2:11–22). There is "no difference" between us whether we are Jews or Gentiles, whatever our gender or social standing. We are one. None is subject to the Torah. It was "for freedom that Christ set us free" and it is our duty to "keep standing" in that freedom as a testimony to the finished work of Christ (Gal. 5:1). We Jewish Christians may not obscure the freedom we have in Christ (Gal. 3:23–4:11, 21–31).

The Mosaic Code—the Torah—included obligations meant for Israel alone. Beyond the ceremonial and civil aspects of the law, there were moral obligations which are reflections of the eternal nature of God himself: the proscription of lying, stealing, murder, and such, the duty and privilege to love God with all of one's being, the duty and joy of loving one's fellow human as one loves one's self. Joseph knew—without the Mosaic Covenant—that he should not commit adultery and that to do so would be to sin against God (Gen. 39:9). God punished lasciviousness and materialism in Sodom without reservation, long before the covenant was promulgated at Sinai. Sabbath was a duty imposed at creation (Gen. 2:1–3) in which man was instructed to emulate and honor his creator by resting in the finished work of the Eternal One who loved him freely. The principle of one day in seven remains our joy and duty, and shall be for all eternity.

I Am Free, But . . .

Some Messianic Jews insist that Jesus fulfilled the law and that we are therefore no longer subject to it. But, they insist, they have chosen to keep the law as a means to affirm their Jewishness. As Stan Telchin says in the introduction to this book: "We have not been called to affirm our Jewishness. We have been called to be transformed into the image of our Lord Jesus." Instead of being occupied with Jewishness, we should be focusing on Jesus, living for him, learning his word, and seeking the help of the Spirit to become more like him. What kind of Jewishness are we affirming by obeying rabbinic dictum? It is certainly not the biblical Jewishness that leads to Christ.

Jewish Christians are free from the Mosaic Covenant, but are free to keep it so long as they abstain from aspects that contradict the gospel. If they choose to keep aspects of the Mosaic Covenant, they are obliged to make it clear that the law is secondary to Messiah, and that they keep aspects of the law as a national custom, not as a religious duty. Such a message is seldom heard among Messianic Jews. Some, such as Dan Juster, David Stern, Ariel Berkowitz, Joseph Shulam and Rich Nichol, call upon Gentiles to adhere to the Mosaic Law. David tells us in his *Manifesto*: "If a Gentile Christian wants to identify fully with the Jewish people, the New Testament allows him to become a Jew. He should accept the whole Torah as understood by the form of Judaism to which he is converting."[43]

In contrast, Paul's words in the letter to the Galatians are so strongly against promoting the law that I dare quote only portions. For a Gentile to become a Jew is to embrace a "different gospel—which is really no gospel at all" (Gal. 1:6-7 NIV); it is not to be "straightforward about the truth of the gospel" (Gal. 2:14); to render Messiah "a minister of sin" (Gal. 2:17); to act foolishly (Gal. 3:3); to be "severed from Messiah" (Gal. 5:4); to have "fallen from grace" (Gal. 5:4). Conversion to Judaism is never an option for Gentile followers of Jesus. Their love for Messiah, their devotion to God, and their gratitude for the salvation procured for them at so great a price should prevent them from allowing such a thought to enter their mind.

Why would they consider law-keeping? Peter tells us that the recipients of his letters, although mostly Gentile, shared Israel's ancestral prerogatives in accordance with the divine purpose framed before the world began (1 Peter 2:1-10). Scan his two letters. There is not the slightest intimation that Gentiles may or could in any way be advantaged by keeping the Torah or becoming Jewish. There is nothing positive about Jewishness in Peter's letters, only a display of the grace of God in Jesus.

EPHESIANS: ONE IN MESSIAH

The Past Has Passed

There is no need for Gentiles to be Jewish. God has blessed Jews and Gentiles "with every spiritual blessing in the heavenly places in Christ," just as he had them in mind before he made the world, intending for them to be "holy and blameless before Him" (Eph. 1:3-4). God lovingly destined us to be adopted through Jesus so that we would be

> to the praise of the glory of His grace, which He freely bestowed on us in the Beloved. In Him we have redemption through His blood,

43. Stern, *Messianic Jewish Manifesto*, 178ff.

the forgiveness of our trespasses, according to the riches of His
grace. (Eph. 1:6–7)

He lavished that grace on us with utter wisdom, "made known to us the
mystery of His will," a mystery shaped by his kindness and conceived in
himself (v. 9), "summing up of all things in Messiah, things in the heavens
and things on the earth" (v. 10). Jesus is the goal for which everything
was created—Jesus, not Jewishness.

In Jesus we all—Jews and Gentiles—"have obtained an inheritance"
through him who causes everything to work according to his will, so that
we (Jews), who were "the first to hope in Messiah," should be to the praise
of his glory. In him, you (Gentiles) have also, as a pledge, been "sealed in
Him with the Holy Spirit of promise" when you heard the gospel and
believed it (vv. 11–13). That is why Paul tells the Ephesians that, after
hearing of their faith and love in Jesus, he has been giving continual
thanks for them, praying that God will enlighten them to understand
"the hope of His calling," the richness of the joys we inherit from him
together in Messiah, the enormity of the power that is involved in our
transformation—the same power that raised Jesus from the dead and
placed him "far above" everything in all times and locations. That same
power made Jesus to be "head over all things to the church, which is His
body, the fullness of Him who fills all in all" (vv. 22–23).

You (Gentiles) were "dead in your trespasses and sins" (Eph. 2:1). We
(Jews) "were by nature children of wrath" like everyone else (v. 3). But God
loved us both and gave us new life in Messiah. We have been saved by
grace (v. 5). He "seated us with Him in the heavenly places in Christ Jesus"
to display the glory of his grace toward us in Messiah (vv. 6–7). You have
been saved by grace through faith (v. 8). Grace gave you the faith that saved
you. Grace acted with a specific goal in view: that no one could attribute
salvation to himself (vv. 8–9). So, remember that you were "once Gentiles
in the flesh," despised by those who knew themselves to be the people of
God (v. 11 NKJV). You used to be "separate from Messiah, excluded from
the commonwealth of Israel, and strangers to the covenants of promise,
having no hope and without God in the world" (v. 12). You are no longer
strangers to the covenants of promise. You have hope because you have
God. Jesus "broke down the barrier of the dividing wall by abolishing in

His flesh the enmity, which is the law of commandments contained in ordinances" (vv. 14–15).

"Formerly," Paul said. Used to be—now no longer (see v. 19 and following). Formerly distant Gentiles have been brought near by the sacrifice of Messiah. Near to whom? Near to God. The dividing wall between Jews and Gentiles has been broken down. God destroyed the enmity created between us by the distinctions required by the Torah and made of the two one new man. In this way he established peace between us and, at the same time, reconciled us both to himself through the body of Christ, destroying the righteous enmity he harbored toward us due to our sin (vv. 13–16).

Messiah has come. He preached peace with God and with our fellow man to Gentiles and Jews. Through Messiah we "both have access to the Father by one Spirit" (v. 18 NIV). So, Gentiles no longer differ from Jews in terms of relationship to God or with regard to the privileges that flow from that relationship. Gentiles are "no longer strangers" but, with Jews, are founded "on the foundation of the apostles and prophets," Jesus being "the corner stone" (vv. 19–20).

No Longer Strangers

That is why Paul said he was "the prisoner of Christ Jesus for the sake of you Gentiles" (Eph. 3:1), assigned the divine task to declare a once-hidden message, revealed to him so that he might make it known. The mystery is this: Gentiles share with Jews in the inheritance and the promises and belong to the same body in Jesus the Messiah through the gospel (Eph. 3:1–6). Paul said that this privilege was accorded him, the least worthy, "to preach to the Gentiles the unfathomable riches of Messiah and to bring to light [how] . . . the mystery which for ages has been hidden in God who created all things" and which I described above, is to be worked out (vv. 8–9). This is not a departure from the Torah or from the promises of the prophets; it is in full accordance with God's eternal purposes (vv. 10–11).

Living It Out

In light of oft-repeated claims, it is surprising to note that Paul makes no reference in this letter to keeping Jewish traditions or the

Torah. Calling upon Jews and Gentiles to live out their newfound unity in Messiah, he calls them not to live like Gentiles—that is to say—in sin (Eph. 4:17–32). Gentiles are no longer to live as Gentiles, but this does not imply the adoption of Jewish custom but of biblical moral norms, spelled out in what follows.

The new practices which the Ephesians are to inculcate are loving truthfulness, self-control, honesty with regard to material possessions, kindness in human relations, a high work ethic, liberality toward those in need, purity of speech, moral sensitivity (which will assist us not to grieve the Spirit), tender forgiveness, and kindness (Eph. 4:17–31, see also 5:3–6:9). The standard Paul sets is not the Torah, but the example of Messiah (Eph. 4:32, see also 5:23–24, 25–28, 29), for Jesus is the new law. Indeed, Paul says, to imitate Jesus is to imitate God himself (Eph. 5:1–2). Ariel Berkowitz insists: "the relationship of the non-Jewish person to the Torah is one of permission and encouragement. . . . They are entitled to follow Torah."[44] Paul says, follow Christ and in so doing you will fulfill the law.

What would happen if all the Gentiles, or all the Christian Gentiles, observed the Torah? In what way—according to Messianic Jewish views— would Israel be distinct from the other nations? Claude Montefiore was right when he stated: "Judaism's institutions and laws and embodiment are . . . national."[45] Some Messianic Jews insist, therefore, that only Jewish Christians are bound to keep the Torah. But on what grounds do we distinguish between the duties of Jews and Gentiles in Messiah? How can Ariel or David Stern claim that "the elements of Torah which apply to Gentiles under the New Covenant are not the same as those which apply to Jews"?[46] There is no inkling of such a difference in the New Testament.

In terms of spiritual realities, duties, and benefits, there is *no difference* between Jews and Gentiles. No difference because the dividing wall which distinguished between Jews and Gentiles has been destroyed.

Jews who believe in Jesus should not observe the Mosaic Law as a matter of religious duty because doing so is to rebuild what Messiah has destroyed. If keeping the law is not necessary for the spiritual health of Gentiles, why is it necessary for Jews? Either the Mosaic Law conveys

---

44. Berkowitz, *Torah Rediscovered*, 64, 69.
45. Claude Montefiore, *Liberal Judaism and Hellenism* (London: MacMillan and Co., 1918), 303–5.
46. Stern, *Messianic Jewish Manifesto*, 156.

spiritual advantages or it does not. If it does, all the followers of Jesus are obliged to keep it because we are all bound to be the utmost for God, to strive for the highest possible level of spirituality. Either the law conveys spiritual advantage, or such an advantage is the gift of God's grace.

THE ESSENCE OF THE LAW

Morality

Paul speaks in Romans of Gentiles keeping the law. In chapter 2 he speaks of Gentiles, who "do not have the Law" (v. 14), who had not been given the covenant at Sinai and did not know the laws of that covenant. Yet, he says, they "do instinctively the things of the Law" and thereby "show the work of the Law written in their hearts" (vv. 14–15). Paul is saying that the law of God may also be found outside the Covenant of Sinai, and that non-Jews are cognizant of it apart from that Covenant. The reason for this is that the law of the Covenant is a reflection of the image of God in which all men are created.

In chapter one Paul stated that even determined sinners are aware of the law to the extent that "they know the ordinance of God, that those who practice such things [described in the preceding section] are worthy of death" (Rom. 1:32). What is Paul talking about? Do Gentiles instinctively wear a tsitsit (fringes), keep a kosher kitchen, and celebrate Passover? Of course not. Paul is speaking of the moral aspects of the law, found in the Ten Commandments. These are universally and eternally binding because they are reflections of the divine image. He is talking about speaking the truth, respecting other people's property, marital faithfulness, avoiding covetousness, and giving each man his due.

Pharaoh and Abimelech knew the difference between right and wrong apart from the law (Gen. 12:13–19; 26:6–11), and Joseph knew that he should not have another man's wife (Gen. 39:6–9). Jesus permitted the eating of non-kosher foods (Mark 7:18–19). He taught that the preservation and promulgation of the spirit of the Mosaic Law sometimes required its literal transgression. Jeremiah, the priest, bought land (Jer. 32:6–15) although priests were forbidden by the Torah to do so. If the law is treated as an end in itself, it fails to fulfill its important function of leading us to Messiah. Instead, it enslaves us. Treated properly, it is a wonderful instrument of grace.

The moral aspects of the Mosaic Law are to be kept by all. All are bound by God's moral law and always shall be. That is why the Ten Commandments had special status in the Mosaic Covenant. They are a summary of the eternal, moral law of God, a description of how every human must live. That is why they—but no other parts of the law—were written by the finger of God. That is why they—and no other parts of the law—were placed in the ark. All mankind is bound by the moral law of God because to break that law is to disfigure the image of God in man, to rebel against God.

The moral law is a revelation of the glory and holiness of God to which all men are obliged to aspire, and by which all will be measured. It is by the light of that law we learn that we are sinners, in need of saving grace. God's revelation of his holiness and of the holiness he demands of man were enunciated from Sinai and encapsulated in a covenantal form that included rituals and civil arrangements meant for a time, *until* Messiah came.

The Law Is Eternal

The civil and ritual aspects of the law are not essential to the law itself. They are the shadow, not the substance. They were signposts pointing to Messiah, his atoning death and the need for atonement, to his power to transform and to our need for such a transformation. Ritual was never the heart of the law. David transgressed the ritual aspects of the law when he and his men ate bread from the table of shewbread (1 Sam. 21, compare Lev. 24:3–9). The Priests had to work on the Sabbath in the tabernacle: trimming the lights, clearing ashes from the altar, carrying wood for the fire, and watching over the conduct of the tabernacle, yet they were not charged with acting unlawfully.

That is why Paul could say, "circumcision is nothing, and uncircumcision is nothing, but what matters is the keeping of the commandments of God" (1 Cor. 7:19). He is not denying that God commanded the people of Israel to be circumcised. He is saying that the burden of the law is not ritualistic but a call for a morality that is motivated by the fear of God. This was also the main burden of the prophet's message. Ritualistic emphasis at the expense of moral adherence is an abomination in God's sight.

The eternal law of God remains in force apart from the demise of its civil and ritualistic elements. None of us is free to steal, lie, or engage in sexual promiscuity. All are bound to love and honor God. The law was binding before it was promulgated at Sinai. It will continue to bind humanity in the new heavens and the new earth, when God becomes all in all. The substance remains, unchanged, although the mode of administration has been altered. God makes identical demands on all mankind. He does so on the grounds of his divine sovereignty: everything must suit his perfect will. As long as God is God, he will demand holiness from his rational creatures. That is the law that Jesus satisfied for us by his perfect life and his glorious death. That is "the righteous requirements of the law," which his Spirit fulfills in and through us (Rom. 8:4 NIV). That is the righteousness to which our regeneration by the grace of God has bound us (Rom. 6:1–19), and that is the law the apostle repeatedly broke and therefore cried out to God for mercy (Rom. 7:1–13).

Holiness is the product of the Spirit's work in man, accomplished through regeneration. It consists of inner conformity to the righteousness of the law, and it is expressed in deeds worthy of God and his Messiah. The law inaugurates the gospel and is accomplished through the gospel. It sets the standards of God's holiness before man and says, "do this and live."

> You must work your soul to save
> and God's commands be done.
> You must work like any slave—
> If not, you are undone.

Our inescapable failure to meet that standard leads us to recognize our guilt and inability, evoking in us a craving that can be met by nothing but the grace of God. The gospel is the message of God's grace in making up for our lack of law-keeping and in remaking us into his perfect image (Col. 3:10) as reflected in the law. In this way the Torah leads to the gospel; the gospel to fulfillment of the law and to glorifying God. As someone once put it,

> I would not work my soul to save
> for that my Lord has done;
> But I will work like any slave
> for love of his dear son.

We are not under a new law but the old one in a new form. We are no longer bound to the rituals and civil forms in the Covenant of Moses, but its moral aspects frame our moral and spiritual aspirations as we seek conformity to the image of God. The moral aspects of the Mosaic Law have lost none of their authority. They are the rule of life for all who live by grace. That is why the English Puritans and the Scottish covenanters identified so warmly with our forefathers. They longed and prayed for the salvation of our people. They knew themselves to be bound to us by common duties, common hopes, and common aspirations promulgated in the Mosaic Law.

MESSIAH AND THE LAW

The ritual aspects of the law, its symbols, hopes, and expectations, find fulfillment in Jesus. Having been fulfilled, they have lost much of their former value. The shadows have made way for the substance. It is wrong to insist upon shadows as if they were still in force. The Mosaic ritual, the sacrifices, the feasts, the specific form of the Sabbath duties, and the dress code requirements are no longer binding. Some of these remain part of our national culture. But we may not live as if they are still binding. It is our glad and happy duty to demonstrate by our lives, our worship, and our communal behavior that Messiah has come.

The ritual aspects of the law, particularly the sacrifices, intimated God's method of salvation. But salvation was never provided by the sacrifices except as they reflected the sacrifice of Messiah. It was "not possible" that "the blood of bulls and goats" could provide a sufficient sacrifice (Heb. 10:4 NKJV). The promise of forgiveness made in the Torah was dependent on the sacrifice of Messiah. It derived strength from that ultimate sacrifice. To think and live as if the coming of Messiah did not alter our relation to the Mosaic Law is to ignore the biblical message, which declares "the law was given through Moses; grace and truth were realized through Jesus Christ" (John 1:17). This statement contrasts two periods—that of the Law of Moses with that of grace through Jesus, the Messiah.

Leo Baeck was right. In a section titled "The Faith of Paul" he states that in Paul's writings, "The knowledge of God . . . is different from what is meant in Judaism. By proclaiming the risen Christ he proclaimed the presence of God's kingdom: 'Now the righteousness of God without the law is manifested.'[47] On the same page Baeck summarizes the implications of Paul's teaching by saying, "If the days of Messiah have come, those of the Torah have come to their close."[48] To prove his point, Baeck refers his readers to ancient Jewish sources which arrive at the same conclusion, such as Yalkut Isaiah 26:2 ("The Holy One—may he be blessed—will sit (in the Garden of Eden) and draw up a new Torah for Israel, which will be given to them by the Messiah."), Niddah 61b ("the commandments will no longer apply in time to come," i.e., after the resurrection). See also Pesahim 50a.

The apostolic church did not at first realize the broader implications of the teachings of Jesus. The original followers of Jesus never considered proclaiming the gospel to Gentiles. When it was proclaimed, they thought that Gentiles who believed should join the community of Israel and assume the full yoke of Mosaic and rabbinic traditions. Such a misunderstanding was to be expected. Israel had been taught to think of herself as the sole object of God's saving kindness. The law of God, with the temple sacrifices, sacred calendar, and list of forbidden foods, had come to be considered essential to the way God was to be served and what it meant to be Jewish. It was difficult to think in other terms until, in the course of time, the leaven of the gospel impacted their understanding and transformed their attitudes. Peter vacillated between eating with the Gentiles in Caesarea (Acts 10–11) and in Galatia (Gal. 2:12), and refraining from doing so for fear of the group from Jerusalem (Gal. 2:12).

Understanding the fuller import of Messiah's accomplishments came only gradually. As the number of Gentile believers in Jesus increased, issues came to a head and the Holy Spirit enlightened the church. As long as the community of faith consisted largely of Jews, the implications of Jesus' teaching with regard to the law and the traditions did not need to be worked out. As the law was understood in light of Jesus there were differences of opinion that resulted in tensions evidenced in the New Testament.

This was the major issue in most of Paul's letters. We've already looked at Galatians and Ephesians. In a moment we'll review Colossians.

47. Leo Baeck, *Judaism and Christianity: Essays by Leo Baeck* (New York: The Jewish Publication Society of America, 1958), 160–61.
48. Ibid.

We also looked at the letter to the Hebrews. The issue was as simple as it was crucial: is Jesus sufficient or is he not? Are the law (Galatians), spiritual experience (the letters to the Corinthians), Judaism (Philippians) and mystical knowledge (Colossians) necessary to make up for what he left undone? The supremacy of Jesus, the sufficiency of his work, and the unity of the church were but different angles of the same truth. In love with Messiah who loved him and gave himself for him, and motivated by the Holy Spirit, Paul refused to allow anything to arrogate what belongs to Jesus. Will you?

COLOSSIANS: PERFECT IN MESSIAH

In Colossae there were those who, like the mistaken brethren in Galatia, claimed to have found the way to a higher level of spirituality—what they chose to describe as a "fullness" (Col. 2:10 NIV), as "putting off the sinful nature" (v. 11 NIV), or as obtaining a kind of spiritual insight (vv. 2–3). They insisted on obeying a combination of rituals, such as circumcising (vv. 11, 13), avoiding certain foods (v. 21), celebrating religious festivals, the appearance of New Moons and Sabbath days (v. 16), and keeping other regulations. They were fascinated with angels and overt forms of self-humiliation (v. 18). Apparently, mystical concepts (for which Colossae was notorious), combined with aspects of Judaism, had influenced the young church.

Elemental Principles

Paul was concerned by these trends. He warned the Colossian Christians not to be deceived "by fine-sounding arguments" (Col. 2:4 NIV) and called upon them to see to it "that no one takes [them] captive through hollow and deceptive philosophy, which depends on human tradition and the basic principles of this world rather than on Christ" (v. 8 NIV). Note, the source of such views of spirituality is "human tradition," a tradition described as the product of "the basic principles of this world." To embrace these is nothing less than to let go of Christ! Echoes of Paul's argument in his letter to the Galatians are obvious. Paul reiterates in verse 19: whoever follows this tradition "has lost connection with the Head" (NIV), that is Christ, on whom the health and growth of the whole body depends. Instead of going forward to perfection, the Colossians were in danger of receding to basic principles.

What does Paul mean by "the basic principles of this world"? A similar term appears in his letter to the Galatians. The discussion there will help us identify those principles. As you will remember, the problem in Galatia arose because a group from Jerusalem taught that faith in Jesus was not enough. Circumcision and the keeping of the law were required for what they described as "righteousness" (the Jewish version of *fullness*). Paul asked, "Did you receive the Spirit by observing the law, or by believing what you heard? Are you so foolish? After beginning with the Spirit, are you now trying to obtain your goal by human effort?" (Gal. 3:2–3 NIV). He then made his point by saying, "When we were children we were in slavery under the basic principles of the world" (Gal. 4:3 NIV), that is to say, under the Mosaic Law. He asked, "Now that you know God—or rather are known by God—how is it that you are turning back to those weak and miserable principles? Do you wish to be enslaved by them all over again?" (v. 9 NIV). He explained in the following verse: "You observe days and months and seasons and years" (v. 10). The "basic principles of this world" are teachings that require human effort to obtain spiritual progress rather than trusting in divine grace—including efforts couched in terms of the Mosaic Law.

Messiah or the Law

What, then, is the way to spiritual perfection? Paul's reply is concise: The way to be "perfect in Christ" is to focus on Christ: "We proclaim him" (Col. 1:28), declares the apostle. In him are to be found "all the treasures of wisdom and knowledge" (Col. 2:3). We are to continue in Christ on the basis of grace, just as we received him and are rooted and built up in him, because in him "all the fullness of the Deity lives in bodily form" (v. 9 NIV). By grace we have been allowed to share in the "fullness" that is "in Christ."

Rather than in glorying in a circumcision performed by human hands, ours is a spiritual circumcision of the heart, performed by God (Col. 2:11). Paul is referring Israel's call through the prophets (Deut. 30:6; Jer. 4:4. See also Jer. 31:32; Ezek. 11:19) to circumcise their hearts and to the divine promise to do just that for them. God has removed our sinful nature through grace and given us a part in the death, burial, and resurrection of Jesus, as typified in baptism (Col. 2:11–12). We were dead in our sins, but God made us alive in Christ. He disarmed the evil powers arrayed against us and "cancelled the written code, with its regulations, that was against us and that stood opposed to us; he took it away, nailing it to the cross" (v. 14 NIV). The Mosaic Covenant accused us, but its claim died when we were put to death in Messiah. Human tradition placed demands upon us, but they have no hold any longer. Having died by grace with Christ to "the basic principles of this world," we ought not to live as if subject to them (v. 20 NIV). We are no longer to submit to their authority.

Such submission, admittedly, has "an appearance of wisdom," with "their self-imposed worship, their false humility and their harsh treatment of the body" (v. 23 NIV). But the regulations lack the ability to restrain sensual indulgence. In fact, it awakens the very senses it is supposed to subdue. Only grace can change us, and grace comes from Christ, not from keeping Mosaic stipulations or human tradition.

We should be taken up with Jesus. Our hearts should be set "on things above," where Jesus sits at the right hand of God (Col. 3:1 NIV). In Christ we are dead, and our life is "hidden with Christ in God" (v. 3 NIV). Whatever others might tell us, ultimate glory is not to be experienced here and now. "When Christ, who is [our] life, appears, then [we] will also appear with him in glory" (v. 4 NIV). We are to wait with confident joy and labor with eager expectation. Instead of being taken up with matters here on earth (rules about touching and eating, angelic appearances, and the exact dates of feasts), we're to be taken up with him who is our life. Spirituality is found by focusing on Messiah, not on the Torah. At the same time we are to struggle against our love of sin, relying on grace rather than on our efforts (vv. 4-17). That is the only way to spirituality. Jews have no advantage over Gentiles with regard to spirituality because we Jews are sinners no less than the Gentiles. The church is one in this respect as in any other. To deny that oneness is to render Gentiles second-rate citizens of the kingdom.

ACTS 10–11, 15: NO DISTINCTION

Cornelius

The apostolic church did not, at first, understand the unity of the church in sin and in grace. Peter had to defend his right to preach the gospel to the Gentiles and to fellowship with them freely (Acts 10:13; 11:12). Remember? He had spent some days in Caesarea, at the home of Cornelius (Acts 10:48). The charge against Peter and his companions was that they had gone "to uncircumcised men and ate with them" (Acts 11:3). In other words, Peter had not observed the national traditions. He had eaten (non-kosher food) at Cornelius' table. He had not maintained the distinction between himself—a Jew—and the Gentiles of Cornelius' household (see Acts 10:47; 11:17–18; 15:9). Peter's defense refers only to the preaching of the gospel because the gospel overrides everything else and because it is the gospel that made him and Cornelius, his Jewish Christian comrades, and the members of Cornelius' household equals. If God had "made no distinction" between Jews and Gentiles with respect to the gospel, no difference was to be maintained (Acts 15:9; see also 11:15-17).

The brethren in Jerusalem were persuaded when they heard that God had given uncircumcised Gentiles the Holy Spirit in the same manner that he had previously given the Spirit to the Jews (Acts 10:45, 11:17). God had not made a difference, so the issue was settled—at least for a time. If the Gentiles could be converted without observing Judaism, Jews were no longer to maintain the difference between Jews and Gentiles in Christ. The dividing wall between Jews and Gentiles had been dismantled by grace. They were now bound to express and maintain the unity of all believers in Messiah.

In Antioch

The same issue arose when Peter, Barnabas, and Paul were in Antioch. Emissaries from James in Jerusalem demanded that the Gentiles follow their faith in Jesus by being circumcised. We have looked at the letter to the Galatians, where Paul relates the story. Peter and Barnabas had erred by withdrawing from table fellowship with the Gentile believers. Paul challenged them. The two were apparently convinced of their error, mended their ways, and joined Paul in his controversy with the Jerusalemites who had caused such a stir (Acts 15:2, 6–12).

The question could have remained: are the Gentiles in any way obliged to the Mosaic Covenant or to Jewish traditions? Peter's argument later, in Jerusalem, was as passionate as it was logical: God had sent him to preach to the Gentiles and bore witness to Peter's ministry. "He made no distinction between us and them, cleansing their hearts by faith. Now therefore why do you put God to the test by placing upon the neck of the disciples a yoke which neither our fathers nor we have been able to bear?" (Acts 15:9–11). The decision arrived at by the convened church in Jerusalem, apostles and elders included, carried no intimation of spiritual advantage purportedly attached to keeping the Torah or to insights Gentiles could gain if they kept the traditions. Instead, the Gentiles were declared free from all such traditions. They were merely asked to treat their fellow believers from among the Jews with loving patience by abstaining from certain foods and patterns of behavior. Some of these caused offense because they were contrary to God's law (idolatry, for example). Others were the product of long-established habits (dietary restrictions). This latter requirement was the only restriction imposed beyond the moral obligations to which all mankind is bound. This was the product of an effort to take contemporary Jewish Christian sensitivities into account, not to impose a religious obligation.

ACTS 21: HOW ABOUT PAUL?

Did Paul Oppose the Traditions?

The believers in Jerusalem had yet to digest the implications of the death and resurrection of Messiah, but they already understood that there was no spiritual advantage in keeping the law. That was the first step. So long as it was understood that the law was unnecessary for the service of God, the rest would fall into place. The church concluded, as did Paul Liberman in *The Fig Tree Blossoms*, that keeping the ritual and civil aspects of the Mosaic Law is "no longer required."[49] It took time for the church to realize the practical implications of that conclusion, and the apostle was wise enough to accommodate himself to the inability of his brethren. He did not engage in an all-out war against Jewish traditions, nor should we. He did not spend his time calling upon "all the Jews who are among the Gentiles to forsake Moses, telling them not to circumcise their children nor to walk according to the customs" (Acts 21:21). He had better things to do: he was a preacher of the gospel.

A rumor had risen to the contrary. Its credibility came from the simple fact that many of the Jews converted under Paul in fact forsook

49. Liberman, *The Fig Tree Blossoms*, 36.

the traditions. They "lived like Gentiles." Paul did not castigate them for doing so. Delighted with their freedom in Messiah, some might have gone to the extreme of shaking off anything distinctly Jewish. Paul addressed that issue when he wrote to the Corinthians, insisting that Jews remain Jews and Gentiles remain Gentiles because each of these national identities was a calling (1 Cor. 7:17–20, 23). He was anxious to preserve the peace of the church and therefore agreed to participate in the traditional vows (Acts 21:23–26). He would make it publicly clear that he was not opposed to Jewish traditions as such. Seeing him "walk orderly, keeping the law" (Acts 21:24) would show all that there was nothing to the charges against him. This was not an inconsistency. Paul had already taught that circumcision—that most sacred of the symbols of Jewishness—and uncircumcision were unimportant ("nothing," 1 Cor. 7:19). But he would yield for the sake of peace.

You may disagree with my construction but, surely, you must acknowledge that it is at least possible. The customary Messianic way of interpreting Paul's action as described in Acts 21 is open to question. I invite my readers to compare the two views with the rest of Paul's writings and with Luke's narrative in Acts. I am persuaded readers will conclude with me that, in taking on the financial burden involved in the vows the brethren had made, Paul was accommodating his weaker brethren. He was *becoming* as under the law, a Jew to the Jews. Adherents of the Messianic Movement describe subservience to the Torah as a strength. They are mistaken. Law-keeping is not a means to spiritual progress; it is a retrograde.

> Accept him whose faith is weak, without passing judgment on disputable matters. One man's faith allows him to eat everything, but another man, whose faith is weak, eats only vegetables. The man who eats everything must not look down on him who does not, and the man who does not eat everything must not condemn the man who does, for God has accepted him. Who are you to judge someone else's servant? To his own master he stands or falls. And he will stand, for the Lord is able to make him stand. . . .
>
> Therefore let us stop passing judgment on one another. Instead, make up your mind not to put any stumbling block or obstacle in your brother's way. As one who is in the Lord Jesus, I am fully convinced that no food is unclean in itself. But if anyone regards something as unclean,

then for him it is unclean. If your brother is distressed because of what you eat, you are no longer acting in love. Do not by your eating destroy your brother for whom Christ died. Do not allow what you consider good to be spoken of as evil. For the kingdom of God is not a matter of eating and drinking, but of righteousness, peace and joy in the Holy Spirit, because anyone who serves Christ in this way is pleasing to God and approved by men.

Let us therefore make every effort to do what leads to peace and to mutual edification. Do not destroy the work of God for the sake of food. All food is clean, but it is wrong for a man to eat anything that causes someone else to stumble. It is better not to eat meat or drink wine or to do anything else that will cause your brother to fall.

So whatever you believe about these things keep between yourself and God. Blessed is the man who does not condemn himself by what he approves. But the man who has doubts is condemned if he eats, because his eating is not from faith; and everything that does not come from faith is sin. (Rom. 14:1–4, 13–23 NIV)

If it was up to us, none of us would be sanctified. Our salvation and our sanctification are the fruit of God's work for and in us. We are saved and sanctified by grace. Does grace need to be supplemented by works? If it does, it is no longer grace because its fulfillment is dependent on human effort. The grace that saves and sanctifies is the same grace that secures our ultimate glorification: "neither height nor depth, nor anything else in all creation, will be able to separate us from the love of God that is in Christ Jesus our Lord" (Rom. 8:39 NIV). There is no room for human boasting. No flesh can glory in God's presence or attribute the smallest iota of accomplishment to itself. "By *His* doing you are in Christ Jesus, who became to us wisdom from God, and righteousness and sanctification, and redemption" (1 Cor. 1:30).

Following Messiah

Jesus, not the Torah, is the way, the truth, and the life. Jesus does not say, "Follow the Torah" or "Maintain your traditions," but "Follow me." He frequently demonstrated his opposition to any thought of religious obligation toward the traditions, incurring the anger of the Pharisees. If we follow him, we will incur similar anger. We are to love Jesus more than anything else—more than our nation, our spouses, our siblings, our parents, or ourselves. There is no other way to be his disciples. Messiah demands an absolute devotion, shared with none. The way to love God is to esteem his Son above all. We have not understood the gospel properly until we have understood that "every good and perfect gift is from above" (James 1:17 NIV), not as the product of our efforts. That is what biblical faith is all about. It focuses on God in Messiah and rests entirely on him. The gospel rules out anything that man might add.

> Those who want to make a good impression outwardly are trying to compel [us] to be circumcised. The only reason they do this is to avoid being persecuted for the cross of Christ. Not even those who are circumcised obey the law, yet they want [us] to be circumcised that they may boast about [our] flesh. May [we] never boast except in the cross of our Lord Jesus Christ, through which the world has been crucified to [us], and [we] to the world. Neither circumcision nor uncircumcision means anything; what counts is a new creation. Peace and mercy to all who follow this rule, even to the Israel of God. . . .
>   The grace of our Lord Jesus Christ be with your spirit, brothers. Amen. (Gal. 6: 12–16, 18 NIV)

We are free. No law can condemn us, harass our consciences, or command our attention. Our eyes are on Jesus, the originator and completer of our faith. The law brings wrath, but "we have peace with God through our Lord Jesus Christ" (Rom. 5:1). In spite of repeated failures, "in my inner being I delight in God's law" (Rom. 7:22 NIV), yet live, not by the law but "by faith in the Son of God who loved [us] and gave himself for [us]" (Gal. 2:20 NIV). Dead to the law, we live for Messiah, rejecting all glorying but in the cross of Messiah Jesus our Lord (Gal. 6:14), by which we "died to the world," its mocking, its promises, its pressures, and its pleasures, even when they originate from our beloved nation or its vaunted religious leaders.

Hallelujah!

3

Rabbinic Customs

NATIONAL IDENTIFICATION

Jesus never challenged the Torah, although he frequently challenged its traditional rabbinic interpretation. Hagner reminds us, "The difference between the Rabbis and Jesus in their attitude to the law cannot be denied. It is basically this difference that led to the death of Jesus."[1] The Pharisees had little difficulty with Jesus' claim to be the Messiah. What they could not accept was his questioning their interpretations of the Torah. Note what Hagner has just said: what led to Jesus' death, so far as the rabbis were concerned, was his attitude to their tradition. With whom do *we* side? The repeated charge against Paul also had to do with his attitude to the traditions, not with his views of Jesus. To submit now to rabbinic interpretation is tantamount to taking issue with Jesus in his conflict with the Pharisees, to siding against Paul against the same foes.

The conflict between Judaism and the message of Messiah is not one of fulfillment over expectation. It is between Messiah and misguided rabbinical insistence of the Torah as interpreted by them; between redemption by divine grace and the stubborn belief that one is capable of achieving divine approbation by keeping the law; between the divine authority of the Son of God and that of the rabbis. The gospel is not the message of Messiah Rabbinic Judaism; it is its replacement. Judaism as interpreted by the rabbis is not Jewish.

1. Donald A. Hagner, *The Jewish Reclamation of Jesus: An Analysis and Critique of the Modern Jewish Study of Jesus* (Grand Rapids: Zondervan, 1984), 89.

The message of Messiah is the fulfillment of all the biblical hopes nourished in the bosom of God's promises to Israel; it is a denial of the hopes framed by rabbinic scholars in the painful crucible of Jewish existence and of the distorted vision of a distinctly Jewish version of human sin, salvation, and purported ability. It is a message for all mankind, brought to the world through the Jewish people, about a Savior for all nations. It is not about Jewish distinctive, but about the glory of God in the face of Jesus, the Messiah.

Judaism's view of God denies the Trinity and refuses to accord God other glories due him. He is presented as subject to the dictums of the rabbis, effectively absent from the world but for the wider movements of history, and dependent on Israel's good works for the accomplishment of his purposes. Sin is no more and no less than an overt transgression of the Mosaic Law and of rabbinic tradition, particularly in terms of ritualistic practice. (When did you last hear a rabbi preach against moral sin, such as tax evasion?) Obedience as conceived by the rabbis does not require the heart's involvement, although such involvement is considered desirable. It is enough to carry out the ritualistic commandments of the law as interpreted by Israel's religious leaders. Grace and a substitutionary sacrifice are not needed for salvation; we simply need to outweigh our bad deeds with good ones. Unlike the Gentiles, "all Israel have their place in the world to come."[2] In my appendix "Justification in Judaism" you will see how far Judaism has removed itself from the joyful confidence of divine grace in which King David exulted.

Of course, Judaism is eclectic; one can always find a quote that proves the opposite. But the convictions described above are shared by the majority of rabbis and by the overwhelming majority of the Jewish religious population. Judaism contradicts the gospel. Judaism is, therefore, not Jewish because it is not biblical.

Messianic Judaism is united in its insistence upon the necessity of at least a semblance of adherence to rabbinic tradition. The motives for such adherence differ. Some insist it is merely a means of national identification. I have little argument with such a view so long as our adherence is subject to Messiah in more than just words, and so long as the custom to which one adheres is part of the national consensus. If we

2. *Mishnah*, Sanhedrin, 11:1.

follow tradition without attributing to it religious significance beyond the facts of history it celebrates, we are acting as Jews in terms of our culture. But the national consensus that unites Jews does not include, for example, the lighting of candles on Sabbath, keeping kosher, wearing a kippa or a tallit katan, or putting on phylacteries.

Menachem Ben Chaim was a deservedly respected brother in Christ. He served faithfully for many years as the Israel Secretary for the International Hebrew Christian Alliance, and then the International Messianic Jewish Alliance, as it came to be called. I had the joy of meeting him early in my Christian life, shortly after he and his wife immigrated to Israel. Menachem was absolutely right when he quoted Hudson Taylor, who wrote the following, referring to the Chinese scene:

> The chief objection that people have against Christianity is that it is a foreign religion, and that its tendencies are to approximate the believers to foreign nations. But why should a foreign aspect be given to Christianity?[3]

Ben Chaim went on to conclude:

> Messianic Judaism must become truly New Covenant Judaism and call for a dynamic challenge . . . for a transformed Jewish life. We may adopt some aspects of normative Jewish life, and we can still learn from our Gentile brothers and sisters in Messiah. Yet we must remain open to the Spirit in the outworking of the New Covenant within Israel for renewed Jewish and Messianic life.[4]

In spite of his verbal assertions, Menachem did not practice the modern fad by affecting a Jewish lifestyle, as if he was still Orthodox but for his faith in Jesus. He was one of the few supporters of the Messianic Movement from an Orthodox background, yet he lived, ate, clothed himself, and acted like any fellow Christian (he lived, if you please, like a Gentile). Of course, he celebrated the traditional feasts, but did not wear a kippa, and he belonged to a congregation that worships without most of the trappings of a synagogue service. In other words, Menachem called for a cultural attachment on the part of Jewish Christians to "normative

---

3. Menachem Ben Chaim, *King of Kings News* 98 (January 1998).
4. Ibid.

Jewish life," to the Jewish cultural consensus. His lifestyle did not exceed that mark.

Yet even dear Menachem said too much. It is true that one of the main objections "that (Jewish) people have against Christianity is that it is a foreign religion."[5] But that is merely an excuse. The real reason the Jewish people refuse to acknowledge Jesus has to do with what Jews share with all humanity: sin, translated into rebellion against God. That obstacle cannot be removed by cultural adaptations; it requires a work of the Holy Spirit. Menachem should have recognized that. As long as sin reigns in Jewish (or Gentile) hearts, there is nothing we can do to save them. Any accommodation of our message to their terms is to confirm them in their sin.

In defending the right of Jewish Christians to adhere to their national identity by way of the national traditions, Menachem correctly put that privilege alongside the right of other nations to act likewise. I assume Menachem did not intend to draw this conclusion, but it derives directly from his argument: Jewish Christians have the right to do what the Hottentots, the Inuit, and the Magyars may do—no more and no less, and on the same grounds.

Saying One Thing and Doing Another

We need to ensure that our attachment to national customs is sincere, and that it does not spill over into religious observance. Former Shintoists should not attach Christian meanings to their national religious customs, and Muslims who are converted to Christ should not attach Christian significance to theirs. The rabbis know God to no greater extent than a Shinto priest or a Muslim kadi, and their traditions have no more religious force. Our practice of Jewish traditions should be a matter of national custom, no more, and should extend to the limit of the national cultural consensus, no further.

Regretfully, Menachem was not as careful in this matter as he should have been. He became increasingly more stringent in his insistence that Jewish Christians adhere to the national customs. More disconcerting, the grounds of his insistence were increasingly those against which I warn in this book: confusing freedoms with duties and national culture with

5. Ibid.

religious obligation. He was unhappy with me for writing in this vein in the first edition of my book. Our last exchange prior to his death was the product of his unhappiness. Menachem was a fine Christian and a fine Jew. But, with all due respect, the gap between his views of the law and what the Scriptures have to say about the topic grew over the years, while his practice remained better than his theory.

Menachem was not alone in this respect. Most—no, all—of the Messianic leaders that I know, fall short in the same manner. I have yet to meet a Messianic Jew who really follows rabbinic traditions. In spite of their vociferous insistence, I know of none who pray at the stipulated times (Shacharit, Mincha, and Ma'ariv), avoid tearing toilet paper on the Sabbath, or avoid walking more than the stipulated three steps without a head covering. As Rausch puts it, "it is not practical."[6] The majority of adherents to the Messianic Movement do not measure up to their own standards.

An Affectation of Judaism

An overwhelming number of adherents to the Messianic Movement are Gentiles who have no business embracing Jewish national customs. Most of the Jewish people in the movement were assimilated Jews with no interest in the customs prior to their conversion. Theirs is not a case of previously cherished cultural norms, but of customs learned and applied, and which they are encouraged to adopt for purported spiritual advantages. Why should the faith of Jesus lead to national custom? Jeff Wasserman is right when he describes much of what goes on in messianic congregations as an "affectation of Judaism" and notes that "an observant Jew from any of the three major American Jewish traditions would find much of what passes of Messianic Jewish worship to be aberrant at worst and unfamiliar at best."[7] He cites examples.

Something is wrong. Jewish national traditions should be adhered to out of informed respect. If we empty tradition of its intended meaning, substituting Christian content, are we treating that tradition with respect? To what extent can we insist we are following truly Jewish

---

6. David A. Rausch, *Messianic Judaism: Its History, Theology, and Polity* (Lewiston, NY: The Edwin Mellen Press, 1982), 227.

7. Jeffrey S. Wasserman, *Messianic Jewish Congregations: Who Sold This Business to the Gentiles?* (Lanham, MD: University Press of America, 2000), 157.

tradition? Dan Juster would have us believe that "Jewish observances point to Yeshua,"[8] that Jesus "lived out the true meaning of Judaism,"[9] and that "it is of spiritual value to mark off the day (Saturday) from other days by a special Friday evening meal, the lighting of candles and prayer."[10] He does not hesitate to declare in the presence of God, "As (thy people) place the prayer shawl upon themselves, they return to their first love."[11]

Paul Liberman makes similar statements when he says that "ritual and tradition were previously obligatory. They now take on a higher meaning. They are seen as the foreshadowing of God's overall plan."[12] This is well illustrated by what Paul has to say about the Passover Seder, insisting that Messiah is hidden in the Passover traditions:

> People often forget the word "holiday" is derived from "holy day." In many ways these solemn assemblies have lost much of their original meaning. By celebrating these holy convocations, Messianic synagogues not only can observe them in the traditional sense, but the New Covenant also gives them a higher meaning. Thus, otherwise meaningless ritual can be seen as a foreshadowing of future events.
>
> Much of the ceremony of these occasions was prescribed in the Old covenant. However, over the centuries the Rabbis have added embellishments. Messianic Judaism believes the biblical ordinances of such convocations should be observed and rabbinical additions de-emphasised. God said these feasts "shall be a statute forever throughout your generations." . . .
>
> Exodus 12 gives a full description of the first Passover and its observance as commanded in Leviticus 23:5–7. According to these instructions, the first and last days of this seven-day convocation were to be considered holy. Unleavened bread was to be eaten during this period. Traditionally, this was to commemorate the exodus of Israelites from Egypt. They were so rushed they were unable to wait for the yeast to rise in the bread they were baking. Today, bread eaten on this holiday must be unleavened (matsah).

8. Dan Juster, *Jewish Roots: A Foundation of Biblical Theology for Messianic Judaism* (Rockville, MD: Davar Publishing, 1992), 131.

9. Dan Juster, *Jewishness and Jesus* (Downers Grove, IL: IVP, 1977), 28.

10. Juster, *Jewish Roots*, 214.

11. Ibid.

12. Paul Liberman, *The Fig Tree Blossoms: Messianic Judaism Emerges* (Harrison, AR: Fountain Press, 1977), 2.

In the New Covenant, the Messiah compared Himself with this bread when He celebrated the Passover. The parallels are worth noting. Yeast is a symbol of sin. It swells, ferments and decays. The Messiah was not puffed up; neither was the matsah. Both have holes from having been pierced. The stripes on the matsah are reminders of the stripes on the Messiah's back from the whippings he suffered. During the Passover Seder (supper), three pieces of matsah were placed in a cloth. The middle piece was broken, as was the Messiah's body. Half of the matsah is hidden and awaits discovery. Isn't this how it is with the Messiah? Anyone truly seeking him will find him. The middle piece is called the afikoman. Afikomenos in Greek means "I have come." It also means "I will return."[13]

We should not attach Christian significance to national custom. The rabbis who invented the afikoman were not inspired by the Spirit and no hint of Messiah is hidden in the afikoman. A word of explanation may be necessary for the uninitiated: the afikoman is the middle of three layers of unleavened bread in the Passover meal. It is hidden at the beginning of the evening and must be found (usually by one of the children) before the festive meal can end. It is redeemed by way of a gift from the leader of the Passover meal. Some have taken to identifying the afikoman with Messiah, the second of the three persons of the Godhead, smitten and pierced for Israel and now hidden from the people. Those who "find" him are rewarded with the gift of salvation. David Stern's insistence that "many scholars believe that these customs were started by Messianic Jews and invested with the meanings we have noted here, but somehow the customs were absorbed into non-Messianic Judaism"[14] is contrary to fact. There are no such scholars and there are no grounds for such an assertion. Nor are we treating Jewish custom with the respect it deserves when we make it convey a Christian message.

A no less unhappy example of messianic efforts to find biblical grounds for rabbinic tradition is to be found in the words of Russ Resnik in his article *Torah for Today*, in the March–April 1999 issue of *The Messianic Jewish Life*:

13. Ibid., 90–93. Used by permission.
14. David H. Stern, *Messianic Jewish Manifesto* (Jerusalem: Jewish New Testament Publications, 1988), 171.

The sages ask, "where is there an allusion to the book of Esther in the Torah?" (Chullin 159b). They answer with a reference to the warning of exile in Deuteronomy 31:18, "and I will certainly hide my face." In Hebrew this reads, "anochi haster astir panai." Astir—hide—sounds like the name Esther. The term *haster panim*, to hide the face, describes . . . conditions that dominate the story of Esther.[15]

This is not biblical interpretation but playing fast and loose with Scripture to make it support our convictions.

Again, Barney Kasdan writes that there are "spiritual lessons" to be found in the rabbinic traditions surrounding the Passover feast. "These customs may seem strange to the uninitiated but the deep spiritual truth will be evident to discerning believers in Yeshua."[16] Note Kasdan's use of the term "spiritual truth." Discerning believers know his statement to be untrue. It is invalid to intimate spiritual legitimacy to human inventions. Legitimacy implies authority, and if the authority of the rabbis is considered to be the will of God for the Jewish people and advantageous to non-Jews, why not submit to their authority when they affirm as they have for two millennia that Jesus is not the Messiah?

How can we persuade our people of the sincerity of our attachment to the traditions when we emasculate them by attributing to them new and foreign meanings?

Drawing a Line

Many in the Messianic Movement have not taken the necessary steps to ensure that attachment to Jewish national custom does not spill over to religious observance. One of my correspondents wrote, "Most of the believers who adopt Jewish practices do so because it is drawing them personally closer to God, because they are finding richness in practising some of the things that are considered (Jewish) Orthodoxy." This is the crux of the matter. If I am persuaded that lighting incense, praying before an icon, or gesticulating "draws me personally closer to God," am I entitled to practice these customs? If not, why adopt rabbinic customs,

15. Russell L. Resnik, "Torah for Today: The Festival of Exile," *Boundaries* (March–April 1999).

16. Barney Kasdan, "Passover and the Feast of Unleavened Bread," *Messianic Jewish Life* 72, no. 3 (July–Sept. 1999), 6.

or adhere to biblical customs that are but shadows of the reality now to be enjoyed? If yes, then why not use icons, incense, and other religious paraphernalia?

Recall how much God hated the introduction of invented means of "drawing closer" to him in the Old Testament, and how he punished our forefathers for the adoption of such measures. When Aaron presented the golden calf, he said, "This is your god, O Israel, who brought you up from the land of Egypt" (Ex. 32:4). The calf was not meant to draw the people away from God but to help them draw near, yet the divine response was terrible. We must avoid introducing into the worship of God anything but what he has commanded. No human invention is permitted. Moreover, how can we know if this or another practice draws us closer to God? Feelings can be terribly deceptive. The only reliable measuring rod we have is the Bible, and the Bible does not justify the use of Jewish cultural customs to draw near to the Almighty.

God has shown the way to draw near to him: self-effacing faith in Messiah, prayer, disciplined holiness, a cultivated spirituality that expresses itself in loving obedience, sincerity guided by the word of God, and an acknowledged dependency upon God. These are the means by which we draw near. Kissing a Torah scroll, celebrating Purim, or eating unleavened bread will not bring us one millimeter closer to him who is a consuming fire. They may accord us an emotional experience, but not all emotional experiences are of God.

To insist that Jews in Messiah are required by God to follow rabbinic injunction is to play into the hands of those who oppose the gospel, and to accord them a level of religious authority to which only God has the right. It is an exclusively divine prerogative to oblige man's conscience. To attribute such authority to the rabbis is to concede their claim to determine the content and confines of Judaism. It is to accept their claim that Judaism as a religion and Jewishness as a national entity are identical, and that their theory of Judaism is right. In other words, it is to give credence to their denial of Jesus. Should we make such a concession?

Paul expressly teaches that a man who prays to God with a head covering "dishonors his head," that is, Messiah (1 Cor. 11:4 NIV). The adoption of male headgear (such as kippot) in worship is a deviation from the biblical norm. The Messianic practice to accord the Torah prominence over other portions of Scripture (by placing a Torah scroll in the sanctuary, by celebrating Simchat Torah, kissing the Torah scroll, and the like) is a tacit acceptance of rabbinic norms that fly in the face of Scripture (Heb. 8).

Daniel Juster wishes to call us back to what he describes as a "biblically consistent Judaism."[17] There is no such thing. On many fundamental points, Judaism is a direct contradiction of biblical teaching. Some 2000 years ago, following the destruction of the temple, a branch of Judaism hijacked Jewish national identity. Under the leadership of Rabbi Yochanan Ben Zakkai, the Pharisees had the foresight others lacked and thereby became the recognized guardians of Jewishness.

Hengel states,

> The former pluralism [which existed within Judaism prior to the destruction of the temple] gave way to the pursuit of unity, to a period of consolidation, which began with quick success, was interrupted by the Bar Kochba revolt, and ended with the redaction of the Mishnah at the beginning of the third century; this affected a deep change in Judaism that has stamped its further history up until the reforms of the nineteenth century and even until today.[18]

BLIND GUIDES

Well before these rabbinic misconceptions were adopted, we hear Jesus describing the rabbis as "blind guides of the blind" (Matt. 15:14). Paul did not hesitate to say that the minds and hearts of our people, rabbis included, have been

> hardened; for until this very day at the reading of the old covenant the same veil [described in the preceding verses of Paul's letter] remains unlifted, because it is removed in Messiah. But to this day whenever Moses is read, a veil lies over their heart; but whenever a person turns to the Lord, the veil is taken away. (2 Cor. 3:14–16)

Is this a coincidence? Is it a divine afterthought? Not at all. Apart from those within Israel whom God reserved for himself (Rom. 11:2–10), the people

---

17. Juster, *Jewishness and Jesus*, 34.
18. C. K. Barrett and Martin Hengel, *Conflicts and Challenges in Early Christianity*, ed. Donald Hagner (Harrisburg, PA: Trinity Press International, 1999), 34.

have been blinded and their ears stopped by God "lest they see with their eyes, and hear with their ears, and understand with their heart, and convert, and be healed" (Isaiah 6:10 KJV, compare Rom. 11:8–10). That is exactly what God said he would do. In Isaiah 29:13–14 he warned the people: "Because this people draw near with their words and honor Me with their lip service, but they remove their hearts far from Me and their reverence for Me consists of tradition learned by rote, therefore behold, I will once again deal marvelously with this people, wondrously marvelous; and the wisdom of their wise men shall perish, and the discernment of their discerning men shall be concealed."

Earlier he said,

> Be delayed and wait,
> Blind yourselves and be blind;
> They become drunk, but not with wine,
> They stagger, but not with strong drink.
> For the LORD has poured over you a spirit of deep sleep,
> He has shut your eyes, the prophets;
> And He has covered your heads, the seers.

> The entire vision will be to you like the words of a sealed book, which when they give it to the one who is literate, saying, "Please read this," he will say, "I cannot, for it is sealed." Then the book will be given to the one who is illiterate, saying, "Please read this." And he will say, "I cannot read." (Isa. 29:9–12)

Happily, this is not all Isaiah had to say. God revealed to him that the day would come when the veil will be removed.

> On that day the deaf will hear words of a book,
> And out of their gloom and darkness the eyes of the blind will see.
> . . . .
> Those who err in mind will know the truth,
> And those who criticize will accept instruction. (Isa. 29:18, 24)

Paul spoke of this too, when he spoke of "the veil" being removed in Messiah, when "a person turns to the Lord" (2 Cor. 3:14, 16).

This has not yet happened. The typical rabbinic attitude toward Jesus testifies to their ongoing blindness. Our Lord's assessment remains true: they are not reliable guides to an understanding of the Torah. In spite of their learning and their rich Jewish background, they are "blind leaders of the blind." They should not be accorded the high status that Messianic Judaism accords them.

OFF WITH THE SHACKLES!

It is time we threw off the distorting shackles of rabbinic tradition. Rather than affirming rabbinicism, we should challenge it by presenting the only viable alternative: the gospel. Rather than submitting to rabbinicism, we should challenge its claim to be the interpreter of God's will for our nation. God's will is that Israel believe, love, and serve Jesus. Jesus is the essence of true Jewishness, not rabbinicsm. Moses, King David, Isaiah, and the prophets would feel out of place in a Jewish synagogue. They would lose their way through the maze of rabbinic traditions. They would not be comfortable with what now passes as Judaism.

The Jewish religious leaders who lived when rabbinic Judaism was framed were heartless in their attitude to Jews who did not accommodate themselves to their standards. Jewish Christians were relentlessly persecuted in those years. During the Bar Kochba revolt (133–35), Jewish Christians were hunted and slain because they refused to fight under the banner of a false Messiah who enjoyed the support of prominent rabbis. That misguided support led to one of the most horrific catastrophes in the history of our nation, yet Jewish folklore glories in the error of those days.

Throughout the Middle Ages, Jewish Christians were thrust out of the nation, into the arms of a waiting church, and then accused of losing their Jewish identity, like the man who murdered his parents but asked the judge for clemency because he was an orphan. In the 1960s, thousands of Jews arrived in Israel from India. The rabbis questioned their millennia of devoted sacrifice and demanded that they undergo a "minor conversion." When the Ethiopian Jews arrived, they were treated likewise, although their traditions had clear biblical foundations and had preserved their Jewish identity for over 2500 years. Both communities faced the choice of being declared non-Jewish or accepting the yoke of rabbinic authority, which is far removed from biblical sources these ancient communities obeyed.

Rabbinic totalitarianism has been repeatedly challenged among Jews since the European Emancipation in the nineteenth century. Reformed and Conservative Judaism in Israel and abroad is challenging it today. We Jewish Christians ought to challenge it even more specifically saying, "Your tradition has contributed greatly to the preservation of Jewish existence. In that respect, we owe you sincere thanks. However, as interpreters of God's word you have failed. You are guilty of distorting Jewish identity. You denied and rejected the Messiah. You have focused on rites and neglected internal devotion. You have cultivated a religion of self-achievement in the face of contrary biblical testimony. Repent and believe the gospel!"

We need to recognize the truth of Jocz's statement, that Judaism "exists by virtue of its negation of the Christian Faith—[the] affirmation of Christianity would have meant the dissolution of Rabbinic Judaism."[19] The infamous Birkat HaMinim—a malediction upon sectarians inserted into the Eighteen Daily Benedictions shortly after the destruction of the temple, when Jewish Christians were many and the gospel was spreading throughout the world—requests

> For apostates let there be no hope, and uproot the kingdom of insolence spreading in our days. Cause the Christians (Notsrim) and the heretics (Minim, an inclusive term which had as its focus the Jewish believers in Jesus) to perish in a moment. Blot them out of the Book of Life and write them not among the righteous. You are blessed, O, Lord, who humbles the insolent.[20]

JUDAISM REJECTS JESUS

Paul Liberman reminds us: "The New Covenant tells of conflicts (between Jesus and the Pharisees) centering on such things as the various traditions. Messiah's opposition to pharisaism led to the Pharisee's rejection of him and, ultimately, to his crucifixion."[21] Judaism today is a consciously determined rejection of Jesus. There is no way faithful

---

19. Jakob Jocz, *The Jewish People and Jesus Christ: A Study in the Controversy between Church and Synagogue* (London: S.P.C.K., 1962), 145–46.

20. William Horbury, *Jewish Christians: In Contact and Controversy* (Edinburgh: T & T Clark, 1998), 67. See also Jocz, *The Jewish People and Jesus Christ*, 51–57.

21. Liberman, *The Fig Tree Blossoms*, 35.

disciples of Jesus can accommodate their faith to such a rejection. There is no way we can appear Jewish to our people so long as we believe in Jesus, until we successfully challenge rabbinicism's hold on our people.

One of my correspondents insisted: "Overall, the movement is striving to express a Judaism and faith in Jesus the Messiah which is entirely biblical, not Rabbinic." Messianic Jews are sincerely seeking to do what they believe is biblical. However, what distinguishes Messianic Jews from their fellow believers who are not Jewish is, primarily, not biblical custom but rabbinic practice. Sabbath candles, Yiddish phrases, prayer shawls, and other such paraphernalia have no basis in the Bible. This is also true of many customs associated with the festivals. Ariel Berkowitz is mistaken when he fails to distinguish between rabbinic Judaism and the biblical Jewishness of the patriarchs by claiming that "Judaism began with Abraham when God entered into a covenant [with him]."[22]

Dr. Richard C. Nichol, puts it succinctly. Replying to the question posed by the title of his article, "Messianic Judaism—So What Exactly Is It?", he says that Messianic Judaism has to do with maintaining Jewish identity "through rabbinic traditions."[23] Such practice is fundamentally wrong because Judaism is no more the religion of the Old Testament than Catholicism is the religion of the New.

RABBINIC TRADITIONS

God never commanded rabbinic practices. He did not command Jewish people to wear phylacteries or place mezuzahs on their doorposts; Israel was commanded to place the law on its heart and as a frontlet between the eyes, to tie the commandments of God on their hands, post them on the doorposts of their homes and talk about them as they come in and go out (Deut. 6:6–9). These are simply homey ways to say that the people of God should be preoccupied with his word, that the Scriptures should guide their every step. In no way can we satisfy such a commandment by placing a box with a text on the doorposts of our homes or on our foreheads. Dan Juster is, therefore, mistaken when he

22. Ariel and Devorah Berkowitz, *Torah Rediscovered* (Littleton, CO: First Fruits of Zion, 1996), 66.
23. Richard C. Nichol, "Messianic Judaism—So What Exactly Is It?", *Messianic Jewish Life* 72, no. 3 (July–Sept. 1999).

describes the use of phylacteries as "a meaningful way of worship."[24] Traditional rabbinic interpretations miss the point. They are false to the meaning of the text, which calls us to be engaged with the word of God at every juncture of life. Judaism is not biblical. Jewish believers in Jesus should not accord that tradition any part of their obedience to God.

Rabbinic legalism has destroyed the spirit of the law and rendered it ineffective, transforming it into a means by which man seeks to satisfy God. Instead of exposing man's sinful weakness and teaching him to seek the mercies of God, Judaism has persuaded its adherents that they have the ability to storm the walls of their sinful inclination and overcome it by the power of their devotion. This is nothing less than the flesh sanctifying itself—a moral and logical impossibility.

The law is understood by Judaism in terms of a legalistic literalism that removes it from the realm of morality and transforms it into a commercial transaction: if I do that for you, then you do this for me. Judaism has lowered the moral standards of the law of God, according man a false sense of security instead of teaching him to flee to Messiah for refuge.

For example, God forbade our forefathers to harvest the fringes of their fields. Instead of allowing each individual to contend with his own heart before God in light of his neighbor's need, as do the Scriptures, the rabbis defined the exact width of a fringe. Now, without a shred of moral reflection, a Jewish farmer may harvest his field up to the extremities of the rabbinic fringe. So long as he does not exceed the stipulated boundaries, his conscience is free without giving a thought to the needs of those around him. What if the needs of his neighbors exceed the amount he has left? Tough luck. Our farmer has fulfilled his obligation to God and, unless his heart is kinder than is his legalistic mind, he is free to go his happy way without a thought for the needy. The law has been stripped of its ability to educate toward a sensitive, heartfelt morality that fears God and loves one's fellow human.

The prophets frequently challenged the people's adherence to the letter of the law instead of its spirit. The people's ritualism, void of moral import, earned God's judgment. In these and many other ways, rabbinic Judaism and its traditions constitute a massive intrusion into the relationship between God and man. Human opinion has been enthroned above the word of God.

24. Juster, *Jewish Roots*, 215.

It might surprise some to note that rabbinic Judaism is closer to Roman Catholicism than to the Bible. Its views of the role of holy men, the authority of tradition, the place of the Scripture in a believer's life, and the right of private interpretation of sin, salvation, grace, the value of human effort, and religious ritual are all as contrary to what the Bible teaches as they are reminiscent of Catholicism.

JUDAISM IS NOT JEWISH

Measured by what the Bible teaches, rabbinic Judaism cannot be considered biblical. Some claim that the only real difference between Judaism and the gospel is whether or not Messiah has come. This is grossly incorrect. Some speak of "returning to the roots of the faith" by returning to Judaism or an observance of its traditions. The Finnish Shorashim Fellowship is characteristic of messianic groups:

> Shorashim is the Hebrew word for roots. The name describes a new effort in Helsinki to gather together believers who wish to *grow deeper in their Hebraic-Jewish roots*. Our purpose is . . . to increase Christians' realisation of the richness of our Hebraic-Jewish *Roots* and how *this may deepen our relationship with God*. The goal is *to win the prize offered by God's upward calling in the Messiah Yeshua* (Philippians 3:14). Specific objectives of this fellowship are . . . home meetings on Friday evenings (Erev Shabbat) for food, fellowship, fun, song and dance, focus on Messiah and God's teachings (Torah) and meeting family needs.[25]

The faith of Jesus is rooted in the Scriptures, not in rabbinic tradition. The apostles and the rabbis disagreed as to how the Old Testament is to be understood. What is more, the Judaism of today is not that of the apostolic period. Before, Judaism was of various kinds. Movements within Judaism contended for priority. Judaism today has become monolithic, permitting thought only within a highly restricted framework. It is not biblical to say, "Let's prove our Jewishness by submitting to the injunctions of the rabbis." Faith in Jesus is rabbinic Judaism's alternative, not its ally.

25. Introductory brochure produced by Shorashim, Liusketie 16 L 67, 00710 Helsinki, Finland (emphases added).

Some Messianic Jews defend their observance of rabbinic tradition by claiming that Jesus adhered to that tradition. Of course he kept the traditions! He was born "under the law" (Gal. 4:4). He lived among a people that had not been enlightened by the gospel and at a time when the gospel was not known. But he was also repeatedly accused of transgressing the traditions of the Elders by healing on the Sabbath, defending the disciples' right to pluck, peel, and eat grain on the Sabbath, and allowing them to eat without the ritual washing of hands. He was better known for his transgressions of tradition than for keeping it.

Jesus chastised the Pharisees because their customs transgressed the word of God (Mark 7:6–13). When challenged as to why he and his disciples did not observe the pharisaic tradition of fasting on Mondays and Thursdays, he replied that he had not come to improve on rabbinic tradition or mend what was wrong with it. He came to replace it altogether (Matt. 9:14–16). The new wine of life that Jesus imparts cannot be contained in the old wineskins of rabbinic tradition. It needs a completely new framework (Matt. 9:17). Jesus said so, dare we disbelieve him? There is no point in trying to fit the new wine of life in the Spirit into the constraints of Judaism. We need to put new wine into new wineskins.

MATTHEW 23: RABBINIC JUDAISM IN JESUS' DAY

In Matthew chapter 23 Jesus provided the most extensive treatment of rabbinic Judaism to be found in the New Testament. At this early stage, rabbinicism had already evolved into a system that conflicted with the fundamental principles of God's revelation. Some seek to soften the harshness of our Lord's words by insisting that he was not speaking of pharisaism as such, only of some among the Pharisees. They fortify their view by references to similar passages in Jewish writings of the time. This is incorrect on two accounts.

First, Jesus expressly speaks of the Pharisees in general, not of a group among them. He accords them the unsavory epitaph, "hypocrites" (vv. 13, 15, 23, 25, 27, 29)—not those among the scribes and Pharisees who are hypocrites but "scribes and Pharisees, hypocrites." He speaks of those who "have seated themselves in the chair of Moses" (v. 2), indicating the Pharisees as those who had arrogated the right to legislate for Israel.

There were exceptions, but the general trend of pharisaism emphasized the symbolic and external aspects of religion rather than spiritual motivation and morality. In Matthew 23, Jesus challenged the trend as a whole, not its more extreme examples.

The second reason we must reject the view that Jesus spoke in Matthew 23 only of some among the Pharisees has to do with the nature of the criticisms he raised. His criticisms were true of pharisaic Judaism as a whole, not just of its fringes. A traditionally Jewish emphasis on the symbolic and the external encourages people to appear to be devout when they are not. Large phylacteries, loud prayers, and long tassels become the order of the day. That is why so many of the Orthodox today wear their religious garb in a provocative and visible manner.

In Matthew 23:6–12 Jesus speaks against honoring man in a way that should be reserved for God alone. It is disconcerting to see how the hands of rabbis are kissed today, their clothing deemed sacred, their presence viewed as the presence of God, their graves visited, and their dead bodies addressed in prayer. Verses 13–15 make Jesus' view of pharisaism clear: rabbinic Judaism shuts the door to the kingdom of God. It transforms a convert into what Jesus calls "a son of hell."

Why such language? Because pharisaism shuts the gospel out by inculcating contrary views. The gospel says that no man can meet God's just and perfect requirements; Judaism insists that a man's good deeds can outweigh his moral failures.

Jesus called the Pharisees "blind guides" (v. 16) and showed, in verses 15–24, how their priorities are mistaken because they emphasize the visible, the symbolic, and the ritualistic; pharisaism attaches importance to incidentals while neglecting the "weightier provisions of the Law: justice and mercy and faithfulness" (v. 23)—all aspects of the moral law, not of ritual.

Jesus goes on to say (vv. 25–28) that an emphasis on externals leads to a covert immorality in which individuals become like whitewashed graves "which on the outside appear beautiful, but inside they are full of dead men's bones" (v. 27). They appear to be exemplary, "but inside they are full of robbery and self-indulgence" (v. 25). In light of its insistence on the need to obey the Torah, one would expect Jewish religious Orthodoxy to excel in moral achievements. The truth is that a sinful corruption underlies Orthodoxy no less than it underlies all human effort.

In verses 29–36 Jesus charges pharisaism with the death of the prophets and prophesies that rabbinicism will not change in this respect. "I am sending you prophets and wise men and scribes; some of them you will kill and crucify, and some of them you will scourge in your synagogues, and persecute from city to city" (Matt. 23:34).

We Jews are eminently adept at castigating the Gentiles for their (unquestionably shameful) treatment of our people over the centuries. But rabbinicism has treated the disciples of Jesus with an equally consistent hatred: Jewish Christians were forced out of the nation, cursed in the synagogues, refused the rites of marriage and burial, and, where opportunity permitted, physically persecuted. During the Holocaust, Jewish authorities—even in the ghettos and concentration camps—refused to succor Jewish Christians, leaving them to the wrath of their Nazi persecutors. I would dread to think what would happen in Israel today if the religious establishment were free to act according to their convictions. The present infrequent but violent activities of semi-official organizations against Jewish Christians in Israel, often openly supported by the religious establishment, would become everyday occurrences.

Jesus brought about a revolution. On the one hand, he deepened and widened our comprehension of the demands of the law. On the other, he challenged Orthodox tradition because it is a human imposition. We dare not attribute authority to a tradition Jesus opposed. We dare not follow a Judaism which chose to reject him almost as firmly as he rejected it.

Some might contend that Jesus never rejected rabbinical teaching. After all, he said: "The teachers of the law and the Pharisees sit in Moses' seat. So you must obey them and do everything they tell you. But do not do what they do" (Matt. 23:2–3 NIV). A superficial reading of this text, divorced from its context, might lead to such a conclusion. But a careful reading shows that this is not the case. Jesus explicitly rejected the rabbis' demand that they be addressed as "father" and "teacher" (vv. 9–10 NIV). He described them as "teachers of the law" who "shut the kingdom of heaven in men's faces" (v. 13 NIV). He went on to give examples, referring to what the rabbis taught about swearing (vv. 15–22) and the relative importance of matters of the law (vv. 23–24). Are we to follow the rabbis all the way to heaven's closed gates?

What could Jesus have meant when he told his disciples to act as the Pharisees required? Quite simply, he states that they "sit in Moses' seat."

That is to say, regardless of what they do or the errors of their teaching, they are in a position of authority and should be obeyed in the general conduct of society. A parallel can be found in Paul's inspired words about rulers in Romans 13. They, too, possess authority. To rebel against them is to rebel against God (Rom. 13:1–2). The apostle then goes on to describe them as those who "hold no terror for those who do right, but for those who do wrong" (v. 3 NIV). It is worth remembering that the ruler of the day was the infamous Nero, a blot on human history no shame can erase. Yet Paul goes on to describe him as one of "God's servants" (Rom. 13:6 NIV) to whom honor is due (v. 7) and who should be obeyed (v. 5).

A qualification is implied in Paul's words, as is implied in the words of Jesus concerning the Pharisees. Paul says that believing citizens should "do what is right" and thereby earn the right to receive commendation from their ruler (v. 3 NIV). The ruler is a servant of God, not a free agent. So long as he commends and rewards those who do right, he is fulfilling his role and should be obeyed, have taxes paid to him, and have honor accorded to him. In a similar way, Jesus says in Matthew 23 that the Pharisees "sit in Moses' seat." So long as they teach the truths enunciated by Moses, they are to be obeyed. But when they abuse their authority and teach what Jesus denounces in this chapter, they are to be disobeyed.

There seems no room for doubt that Jesus rejected the Pharisees' claim to represent biblical traditions. The rabbis' efforts to interpret the commandments of God were a dismal failure. They misconstrued the word of God, rendered the primary secondary and the secondary primary. Their interpretations created an ever-increasing gap between the believing heart and Scripture, forcing those who would serve God to depend on their traditions. Rabbinic interpretations are described by them as "a hedge to the Torah," devised to safeguard Jews from transgressing the laws of God. But such a hedge is a barrier between believers and their God. Man has injected himself into the relations between God and his creatures.

Is this valid? Is it biblical? A thousand times no. Human inventions cannot cultivate spiritual love for God. Only God can do that by his Spirit, and he does so through his powerful, living, transforming word. None but the Holy Spirit can draw us closer to God, and none but God can tell us how to worship him in spirit and in truth.

Did the Apostles Keep Jewish Traditions?

Juster states, "It was assumed [by the early church] that Jewish Christians will maintain their heritage in a biblically consistent way as Jews,"[26] that is to say, according to the traditions. There is no biblical evidence to support such a statement. The most that can be said is that some in the early church continued to think in rabbinic terms. This group never succeeded in persuading the apostles of their opinion. We cannot even say that James supported them, although some sent by him to Antioch were of the opinion that both the Torah and the traditions should apply to believers. There is not a single apostolic statement to the effect that believers, Jewish or otherwise, are obliged to maintain the traditions.

Some continued to observe the traditions. These were to be borne in loving patience until the light of the gospel impacted their thinking and they understood the gospel better. In Romans chapters 14–15, Paul addresses Gentile believers, calling them to bear the weaknesses of those among their Jewish brethren who retained dietary restrictions. He describes such qualms as a weakness (Rom. 14:1, 15:1). As for himself, he declares, "I know and am convinced in the Lord Jesus that nothing is unclean in itself" (Rom. 14:14). *Nothing*? Even pork? Even a young goat in its mother's milk? Yes, everything is kosher; everything is to be eaten with thanks to God, the gracious Provider (see 1 Tim. 4:4). Whatever may have been the qualms of Jewish believers in Rome, Paul's above quoted statement is clear. Dietary restrictions are no longer binding (see also Mark 7:14–19). Nothing is unclean in itself.

The strong should not ride roughshod over the sensitivities of the weak, but take them into consideration. We should not wound the oversensitive and misinformed conscience of our brethren by demonstratively partaking of foods considered to be forbidden (Rom. 14:15). This is an example of Paul's earlier statement to the effect that both circumcision and uncircumcision (or eating and not eating) are of no account. What is important is faith working in love (Gal. 5:6).

The fact that Paul wanted to be in Jerusalem to celebrate the feast (Acts 18–21) does not prove that he followed the traditions; he spent many a year without going to the feast. In fact, he did not arrive in time for Passover—the main feast—but arrived for Pentecost. Upon his arrival,

26. Juster, *Jewish Roots*, 74, 82.

James requested that he take part in a traditional ritual. The reason for James' request is instructive. Note how he describes a party in the Jerusalem church (from whom he excludes himself): "You see, brother, how many thousands there are among the Jews of those who have believed, and they [not "we"] are all zealous for the Law" (Acts 21:20). By following national tradition, Paul was to demonstrate he did not oppose the traditions as such, that he could as freely keep them as he was free not to do so (Acts 21:24). In this way, it was hoped, an end could be put to the rumor that Paul had embarked on an anti-Torah campaign, "teaching all the Jews who are among the Gentiles to forsake Moses, telling them not to circumcise their children, nor to walk according to the customs" (Acts 21:21).

Paul preached the gospel to "all the Jews who are among the Gentiles." His efforts caused them to be driven out of the synagogues. Their faith brought them into close and constant fellowship with their fellow believers among the Gentiles. In other words, as a result of his efforts, Jewish Christians learned not to distinguish between Jewish and Gentile believers. But he was not engaged in a concerted effort against Jewish tradition. His concern was for the gospel. On the other hand, the apostles continued to make their way to the temple (Acts 3:1; 5:25) at the times of public prayer (Acts 3:1). But we do not read that they participated in the temple worship. Worship in the temple focused on public sacrifice, and the New Testament never portrays the apostles offering sacrifice. We do know that they proclaimed the gospel when they visited the temple; there was no better place and no better time to do so, just as Paul could find no better place to preach than at the local synagogue or marketplace (Acts 9:20; 13:5, 14–17ff; 14:1).

The council in Jerusalem (Acts 15) set no bars to fellowship between Jews and Gentiles in Messiah. It did not call upon Gentiles to maintain Jewish religious tradition because "there is a glorious and beneficial dimension to some of the traditions of Judaism," as modern day Messianic Jews claim. Paul circumcised Timothy because his mother was Jewish (Acts 16:1–3) and "because of the Jews who were in those parts" (v. 3), not for religious or spiritual purposes. On the other hand, his refusal to circumcise Titus—a Gentile—was squarely founded on religious grounds.

Messianic congregations should not adhere to rabbinic traditions. Distinctions between the duties of Messianic Jews and those of their

Gentile brethren are barriers to fellowship. If, to be accepted as an equal, I am required to do anything beyond believing in Jesus and obeying him, my fellowship is restricted. Paul had interesting things to say about the Judaism of his day. Like Jesus he addressed the issue long before Judaism had become the determined rejection of Jesus it now constitutes. In chapter 3 of his second letter to the Corinthians, Paul contrasts the divinely inspired religion of Moses with the equally divinely inspired religion of Jesus. He goes on to reflect briefly on rabbinic Judaism. He describes the faith taught through Moses as "the ministry of death . . . engraved on stones" (2 Cor. 3:7) and as "the ministry of condemnation" (v. 9) whose glory fades away (v. 11), under which there is now a hardening of minds (v. 14) and hearts (v. 15).

In consequence, although Moses is regularly read in the course of synagogue ritual, instead of spiritual insight there is blindness; a veil has been spread over the minds and hearts of the readers. Rather than spiritual insight, Paul attributes to Judaism a terrible blindness. This blindness can only be "removed in Christ" (v. 14), not through the Torah but "whenever a person turns to the Lord" (v. 16), who sends his Spirit to remove it. Then, "beholding as in a mirror the glory of the Lord" revealed in the Torah, we are steadily "transformed into the same image" by the powerful workings of the spirit, "from glory to glory" (v. 18). Spiritual progress is a work of the Spirit of God, resulting in ever-increasing moral similarity to Messiah.

Rabbinicism and National Custom

It is a matter of considerable embarrassment to note that the overwhelming majority in messianic congregations throughout the Diaspora is, in fact, non-Jewish, including a sizeable part of its leadership. The basis of their fellowship is a common attachment to Jewish tradition, but fellowship on the basis of Jewish custom is not true Christian fellowship. Fellowship in Messiah connotes unconditional equality, not the superiority of custom or ethnic identity.

That was Paul's argument regarding Peter's behavior in Galatia (Gal. 2:12). If we cannot walk into the home of a non-Jewish believer and eat whatever he serves, fellowship is compromised. To insist that we are obliged to keep the traditions is to say that we cannot eat freely. We cannot have our proverbial cake and eat it. Either we are subject to the Mosaic Covenant or we are not. Either the body of Messiah is one, or it is divided.

Rabbinic traditions form much of Jewish culture. They are part of the national consensus by which Jews identify themselves. They are Jewish cultural norms. These traditions determine which holidays we celebrate and, to a great extent, how we celebrate them. Jewish holidays have become national distinctives, accompanied by a perfunctory nod toward the religious aspects of the tradition. There is nothing wrong with Jewish Christians celebrating the feasts as a matter of culture. But they are not to be viewed in terms of religious duty or a means to spiritual advantage. Religious observance of rabbinic custom cannot consistently be limited to outward symbolism. Rabbinical Judaism is designed to affect life as a whole. It encompasses all of an individual's waking hours: what he eats, the first thing he does in the morning, what kind of toilet paper he buys, when he uses his car—there is no end to rabbinic injunction. If followed faithfully, no area of life remains unaffected.

The essence of our faith is inevitably affected by our practice. In defending the validity of Jewish religious tradition, Dan Juster goes so far as to say, "at no time can we biblically draw a line and say, 'from this time forward, if a Jew hasn't accepted Yeshua, he is lost.'"[27] Jews can be saved from the wrath of God "through natural revelation or the Abrahamic covenant. . . . We cannot preclude the possibility of Jews responding in faith to God's revelation in the Tanach even if they reject and deny Jesus the honor that is due him as Lord, Savior and Messiah."[28] Mark Kinzer's book intimates a similar disconcerting conclusion. Is this not a denial of the necessity of the atoning death of Messiah, the need for faith and repentance, and for the regenerating work of the Holy Spirit?! Biblical notions have been replaced by non-biblical notions of an "unconscious" or "incipient" faith in Messiah. Do Jews believe in Jesus by the force of "God's revelation in the Tanach," without knowing in whom they believe? If Jews can be saved by virtue of such a faith, why can't Gentiles be saved in the same way? If they can, Jesus' death was an unnecessary waste (Gal. 2:21)—cursed be the thought! In rejecting conscious faith, repentance, and a recognition of the uniqueness of

27. Ibid., 17ff, 172.
28. Ibid.

Jesus as the way to salvation, Messianic Judaism is in danger of losing the gospel and becoming a cult.

Jewish rabbinic customs can serve Jewish Christians. However, their practice must be subject to careful scrutiny to ensure their doing so does not blur the gospel. Messianic Judaism is not guided by biblical standards in its attitude to Jewish tradition. The extent to which I have succeeded in proving this is the extent to which Messianic Judaism should be rejected.

We Jews in Christ do not cease to be Jewish by virtue of our faith in Jesus, nor ought we. If believing in Jesus amounted to a termination of our Jewish identity, it would also amount to a denial of the Old Testament and to Jesus' claim to be the Messiah of Israel. The difference between Jews in Messiah and their Gentile brethren is not one of religious duty. It is one of culture and national identity. But those differences should not be allowed to divide the church.

Jewish Christians are Jews. Most of us wish to remain Jewish. We identify with our people, celebrate the feasts, delight in the existence of our State, enlist in Jewish causes, and maintain those aspects of our tradition that form the national consensus. But we are free from the Mosaic Law and from rabbinic authority, and we refuse to submit again to that yoke of bondage. Messiah is more than all we need. We freely confess, "Nothing in my hand I bring, simply to thy cross I cling."[29] In so doing, we find life.

EVANGELISM AND CONGREGATIONAL LIFE

How to Become More Effective

One of the main justifications offered for Messianic Judaism is the desire to promote faith in Jesus among the Jewish people. David Stern explains that Messianic Judaism is designed for "sparking the salvation of the Jews and the fulfillment of the church's great commission."[30] He insists: "Messianic Judaism will not make significant inroads in the Jewish community without interacting seriously with the Judaism that exists today."[31] Paul Liberman states, "For nearly two thousand years the

29. Augustus Toplady, "Rock of Ages Cleft for Me," 1776.
30. Stern, *Messianic Jewish Manifesto*, 10.
31. Ibid., 174.

Christian church has missed chances to fulfill its mission to bring the good news of the coming of the Messiah to the world's Jewish population. A time for change has come."[32] The change called for is described: "by [our] becoming better Jews . . . traditional Judaism no longer can justify the claim that acceptance of the New Testament is an attempt . . . to assimilate."[33] "This adds credibility to Jewish believers in the New Testament. . . . Thus, the existence of completed Jews forces the fair-minded traditional Jews to examine his criteria for determining what a Jew is."[34] He concludes, "If you want fewer Jews to accept the Messiah, make the faith less Jewish. If you want more Jews to accept him, then reinforce the Jewishness of the faith."[35]

We already noted that the Messianic Movement has attracted more Gentiles than Jews. It has failed in promoting the gospel among the Jewish people and has not gained acceptance by the Jewish community. These facts should move every sincere lover of God in the movement to reconsider his position.

The Messianic Movement is right: it is best "that Jews are able to hear [the gospel] message from Jewish lips in a Jewish idiom."[36] But the Jewish people need to hear *the gospel*, not an unintelligible message that focuses on Jewishness and on the Messiahship of Jesus. The crux of the gospel is man's sinfulness and God's grace in Jesus. The gospel is God's power to save, not our presentation methods. That is where David Stern and Paul Liberman fall short. "Sparking the salvation of the Jews and the fulfillment of the church's great commission"[37] is something that God has promised to do by the power of the gospel. It is a work he has reserved exclusively for himself because only he can do it. Our duty is to proclaim the gospel because "faith comes from hearing, and hearing by the word of Christ" (Rom. 10:17).

We need to believe in the power of God through his word. It is our duty to preach the gospel faithfully, not effectively. Our sufficiency is from God, not from what we can do. The human heart is so infected with sin

---

32. Liberman, *The Fig Tree Blossoms*, 2.
33. Ibid.
34. Ibid., 6.
35. Ibid., 70.
36. Jocz, *The Jewish People and Jesus Christ*, 215.
37. Liberman, *The Fig Tree Blossoms*, 70.

and so enslaved to it that we cannot convince man to turn to God. That is the work of the Spirit. God himself must work to free our people from the bondage of sin. Only then will our people look upon him they have pierced and turn to him in repentance. Any other kind of "conversion" is no conversion at all. In things that pertain to God, there is no such thing as a "fair-minded" Jew or Gentile. Our minds, wills, and emotions are affected by sin. We are inherently prejudiced against the gospel to the point of hostility (Col. 1:21). People need to be born again, from above, by an act of God. Until that happens, Jews will continue to object to the gospel and charge Jews who believe in Jesus with going over to the enemy.

We do not need to become better Jews, but better Christians. The holiness of our lives will count far more than a self-defeating effort to persuade an unwilling Jewry that we are Jewish. We should declare the gospel to our people with confidence. God stopped Paul dead in his tracks and transformed him into a preacher of the gospel. He can do it again, and again, and again. It was not someone's Jewishness that persuaded Paul but the power of God. Conversion always is an act of divine power. Instead of looking for more effective ways to win the hearts of our people, we should have more confidence in the Spirit of God and in his ability to change the heart of all and any. God is the Savior. We are merely heralds of his word.

We need to preach to our people more than that Jesus is the Messiah and that the gospel is Jewish. We need to follow the example of the Scripture and preach about sin, righteousness and judgment to come. We need to call our people to turn from their sin, their self-reliance, and their determined rejection of Jesus. They must acknowledge him as God our Savior, the only sufficient atonement for our sins.

Authentic Judaism?

Messianic Judaism has sought to justify many of its practices by their purported evangelistic appeal. There is an important difference between evangelism and congregational life, often overlooked in discussions of the Messianic Movement. As we have seen from 1 Corinthians 9:20 and Acts 17, Paul accommodated himself to his respective national audiences when presenting the gospel. But he never founded ethnic- or culture-based congregations. He acted the opposite. Acts shows that the congregations he founded were mixed (Acts 13:43, 48; 14:1). The apostolic epistles evidence congregations of Jews and Gentiles (Rom. 2:17 and 11:13; Gal. 2:11–12, for example) in spite of the difficulties that arose as a result. Many of the New Testament letters are the product of those difficulties.

Naturally, congregations will take on the cultural flavor of their respective surroundings and of the majority of their congregants. Culture is, after all, a language, and people are expected to speak their own language. There is no need to learn Hebrew, Latin, or Esperanto in order to worship God, unless those are the languages of the nation or people we seek to address. Nor is there need to take on a "universal culture"—as if there is such a thing. Jews in Messiah remain Jews and Gentiles in Messiah remain Dutch or Chinese, French or Hottentot. They identify and express themselves by their culture, including the culture of their worship. Where a congregation is largely made up of Greek or Hindu speakers, the language of worship will be Greek or Hindu. But Messiah must be the focus, not culture or national identity. Jesus must have the prominence, the praise, and our attentive obedience.

The modern emphasis on ethnicity, epitomized in the Messianic Movement, is an expression of (national) individualism and is far less biblical than we think. The individual indeed has worth—Messiah died for individuals. But he also died to make Jew and Gentile into "one new man" (Eph. 2:15). Our oneness is at least as important as our individuality. The Messianic Movement is an expression of Jewish Christian insecurity and of a desire to find a sense of individual worth through acceptance. For many Gentiles, the movement provides a sense of belonging.

I was flabbergasted to find, during a visit to Namibia in 2001, a messianic group wholly made up of African Gentiles. Imagine: in the middle of nowhere, with the African sun beating down on their heads and the Namibian desert around them, a group of Gentiles had found a shortcut to God. Someone there with me enthusiastically described the practice of the group: "It's wonderful. They sit there, light the Sabbath candles, and enjoy the presence of God." If this is not paganism, I do not know what is!

In fact, it is surprising to discover how much of Jewish national tradition has pagan roots. One example is the belief that, in the period between Rosh HaShanah and Yom Kippur, God determines the fate of individuals for the coming year, or that the blowing of a ram's horn conveys spiritual power. The celebration of a Feast of Lights at the end of December is another. Pagan overtones have been lost in antiquity, but they are there. We celebrate Hanukkah, the Feast of Lights, to commemorate the Maccabean victory over Antiochus Epiphanes. The fact that we do so on the shortest day of the year and that many ancient nations celebrated their own Feasts of Light for the same reason and on the same day has been forgotten.

Returning to the issue of personal worth, no individual or group is void of worth. True worth comes from God in Messiah. But Jesus taught that we find ourselves by losing ourselves, not by self-assertion. We are granted life when we fall into the ground and die, denying ourselves, not when we assert our identity and impose it on others. Being Jewish (or Gentile) will not get us far in the kingdom of God. It is Christ we should be promoting, not our identity. In an effort to be Jewish, Messianic Judaism has created liturgical practices that are in no way Jewish, although a large and still-growing Gentile populace seems to think they are. Most of so-called "messianic music" has little Jewishness about it. It is simply modern chorus singing, often in truncated Hebrew ("Arkhamchana Adonai") or with a heap of garbled Hebrew words that make no semantic sense such as "Baruch Hashem, Adonai Yeshua."

Messianic Judaism does not identify with Judaism at its core but with those external forms of Judaism that developed in Eastern Europe (chicken noodle soup on Sabbath eve, corn beef sandwiches, and Jewish delicatessen foods), or in Israel (dancing the Hora, eating Tehina and Humus, singing Hava Nagila). As to "davidic dancing"—I invite any of my readers to perform such in a synagogue, or allow women carrying banners to prance about in the synagogue aisles. They will soon discover how un-Jewish such practices are.

Is there inherent spiritual value in singing in Hebrew or using Hebrew phrases? Ought we not to sing with the understanding as well as with our hearts? Ought we to worship in Hebrew when no one understands what is being said, much like the Catholic Church when it restricted its worship to Latin? Is Hebrew more sacred than Hungarian, Hakka, or Hutu?

Congregational Practice

What has happened to us? Have we forgotten the Reformation? Have we forgotten the prophetic call to do away with empty rituals that sidestep the mind? Should we not ensure that our people are addressed in a language they can understand? Can worship exist without understanding? God is a spirit and, as such, must be worshiped in spirit and in truth. "Spirit" in biblical terms is not equal to emotion even when it includes emotion. Spirit is the innermost part of man. Worship in spirit is a heartfelt response to truth understood, loved, and experienced. As we hear, speak, or sing of the majesty of God and his unfathomable love, our spirits are stirred to worship. The more we discover of his glorious holiness and understand the sinfulness of our nature, the more are we enabled to discover the wonder of God's grace. This moves our hearts to worship. "Spirit" is always linked to "truth."

Paul Liberman asks, "Isn't it much more reasonable . . . to speak Hebrew when talking to a Hebrew?"[38] Of course—if he knows Hebrew and is comfortable in that language. It is always right to present the gospel in the language of the people, taking into account their sensitivities, prejudices, and fundamental concepts. But the average Jew in America knows just about as much Hebrew as he does French. Why speak or sing in Hebrew when our hearers can better understand English, Chinese, or Russian? Paul Liberman penned those words when he could not converse in the language for which he was contending. What is the point?

Evangelical churches should rid themselves of the anti-Semitism that has crept into their thinking. Jewish Christians are often discomforted by anti-Jewish sentiment in both pews and pulpits, however evangelical and however unintended. More effort needs to be made to ensure Jews in Christ know they are welcome. The solution is not to establish separate congregations. It is wrong to make ethnicity the focus of congregational life, to establish congregations whose sole distinction is cultural. This is all the more true when the majority of those living in the area do not share that culture. Paul spent most of his Christian life opposing such tendencies because they threaten the delicate fabric of unity in Messiah. Worse, they displace the Lord of Glory by placing national culture at the center. Why should a Sikh Christian imbibe

38. Ibid., 5.

Hindu cultural norms when living among his own people? Why should a Gentile Christian take on Jewish cultural trappings? Jews should remain Jews and Gentiles, Gentiles (1 Cor. 7:18).

A CHURCH AMONG THE JEWS—THEOLOGICAL REFLECTIONS

God over All

This is God's world. Everything should be guided by his word (Isa. 8:20). He alone may determine what is godly, wise, or just, because he alone is wise, just, and gracious beyond comprehension. He is the object of the angels' eternal praise. Human wisdom is insufficient for the management of this world. It is foolishness in comparison with the wisdom of him who made all things (Isa. 55:8–9).

Everything that purports to be biblical should have Jesus, his glory, his deeds, his teaching, and his accomplishments as its ground and its focus (Col. 1:16). No other name, no other authority, no other interest, may be the focus of our lives. God's word has Jesus as its object (Luke 24:27, 44–47), and the glory of God in and through Jesus as its eternal goal. Scripture leads to him.

These principles should be doubly clear when we reflect on our theme, "A Church among the Jewish People." Our task is not to seek a cost-effective or socially acceptable means to promote our message, but to engage our society with the message of Messiah. If this means calling upon our people to bear the price of discipleship by going outside the camp, where the lepers and the unclean were sent, so be it. We have no right to try to improve on the gospel. Our duty and our delight is to obey.

4

The Biblical Argument

WE ARE GOING to spend a long time together in the letter to the Ephesians, especially in chapter 2. To get the gist of that chapter we'll look elsewhere in Ephesians and in Paul's writings. But we'll come back to Ephesians 2 because it is central to the theme of this book. Here is the text:

> You were dead in your trespasses and sins in which you formerly walked according to the course of this world, according to the prince of the power of the air, of the spirit that is now working in the sons of disobedience. Among them we too all formerly lived in the lusts of our flesh, indulging the desires of the flesh and of the mind, and were by nature children of wrath, even as the rest. But God, being rich in mercy, because of His great love with which He loved us, even when we were dead in our transgressions, made us alive together with Christ (by grace you have been saved), and raised us up with Him, and seated us with Him in the heavenly places in Christ Jesus, so that in the ages to come He might show the surpassing riches of His grace in kindness toward us in Christ Jesus. For by grace you have been saved through faith; and that not of yourselves; it is the gift of God; not as a result of works, so that no one may boast. For we are His workmanship, created in Christ Jesus for good works, which God prepared beforehand so that we would walk in them.
>
> Therefore remember that formerly you, the Gentiles in the flesh, who are called "Uncircumcision" by the so-called "Circumcision," which is performed in the flesh by human hands—remember that you were at that time separate from Christ, excluded from the

commonwealth of Israel, and strangers to the covenants of promise, having no hope and without God in the world. But now in Christ Jesus you who formerly were far off have been brought near by the blood of Christ. For He Himself is our peace, who made both groups into one and broke down the barrier of the dividing wall, by abolishing in His flesh the enmity, which is the Law of commandments contained in ordinances, so that in Himself He might make the two into one new man, thus establishing peace, and might reconcile them both in one body to God through the cross, by it having put to death the enmity. And He came and preached peace to you who were far away, and peace to those who were near; for through Him we both have our access in one Spirit to the Father. So then you are no longer strangers and aliens, but you are fellow citizens with the saints, and are of God's household, having been built upon the foundation of the apostles and prophets, Christ Jesus Himself being the corner stone in whom the whole building, being fitted together, is growing into a holy temple in the Lord, in whom you also are being built together into a dwelling of God in the Spirit.

GENTILES AND JEWS—PAST AND PRESENT

In chapter 1 of his letter to the Ephesians, Paul focused on the centrality of Christ in history. God, he says, has determined to sum up "all things in Christ, things in the heavens and things on the earth" (Eph. 1:10). The salvation of man is not an end in itself. It is part of a wider plan. In chapter two Paul describes how God has worked for the accomplishment of that plan. In verses 1–2 Paul speaks of the Gentiles ("you"), dead in trespasses and sins, captives of the devil. In verse 3 he speaks of the Jews ("we") as no better off. In spite of the repository of divine grace granted to us, we were "by nature children of wrath" like the others. Gentiles and Jews differed little with regard to sin and therefore to God, and they differ to no greater degree in Christ. By grace, both are made "alive together" in Christ. That togetherness forms the substance of God's dealings with both Israel and the nations, and is part of the eternal plan Paul indicates in verse 10.

Why, then, does Paul speak of two groups? In order to indicate the unity God has created in Christ, incorporating "all things"—in this case, Jews and Gentiles—"in Christ." Paul repeatedly uses the term "in Christ" because it points to God's eternal plan. Jesus is the focus of eschatology. God has reversed the state of Jews and of Gentiles.

> God, being rich in mercy, because of His great love with which He has loved us [Jews and Gentiles], even when we were dead in our transgressions, [God] made us alive together with Christ . . . and raised us up with Him, and seated us with Him in the heavenly places in Christ Jesus, so that in the ages to come He might show the surpassing riches of His grace in kindness toward us in Christ Jesus. (Eph. 2:4–7)

Paul praises God for the wonder of his grace. He prays that his readers would be enabled to comprehend that grace in its boundless power, by which grace God is glorified in Christ and by which individual sinners, dead in their sins, are made "alive together." *Together* is the issue: Paul rejoices in the way the gospel brings an end to differences between mankind, uniting members from all parts of the human race.

Remember (vv. 11–12)

"Therefore," says Paul, in light of the glorious grace of God in Christ to Gentiles and Jews, "remember." The church has long forgotten what Paul called upon her to remember. The church was taken over by Gentiles who arrogated to themselves privileges and attributed to themselves qualities over the Jews. While it is true that Jewish pride is no more commendable than Gentile pride, Gentiles in Christ should have known better. "Remember that formerly you, the Gentiles in the flesh, who are called 'Uncircumcision' by the so-called 'Circumcision,' which is performed in the flesh by human hands" (v. 11). The Jewish people divide mankind into two groups: "them" and "us"—Gentiles and Jews. Paul rejects this division. His mind has been transformed by Christ.

Gentiles in Christ are only called the uncircumcision. They are no longer such because they have been circumcised in heart. They are called the "Uncircumcision" by those who are the "so-called 'Circumcision,'" who have no more than a circumcision "performed in the flesh by human hands." Instead of despising others, the "so-called 'Circumcision'" should have sought the circumcision of the heart promised by the prophets (compare Phil. 3:2–3).

"Remember that you were at that time separate from Messiah, excluded from the commonwealth of Israel and strangers to the covenants of promise, having no hope and without God in the world" (v. 12). These words are expressive of the New Testament view of man without Christ, but they are intended here to describe the state of the Gentiles outside Christ. Those who do not belong to the commonwealth of Israel are without hope, without a Messiah, and without God in the world, regardless of the originality of their thought, the beauty of their ethics, the cost of their sacrifices, or the sincerity of their convictions. Only to Israel did God give hope of a Messiah through the covenants of promise.

In the Old Testament, the world was also divided in two: the people of the covenant, and all the rest. Israel, in covenant with God, had the promises of his presence, protection, and guidance, the wisdom of his commandments, the privilege of his worship, and the assured hope of the Messiah. Others had none of these. The only way they could possess them was to become part of Israel. The distinction was starkly drawn. Faithful Jews did not sit at table with Gentiles, let alone worship with them. In New Testament times, this division was epitomized by an inscription placed at the entrance of the temple court, by the gate that led from the court of the Gentiles to the court of Israel: "No Gentile may enter within the wall which surrounds the sanctuary and its enclosure. Anyone caught doing so will be guilty of his ensuing death." The partition was firm and final.

The Past Is Past Already (vv. 13-14)

But, once again, in verse 13, God has reversed the situation. "Now in Christ Jesus you who formerly were far off have been brought near by the blood of Christ. For He Himself is our peace, who made both groups into one and broke down the barrier of the dividing wall." In Christ, there are not two groups of humanity. God has made the two into one. He has destroyed the wall that divided them. In Christ, God has destroyed the differences. Whatever differences exist in any other context, in Christ there is "no difference." Now, in Messiah Jesus, "you who formerly were far off have been brought near by the blood of Messiah." Contrary to Jewish expectations that Messiah would enthrone Israel over the nations, Messiah brought an end to the separation between Jew and Gentile. He shed his blood for both; he brought them both near. He made them one.

Paul is thoroughly true to the Old Testament. His terminology is taken from the promise to Israel in Isaiah 57:16–19 where, after describing the sin of Israel and its punishment (the people are "far off"), God promised to work savingly for them (they will be "brought near" by his grace). Like the Gentiles, Israel had become idolatrous. But, God promised, "he who takes refuge in Me [Jewish or Gentile] will inherit the land and will possess My holy mountain" (v. 13). In other words, Israel apostatized from God and had become like the other nations. It was put "far off"—as far as any Gentile nation could be. But, Isaiah promises, God is true to his grace and to his covenant. He will bring Israel back by a unilateral act of mercy. Those once "far off" will be "brought near." Hosea assured Israel of similar things, at one moment declaring Israel to be "not My people" (Hos. 1:9) and at another promising that "where it is said to them, 'You are not My people,' it will be said to them, 'You are the sons of the living God'" (Hos. 1:10, cf. 2:23).

Paul is saying that Gentiles and Jews were "formerly . . . by nature children of wrath" (Eph. 2:3), but God has saved them both by grace, making no difference between them. He has brought both "near by the blood of Messiah" (v. 13). Jesus levels mankind. All are equal before him in sin and by the grace of his sacrifice.

The Means (vv. 14–18)

He himself is our peace, who made both groups into one and broke down the barrier of the dividing wall, by abolishing in His flesh the enmity, which is the Law of commandments contained in ordinances, that in Himself He might make the two into one new man, thus establishing peace, and might reconcile them both in one body to God through the cross, by it having put to death the enmity. And He came and preached peace to you who were far away, and peace to those who were near; for through Him we both have our access in one Spirit to the Father.

God achieved this unity "by abolishing in His flesh [by the sacrifice of Messiah] the enmity, which is the Law of commandments contained in ordinances" (v. 15). Paul is referring to the role of the Torah, given to draw a clear distinction between Israel and the nations. That distinction created mutual enmity. Israel looked upon herself as the chosen nation and held herself aloof from the rest of mankind. Had God not shown the people of Israel his favor, given them his law, and granted them his presence? Had they not received the covenants of promise, including the promise of a Messiah, and been given reason for hope in God? Were the Gentiles not strangers to all this? The nations were offended by such arrogance and responded with understandable enmity. Who do these Jews think they are? They will not even eat with us! They despise our customs, reject our idols, and refuse to mingle with us as equals. Surely, this arrogance is to be rejected, despised, and hated.

But now, says Paul, now, things are different. Those "far off" have "been brought near by the blood of Christ" (v. 13). The dividing wall of commandments has been fulfilled in Christ and is consequently "abolished"—set aside as accomplished.

It is worth spending a few minutes clarifying the meaning of the Greek term translated "abolished." Walter Bauer informs us that κατργεω means to "make ineffective, powerless, idle, nullify, abolish, wipe out or to set aside."[1] In Romans 7:2 the meaning is "to be released from an association, have nothing more to do with." Paul is saying that the law has been nullified, abolished, wiped out, or set aside. These are strong words; can they be justified by the apostles' use of the term elsewhere?

Paul employs the term κατργεω extensively in his letter to the Romans. For example, he tells us that the faithlessness of Israel cannot abolish God's faithfulness (κατργησει, Rom. 3:3); that if salvation may be obtained through the law, faith is rendered ineffective (κατηργηται, Rom. 4:14, cf. Gal. 3:17); that the death of a woman's spouse releases her from obligation toward her dead husband (κατηργηται, Rom. 7:2). This is precisely what the death of Christ has accomplished on behalf of the redeemed with regard to the law (κατργηθημεν, Rom. 7:6). In other words, what the law could not do to faith, faith has done to the law: the law has been abolished, nullified, set aside as to its authority. It no longer regulates the relationships between God and man.

Why has God abolished the law? "That in Himself He might make the two into one new man, thus establishing peace" between Israel and the nations by dealing with the enmity between them (Eph. 2:15). Further, God has so worked that he "might reconcile them both in one body to [himself] through the cross, by it having put to death the enmity," (v. 16)

1. Walter Bauer, *A Greek-English Lexicon of the New Testament and Other Early Christian Literature*, trans. William F. Arndt and F. Wilber Gingrich (Chicago: University of Chicago Press, 1957).

which constituted both Jews and Gentiles, the "children of wrath" (v. 3). Gentiles and Jews are reconciled to God by the cross as well as to each other. Their mutual enmity is set aside by the sacrifice of Christ. "He came and preached peace to you [Gentiles] who were far away, and peace to those [Jews] who were near; for through him we both [Gentiles and Jews] have our access in one Spirit to the Father" (vv. 17–18), and mutual access is possible because "the barrier of the dividing wall" in the temple (v. 14) has been "broken down."

The peace of which Paul speaks is of two kinds. The first has to do with the enmity created by what Paul describes as "the Law of commandments contained in ordinances" (v. 15). This law served as a dividing wall between sons of the covenants and those outside the covenants. It served in the same way as did the inscription on the temple court wall, dividing Jews from Gentiles. The law was not meant to create enmity, but it did. Human pride is always xenophobic: it resents and rejects those who differ. The Jews, exulting in their law, considered the Gentiles to be "dogs," soulless pagans. The Greeks and Romans despised the Jews for their strange dietary traditions, their avoidance of sports, and their other national habits. That enmity has now been dealt with because God "broke down the barrier of the dividing wall" (v. 14). He has abolished "in His flesh the enmity" (v. 15). By one atoning sacrifice both Jews and Gentiles are "brought near" (v. 13) to God and thereby also to each other. By one Spirit they both now have access (v. 18) and belong to the one body of the redeemed (v. 16). God has made Jews and Gentiles "one" (v. 14), "one new man" (v. 15)—"establishing peace" between them (v. 15).

The other kind of peace is more fundamental, having to do with God's enmity toward man, because even the sons of the covenant disobeyed God's commandments and rejected his Son. That enmity has also been "put to death" through the cross (v. 16). Sinners are now reconciled in the eyes of God (v. 16) and peace is preached to them (v. 17). They both have access to the Father (v. 18).

Important as the atonement is in terms of its restoration of the relationship between God and man, Paul is emphasizing another aspect of that work of God. He is stating that the atonement has restored relationships within mankind. Man, in rebellion against God, hated his fellow man. Man, in Christ, is now relieved of that defiling burden and united with his fellow man by the recognition of his shared sin and of a shared saving grace. They are made into one body. They share in the benefits of one sacrifice, one Spirit of God, and access to the one Father.

One in Him (vv. 19–22)

> So then you [Gentiles] are no longer strangers and aliens, but you are fellow citizens with the saints, and are of God's household. (v. 19)

God has done away with the distinction between Jews and Gentiles. The cross has made them equal. The Gentiles are "no longer strangers"; they are citizens—no, fellow citizens—with the Jews. Paul uses repetition to get the message across. Redeemed Gentiles belong to "the household of God," as do redeemed Jews, "having been built upon the foundation of the apostles and prophets, Messiah Jesus Himself being the corner stone" (v. 20). Jews and Gentiles in Christ are established together on one foundation. The revelation is shared, as is whatever tradition may develop from it. Jews and Gentiles share a common foundation in the apostles and prophets, Messiah himself being the cornerstone according to which the building is constructed.

That is not all! A glorious process is taking place. In Messiah, God is still at work. He is drawing Jews and Gentiles to his Son, freeing them from the tyranny of sin, and weaning them from sinful habits. God is active in the church in ways that he is not active anywhere else. Slowly but steadily, Jews and Gentiles are being remade into the image of Messiah individually and as a body. He is present in the church, united by the blood of Christ, in ways he is not present anywhere else. "The whole building, being fitted together, is growing into a holy temple in the Lord" (v. 21). It is wonderful to belong to the body of Messiah!

God dwells among people who are united in Christ. He dwells among those divested of their intolerance and enmity. "Being fitted together," the body is "growing into a holy temple in the Lord." Paul stretches the limits of imagination by using mixed metaphors. From the metaphor of a building being constructed he goes on to speak of a living, growing body. The temple of the Lord is alive with human life, sanctified by the blood of Christ, and changed with the work of the Holy Spirit. Returning to his original metaphor, Paul concludes, "in whom," that is to say, in Messiah, "you [Jews and Gentiles] also are being built together into a dwelling of God in the Spirit" (v. 22). God is the builder, and Christians from every nation are the building blocks.

Paul wants his readers to aspire to glorious things. He wants them to yearn to be "a dwelling of God through the Spirit," where God is present, known, loved, adored, and served. It will be a dwelling where humans, formerly locked in conflict, live together, united by the gospel. They can only achieve this together, as Jews and Gentiles in Christ, united into one body by an eternal bond nothing can sever. Such is Paul's inspired view of the church: not a conglomerate of humans united by shared sorrows, conflicts, or interests; not primarily a sanctuary where wounds are healed. Above all, the church is a temple of God in which he is the focus. Such a wonder will never come about if we choose to be occupied with the differences between us.

God dwells in the sanctified unity established by the sacrifice of his Son. It is a unity focused on him, grounded in the saving work of Christ and the regenerating power of the Holy Spirit, and expressed in a courageous, determined dedication to live by the truth of God's word.

THE CENTRALITY OF CHRIST

From the moment Jesus revealed himself to Paul on the road to Damascus (Acts 9), the apostle was taken up with Jesus. His longing was to know him and be found in him, even at the expense of his Jewishness (Phil. 3:9–10).

Jesus was the sum of what Paul had to say. Luke describes Paul's preaching by saying he "proclaim[ed] Jesus" (Acts 9:20). This was also the apostle's own summary of his message: "We preach Christ crucified" (1 Cor. 1:23; see also Acts 5:42; Phil. 1:15). Jesus, sent by God for the salvation of the world, crucified, risen, reigning in glory, and coming again, filled the horizon of the apostle's message. This should be the sum and focus of our message and of our congregational life. Paul perceived Jesus to be the sum of God's gifts. Those redeemed by Christ's blood and granted true faith are "complete in Him" (Col. 2:10 NKJV), in whom the whole fullness of the godhead dwells (Col. 1:19; 2:9), of whose fullness we have received (John 1:16) and into whose fullness we should grow (Eph. 4:13). It is not, therefore, surprising to discover that Paul summarized the

Christian life as being "in Christ." Christians believe in Christ (Eph. 1:1, 13), are blessed in Christ (Eph. 1:3), chosen in Christ (v. 4), redeemed and forgiven in Christ (v. 7). The whole creation is to be summed up in Christ (v. 10) in whom Jews and Gentiles obtain an eternal inheritance (vv. 11, 13), for which they hope in Christ (v. 12), and in whom they are sealed (v. 13).

Jesus filled Paul's vision because God subjected everything to Jesus, made him to be the head of the church, and established the church as his body, the fullness of him who fills everything (Eph. 1:22). This latter statement is worth contemplating. Paul was not blind to the weaknesses and failings of the church; most of his letters, if not all, were composed to address these. Yet he does not hesitate to describe the church as Christ's fullness—"the fullness of Him who fills all in all" (v. 23)! Jesus should be the focus of every church. His holy, gentle, mighty personality should be expressed, his amazing glory manifested, the wonder of his deeds professed and exemplified, his teachings taught and obeyed, his purposes primary, and his name loved, revered, and promulgated on every occasion. The focus must be on Messiah—nowhere else.

Unity in Christ—Paul's Major Concern

Paul worked for the unity of the body of Christ because Christian unity gives expression to the supremacy of Christ by rendering all other considerations peripheral. Paul's concern for the unity of the church is expressed time and again. In Ephesians he exhorts his readers to conduct themselves in a manner worthy of their calling which, he explains, means that they should be "diligent to preserve the unity of the Spirit in the bond of peace" (Eph. 4:3). He then goes on to remind them that there is but "one body" (Eph. 4:4). Christ died to undo the distinctions within mankind and to create "one new man" (Eph. 2:15).

In Romans 12–16, Paul speaks against those who disturb the unity of the church by contending over secondary matters. He stringently reminds his readers: "just as we have many members in one body and all the members do not have the same function, so we, who are many, are one body in Christ, and individually members one of another" (Rom. 12:4–5). In his first letter to the Corinthians Paul is distressed to hear of contentions in the church over the relative primacy of leading teachers (1 Cor. 1:10–17). He says that such a focus runs contrary to the spirit of the gospel (1 Cor. 1:11–29), and then returns to the theme of unity in Christ while discussing the Lord's Table. "By one Spirit are we all baptized into one body, whether we be Jews or Gentiles, whether we be bond or free; and have been all made to drink into one Spirit" (1 Cor. 12:13 KJV, see also 1 Cor. 10:17 and chapter 12). He raises the issue again in Colossians 3:11, stating that "there is neither Greek nor Jew, circumcision nor uncircumcision, Barbarian, Scythian, bond nor free; but Christ is all, and in all" (KJV).

The letter to the Galatians was composed to defend the unity of the body of Christ, in which there is no difference between duties incumbent on Jews or on Gentiles, nor in the blessings they receive (Gal. 3:28). They are "all sons of God through faith in Christ Jesus" (Gal. 3:26). Paul calls upon the Philippians not to be taken up with earthly distinctions. He refuses to take his Jewishness into account and invites his readers to follow that example because their citizenship is in heaven, from whence they await the reappearance of Messiah (Phil. 2:1–20). They should not, therefore, succumb to the call to be circumcised. In other words, Paul intimates that Jewishness has to do with earthly-mindedness, whereas belonging to Messiah is nothing short of heavenly.

Reflecting Messiah

Jesus, Son of God, Maker and Sustainer of heaven and earth, our Redeemer and only Savior from the guilt and power of sin, should be the focal point of congregational life. Whatever else may be true about a church among the Jewish people, Jesus must be its most prominent distinctive. Jesus, not Jewishness. We must therefore consider the legitimacy of Jewish Christian congregations, even among the Jewish people. Such congregations are obliged by the rationale of their existence to focus on Jewish identity, Jewish custom, Jewish history, and present-day Jewish realities. These are more than enough to occupy the minds and hearts of a congregation. Jewish tradition is so rich, Jewish identity so all-encompassing, contemporary Jewish reality so challenging that they engage the whole of one's energies, leaving little room for Messiah, who should be the heartbeat of Christian congregations.

That is where biblical evaluation must play its determining role. If we are to think biblically about a church among the Jews, we must begin with biblical data. We must derive our thinking from the word of God and shape our congregations according to it. There are no biblical grounds for ethnically focused congregations; a focus on Jesus must have maximal expression in the life of congregations. If "a congregation among the Jews" means in an area where there is a Jewish majority, it is to be assumed that the majority of those owning the name of Christ in the congregation will be Jewish, not by premeditation but due to geography. The flavor of such a congregation will rightly and naturally reflect the flavor of the congregants' everyday life, Jewish or Gentile. This, too, will not be the product of premeditation. A church among the Jews must be, first and foremost, a church. As such, it is the glad and holy duty to conduct congregational life in a way that will enable every redeemed member of the body of Christ to feel at home, without having to act as if he were Jewish, educated, male, rich, white, black, or Gentile. There is, therefore, no room for premeditated Jewish Christian congregations. We must not make ethnicity or culture a test of fellowship.

This is easier said than done. It means that Jesus should be the focus of congregational life even among the Jews. A congregation of Messiah is not to reflect the world, but Messiah in and to the world, calling on the world to forsake its divisive, mistaken ways and join the victorious train of King Jesus. He reigns over all and will continue to reign until his Father makes all his enemies his footstool, after which he will deliver the kingdom to the Father. We may not be preoccupied with anything but Jesus.

One in Messiah

Of course, distinctions remain: Slaves remain slaves (Eph. 6:5–8), the poor are not suddenly enriched, and the rich are not impoverished (1 Tim. 6:17). Jews remain Jews, and Gentiles remain Gentiles (1 Cor. 7:18). The uneducated do not obtain a supernatural education, and the educated do not, by virtue of their conversion, forget what they have learned. Jews and Palestinians do not lose their national identities or become immune to the conflicting interests of their respective people. But their views of those interests will be modified by distinctly Christian concerns, and all their differences will be left at the doorstep of the church. The very mixture that should exist in a local church—in just about every church— helps to safeguard it from serving the world instead of Lord Messiah. Such a mixture is a practical demonstration of the fact that our ultimate citizenship is indeed in heaven, where our ultimate loyalty is to be found; that we no longer regard men "after the flesh" (2 Cor. 5:16 KJV) but after the Spirit. The concerns of Messiah's kingdom must be seen to override those of the world.

Some might ask, "What, then, can be the appeal of such churches?" Their appeal is *Jesus*. God forbid that we should boast in anything but Christ and him crucified. There is no need to beautify the gospel or attempt to render it more attractive. We cannot improve on what God has done. Nor can we make the gospel appealing to sinful man. The gospel is God's power to save. If men and women come to Messiah, it is because they have been moved by the power of God. The gospel itself is that power (Rom. 1:16). Ethnicities, doctrinal issues that do not reflect on the glory of Christ, cultures, and human interests must not be allowed to define congregations. To transgress this standard is to promote a man-centered gospel that places human interests on the throne where God in Christ should be sitting. It is to forsake the biblical focus that should characterize all who seek to serve God.

Tradition . . . Tradition!

A church in which Jewish people are the majority will naturally partake of the majority's culture. Rightly so. You would not expect a church among the French to conduct its services in anything but French. A church among the Koreans will naturally speak the message in Korean. Language is but one aspect of culture. So are ways the congregation shows respect for the Scripture or worships in song. There is no such thing as a cultureless church or cultureless worship. I am not calling for congregational life that is the color of water. I am saying that no culture may be exalted in the church above another.

All cultures have a measure of truth, and all are contaminated by sin. They differ from each other with respect to their ability to communicate aspects of the gospel. No one will deny that some aspects of Jewish culture are better equipped to that end than, say, the culture of the Kikuyu. But these aspects should never be used in a manner that would render any worshiper incapable of meaningful participation.

It is also worth noting in this context that rabbinic Judaism is the most self-consciously reactionary religion on the face of the globe. It was framed in determined conflict with the gospel, premeditatedly designed to serve as a barrier to the gospel. It is therefore incorrect to claim that Judaism is the root of Christianity, or to claim to have found Christ in rabbinic tradition. The roots of the Christian faith are not Jewish; they are biblical. Rabbinic Judaism is not biblical.

Congregants may premeditatedly cherish, maintain, and cultivate their respective cultures outside the framework of the church. They might invite others to share in their cultural activities. But they should never claim divine authority for their cultures or consider them superior ways to obey and worship God.

In the opening paragraph of this section I said, "A church in which Jewish people are the majority will naturally partake of the majority's culture. . . . A church among the Koreans will naturally speak the message in Korean." "Naturally" is the determining word. "Naturally" means non-deliberate, without affectation. Can that be said of Messianic Judaism's attitude to rabbinic Jewish customs?

THE ESSENTIALS

A congregation among the Jews should be as recognizably Christian as a congregation among any other people. With all churches of Christ it should hold to the five Reformation Solas.

- Sola Scriptura
- Sola Fide
- Solo Christo
- Sola Gratia
- Soli Deo Gloria

Sola Scriptura

The Scriptures alone should govern all aspects of congregational life and activity. Truth about how God is to be served is available nowhere but in Scripture. There is no room to interpret Scripture through the authoritative grid of rabbinic tradition, although some historical light can be found in that tradition. We are forbidden to introduce into worship anything but what God has commanded in his word or what we may legitimately infer from his word. This rules out paraphernalia such as icons, incense, idols, prayer shawls, gesticulations, candles, drama, kippot, clerical garb, Torah scrolls, and dancing.

God is to be worshiped and served in spirit and in truth, not by human traditions. Our fear of God must be the result of a personal encounter with him as he is revealed in Scripture, not of man-made precepts. Such an encounter is only possible by the work of the Holy Spirit, who moves in accordance with the written word of God.

Sola Fide

Faith alone, as defined by the Scripture, is the means of our salvation and should be the only grounds for members being accepted into the church. If their faith is evangelical, however imperfect, they are heirs and joint heirs with Christ, children of our father Abraham. No achievement, no keeping of the Torah, no adherence to traditions can advance one in the matters of the kingdom or add to spirituality. There is no room for elitism in the church.

Solo Christo

We are saved and sanctified by Messiah alone, as he is revealed in the Scripture. He should be the focus of church life. His teachings should be reflected upon, imbibed, and obeyed; his example should be studied and followed; his honor should be defended; and his will should be done. We can know and serve God only in Messiah. No more than Messiah is needed. His is a completed work, and our salvation is complete in him. Jesus must fill the horizon of a faithful church's vision and be seen as the sum of a faithful Christian's passion: to know him and the power of his resurrection, to conform to his death, and to love him more than father, mother, brother, or fellow nationals. Nothing can be compared to the thrill of knowing, loving, and serving him. If we choose to live by any other standard, we are not his disciples.

Sola Gratia

Grace alone, God's grace in Messiah, is the grounds of our salvation and should be the grounds of our labors and hope. It must be the only grounds of our relationship with God and should characterize our every human relationship. Faith is a gift of God's grace, leaving no room for boasting (Eph. 2:8–9). Grace impacts the whole of our life, constituting its fundamental fiber. We can—and need—add nothing to what God has done. Sanctification, God's nearness, and our efforts for the kingdom are the fruit of God's grace working in us, recreating us into his glorious image.

Soli Deo Gloria

God alone is to be glorified and recognized as sovereign. He is to be recognized as the author, the overseeing master, and the source of our salvation. His scriptural will is to be esteemed and obeyed. We chose him because he first chose us. He is the goal of our worship. His glory is the desire of our heart, and his pleasure is our greatest ambition. The gospel is all about and all for the glory of God, and so is truly biblical congregational life. It's not about us, but about him!

CONCLUSIONS

> So then you [Gentiles] are no longer strangers and aliens, but you are fellow citizens with the saints, and are of God's household, having been built on the foundation of the apostles and prophets, Christ Jesus Himself being the chief corner stone, in whom the whole building, being fitted together, is growing into a holy temple in the Lord. (Eph. 2:19–21)

Note again the centrality of Jesus. The cornerstone is not only the part on which the structure rests. It is also the basis for the construction of the whole building. Note further the repeated use of the word "together." The church is to grow into "a holy temple" in the Lord only as it is "fitted together"—Gentiles and Jews worshiping and serving God as "one new man."

Paul concludes by assuring his Gentile readers that, along with Jewish believers, they are "being built together in the Lord into a dwelling of God in the Spirit." That is why he pleads with his readers to conduct themselves

> with all humility and gentleness, with patience, showing tolerance for one another in love, being diligent to preserve the unity of the Spirit in the bond of peace. (Eph. 4:2–3)

True spiritual growth will only occur when Christ is accorded his rightful place at the center of congregational life. Gentiles and Jews are to live out the fruits of God's accomplishments in Christ by maintaining a unity that obviates the distinction between the two, bearing each other in love.

How should culture be treated in the context of congregational life? More specifically, how should Jewish culture be treated? Culture is an important aspect of human life and has been since creation. That is the point: cultures must be directed by God. To the extent that they are, they can express the gospel. Every culture it is a valid means for humans to conduct their lives and communicate the gospel. But all men, and therefore all cultures, are tainted by sin. They are, therefore, limited in their ability to communicate the gospel faithfully. Rabbinicism is not a divinely inspired culture and should not be allowed to claim that status. The civil and ritual duties God imposed on Israel are no longer matters of obedience to God, and keeping those duties must never be viewed as spiritually advantageous or superior.

As cultural norms, Jewish traditional practices (with the exception of the sacrifices, the temple worship, the Day of Atonement, and so on) may be practiced. This is also true of customs in other cultures. Mankind has been engaged in a search for and a flight from God, both of which have found expression in the creations of many fascinating cultures. All of these may be enlisted to a greater or lesser extent to communicate the gospel.

There is no discussion of culture as such in the New Testament, but it seems to me that the following may be gleaned from the pages of the New Testament:

1. All cultures are impacted by their religious contexts and convey religious messages. In spite of the significant cultural differences between Israel and the Gentiles, between the relatively primitive Phrygian Galatians and the cultured Athenians, the sophisticated dwellers of Rome and the crass Corinthians, Paul refused to allow culture to intrude into the duties of a Christian life. He maintained a firm, uncompromising stance, relegating culture to the sidelines and exalting the gospel, Christian morality, and church unity over cultural demands and conventions.

    In Galatia, for example, where (Jewish) custom was posited as a religious duty, Paul firmly objected. In no case did he teach adherence to Jewish religious custom. Nor did he call upon his

Gentile converts to replace their cultures and languages with Jewish culture and Hebrew.

2. By choosing to be as a Jew to the Jews and as a Gentile to the Gentiles, Paul demonstrated his freedom from all cultural obligations. In his letters to the Romans (Rom. 14) and the Corinthians (1 Cor. 8), he discussed the rights and wrongs of eating meat bought in the marketplace. He ignored the fact that most such meat had been offered to idols before being sold in the marketplace. Idols are nothing, and there is no God but one (1 Cor. 8:4). No religious overtones are to be attached to the eating of such meat ("all things indeed are clean," Rom. 14:20) unless an unbeliever or a weak Christian makes such an attachment. Then the meat is not to be eaten because of the message such individuals are liable to receive from the exercise of Christian liberty, not from any spiritual import in the meat or its consumption (1 Cor. 8:10).

   The issue, then, is not religious but moral. Neither eating nor abstaining commends us to God (1 Cor. 8:13). What is at stake is our loving consideration of one another. None are to be destroyed by our selfish enjoyment of liberty (Rom. 14:15–17, 20). The evil is in eating and causing offense, rather than in what we eat. Virtue is to be found in our attitude to our brethren (1 Cor. 8: 13), not in our diet. That is why Paul adamantly opposed the circumcision of Gentile believers. He insisted that "neither circumcision nor uncircumcision" (Gal. 5:6) are important in and of themselves.

   Now, the circumcision to which the Galatians were being called was not a cultural matter; it had religious implications. That is why it was forbidden. A Gentile Christian who agreed to be circumcised had "fallen from grace" (Gal. 5:4), rendering Christ "of no benefit" (Gal. 5:2).

3. No one has the right to criticize, look down upon, or boast before another of his national culture or tradition (Col. 2:16). Dietary laws, holy days, and the like are at best shadows that find their substance in Christ (Col. 2:17; cf. Heb. 8:5, 10:1).

4. There is no biblical call to forsake one's (Gentile or Jewish) culture, except where that culture may conflict with the gospel. Converted Jews may remain Jews and practice those aspects of their culture that do not conflict with the gospel. Gentiles may remain true to

their own cultures. No culture is superior to another. No culture should be preferred. There is no room for cultural elitism.

5. There is no room to draw national or cultural distinctions in the church. The church should express its unity in all aspects of its life and witness, regardless of the national backgrounds, social status, or genders of its members. Legitimate differences between Christians should not be the basis of church fellowship.

We conclude, then, that Jewish or Gentile Christians may choose to form fellowships apart from their respective congregations, where they celebrate their feasts, give expression to their shared Jewishness, and reach out to their own people. Such fellowships should never be allowed to supplant the role of the church. Further, we are forbidden to introduce into the worship of God any cultural forms that are to be considered binding or spiritually advantageous to worshipers.

A church among the Jews should partake of all of these traits. It should "be among the Jews" in the sense that it addresses Jewish issues in terms Jews can understand. The cultural language used will naturally be Jewish, and the church will consciously engage Jewish people with the gospel. But such a church ought not to prefer Jews, buy into Jewish self-interest, or submit to Jewish religious tradition. It should exercise a truly prophetic role by calling the nation to repentance and daring to challenge sin adopted in pursuit of national interests.

We should consciously labor for multiethnic congregations that proclaim in both word and deed that Christ is preeminent. Such a church will naturally partake of the majority culture, but constantly subject it to careful scrutiny in accordance with the spirit of the gospel. A church should always reflect the gospel, call with a voice of righteousness to all nations, and show by example what God in Christ does in the life of a community. This church will invite all men to the obedience of faith.

May God forgive our many errors!

5

Making Churches Comfortable for Jewish Christians

THE BELOVED COMFORT ZONE

We are creatures of comfort. We prefer situations in which nothing is liable to surprise or disturb us, or challenge our cozy status quo. This turpitude lies behind a significant part of the modern search for "balance," masquerading as Christian moderation and humility. Our forefathers knew little of such dishonesty. They were anxious for truth and often paid a high price to discover and maintain it. They were not moderate—they were dedicated, courageous, sacrificial. They did not seek balance but the right biblical tension that exists between facets of truth, and they were prepared to die for what they believed. Nowadays, it looks like Muslims are the only ones who are willing to live and die for what they believe to be true. The modern search for balance has often led either to the denial of truth or to the affirmation of one truth at the expense of another. We are unable to see far enough into eternity, where parallel lines meet. We are anxious to have everything within reach.

Knowledge is a kind of control. If we cannot explain how God can be sovereign over the free acts of man, we redefine either God's sovereignty or man's freedom in terms that seem to relieve the tension. If we cannot understand how God can be in covenant with Israel and, at the same time, with the church, we deny or qualify one or another of the covenants. If we stumble at the humanity or divinity of Jesus, we deny one or the other. We affirm the unity of the church, but we tend to evade the tensions such unity would create if we lived it out in practice. We establish churches for different language groups, cultures, and people. There are few blacks in white churches, few Koreans in Chinese churches, and few poor people in the congregations of the rich. It is common for young people to prefer one congregation to another because of the age groups of those attending rather than for biblical considerations. Seeking the comfort zone, we avoid the tensions that a multicultural, multinational, multilingual, multi-layered church would posit.

Shame on us! We act as if it is not worth the effort to preserve the unity of the church in the bond of peace. We redefine the body of Christ as if it meant a kind of communion between churches that does not impact the day-to-day life of congregants. The single remaining restriction on need-based, seeker-friendly churches today is the idea of separate churches for males and females. Such an attitude is a denial of the biblical affirmation that in Christ there is neither Jew nor Gentile, male nor female, slave nor free (Gal. 3:28).

This book is written with a passion—a passion to see the church united, virile, ever-changing in form and ever growing in her intellectual and experiential knowledge of God, his word, and his ways. It is written with a longing to see the church challenge the world rather than become more like it by adopting the prevailing individualistic divisiveness. It is written with the conviction that the unity of the church is a manifestation of the glory of God in the gospel, and of the gospel's power to save and transform.

Some Jewish Christians left churches because they felt or were made to feel uncomfortable. The following is written with the hope that it will serve in some small way to help churches and Jewish Christians serve Christ by serving each other in the context of church life, so that the world might know that the Father sent the Son to be the Savior of the world.

WHY CAN'T YOU BE LIKE EVERYONE ELSE?

The church should do more to accommodate Jewish Christians. Most Jewish people have grown up in non-Jewish environments. They speak the common language, dress as do others, live in similar homes, and send their children to the same schools. They are, therefore, expected to be like everyone else. But Jews are (need I say it?) Jewish, even if they do not look different. Cultural distinctions often become a stumbling block to human relations because we naturally suspect the divergent. Note how the only redhead in class draws negative comments, as if there is anything wrong with the color of her hair. Jewish Christians are repeatedly asked, "Why can't you be like everyone else?!" Would you mind if I asked you, dear reader, just who on earth is "Mr. Everyone Else"? What does he look like? Is he black or white, tall or short? Does he sing like the Welsh, the Thai, or the Latin Americans? How does he dress? What are his social habits? Is he a he or a she?

Many non-Jewish believers assume that since their Jewish Christian friends are so much a part of the general run of things, their Jewish identity has been relegated to the distant past. But we Jews are usually very Jewish and very much aware of our Jewishness. Many of us cringe when introduced as "from a Jewish background." Would you feel uncomfortable if you were introduced as a Christian "formerly French, American, British, or Chinese"? Has your Christian faith erased your national identity? On more than one occasion, even when I was in my twenties, I was introduced as "one of God's ancient people" although I did not feel quite so ancient.

We Jewish Christians are not anyone else. We're Jewish. We're not even like most Jews because we're Christians. We have a warm attachment to the State of Israel, our mannerisms are Jewish, and we are sensitive to jokes that begin with "A Jew, an American, and a Frenchman meet on a bus. The Jew says . . ." Wouldn't you be sensitive if your people had borne the brunt of derision for 2000 years? Of course, Jews aren't only Jews. We're British, Dutch, Swedish, or American—some of us are even Chinese, Occidental, Ethiopian, or Latino. We are loyal to our adoptive countries, yet have an affection for Israel and a concern for our fellow Jews.

One of my correspondents related how she was introduced to a fellow believer who, upon hearing that she was Jewish, reached out to touch her, exclaiming, "Wow! I've touched a Jew!" Others are put on the spot when people say to them, "I love your nation!" as if one was saying, "I love ice cream." Another young Christian, with very little knowledge of the Scriptures, was asked to teach in his church simply because he is Jewish—as if Jewishness could make up for his lack of Bible knowledge. Being Jewish does not constitute us an authority on anything but what we have studied. The best intentions are simply not enough to make Jewish Christians comfortable. Don't treat us like museum pieces.

Another acquaintance was asked to teach the Old Testament "from a Jewish point of view." Why on earth would a church want to hear a point of view that led to the rejection of Jesus? Would you study the Bible from a Muslim point of view? Do fellow believers from among the Gentiles realize that the Judaism of today radically differs from the Judaism of Jesus' day, and that even the Judaism of that day was a departure from biblical truth? An ignorant fascination with things Jewish is a poor substitute for human friendliness.

YEAH, BUT WHAT DOES IT MEAN TO BE JEWISH?

Jews in Christ remain Jews. We have our own culture, our own festivals, and our own ways of doing things. We bear the scars of history. Our brethren in Christ ought not to be put off by our love for our heritage, nor think we are inevitably judaizing. Everybody should love to be what God made him and encouraged to be just that.

Churches should encourage Jewish Christians to be active in the fellowship of the church, leaving room for inner- and intra-congregational fellowships where Jews in Christ can address their special concerns. After all, this is common practice for youth, men, women, and the elderly. Such fellowships should be subject to the supervision of a wise, godly eldership. But a warm welcome and a measure of sincere goodwill promote an awareness of the needs of various church members, Jewish Christians included.

Jewishness often has to do, as another of my correspondents put it, with nature rather than nurture. The sense of estrangement Jewish Christians experience in a church is likely to accompany us into secular life. A strong sense of community, the drive that many Jews invest in their business, the humor we enjoy, our delight in reading between the lines, taking note of legal gaps, and identifying legalistic opportunities—these are national traits developed over a painful and lengthy history, as a necessary means of survival. We can't help being what we are and what many of you, my Gentile readers, made us be. Our non-Jewish fellow believers are sometimes irritated or amused by such traits, at times portrayed in the worse possible light. (I was once asked if I could be "Jewed" into giving a discount for my book). True, the gospel modifies behavior and alters deeply embedded national traits, but it does not erase national identities.

IS THE BIBLE ANTI-SEMITIC?

Many sermons banish the Jewish people from Old Testament texts. Promises are spiritualized and referred to the church while threats and warnings remain, by some form of spiritual alchemy, the exclusive domain of the Jewish people. How would *you* feel if you were Jewish and heard sermons like that day in and day out? Much of the language of the church is offensive to Jewish Christians. We find ourselves writhing under sermons in which the term "the Jews" is used pejoratively, while the term "God's people" is reserved for the faithful. Some preachers imply that "the Jews" are bad and unbelieving, and that God's people are not Jewish. Are there no sinners among Gentiles? What are the grounds for the contrast frequently drawn between "the Jews" on the one hand and "the apostles" or "the early church" on the other? Were the apostles not Jewish? Was the early church not primarily composed of Jews? How can a Jewish person, who loves his people and numbers himself among them, feel comfortable when he and his people are castigated in the name of the gospel?

The only way many Jewish Christians can feel comfortable in a church today is by either absconding from their Jewishness or becoming "token Jews." Neither option serves the cause of the gospel. Nor does either address what it means when we say that the church is truly one. Don't ignore us, but don't make too much of us. Let us be what God has made us, and allow us to make our distinct contribution to the beauty of the body of Christ, in which all worship him on equal grounds with no impositions of human requirements, Jewish or Gentile. Every imposition tends to eclipse the glory of Messiah and establish a competing value. Let's love and serve God together.

INTERIM CONCLUSIONS

- Like all Christians, Jewish Christians are free from the Mosaic Covenant, as we are from rabbinic tradition.
- We are also free to maintain our national identity and should maintain it if we wish to further the best interests of our people.
- The only way to maintain such an identity is to abide by the cultural consensus through which the majority of contemporary Jews maintain their Jewish identity.

- It is vital that we maintain Jewish identity in a manner consistent with the Scriptures. The gospel must never be obscured. Nothing but God in Messiah and his finished work on Calvary may be the focal point of congregational life, worship, or evangelism.
- The unity of the church should be maintained; rabbinic tradition should never be accorded religious authority. God reigns among his redeemed by his word.

May it be so with us.

PART 2

A Practical Assessment

6

Standards

———— ——— ——— ———

THE MESSIANIC MOVEMENT has created its own standards, formulated in terms of goals:

- Achieving acceptance as believers in Jesus within the Jewish nation, in order to
- Impact the Jewish nation with the gospel, and to
- Provide a spiritual home for Jewish believers in Jesus.

We have sought to examine the Messianic Movement in the light of Scripture. We will now evaluate the movement by its goals. Reference to these has been made in previous sections, but it is appropriate to consider them separately.

WHO HAS BEEN PERSUADED OF WHAT?

In an effort to convince Jews of the Jewishness of faith in Jesus, Messianic Jews have chosen to express their Jewishness by way of rabbinic custom in worship and, to a lesser degree, in lifestyle. This is a departure from traditional Jewish thinking, which emphasizes lifestyle rather than modes of worship. It therefore inevitably fails to persuade Jews of the Jewishness of Messianic faith. What is more, it smacks of hypocrisy. Messianic Jews increasingly insist on adherence to Jewish tradition as a matter of religious obligation. They meet in what are often described as synagogues, their preachers are called rabbis, men (and some women!)

wear kippot and prayer shawls for worship, and so on. The movement accords rabbis the right to determine what is Jewish, although the majority of the Jewish people prefer to express their Jewishness in cultural rather than religious terms. Instead of convincing the nation of our Jewishness, the persistent emphasis upon Jewishness confirms doubt in the minds of those we want to reach. Our efforts merely betray the insecurity that underlies them.

Why should we care if the rabbis refuse to recognize our Jewishness? They are wrong. They can claim that we have cut ourselves off from the nation, but we know better and the nation will too in due time. Meanwhile, we are willing to go outside the camp, bearing our Lord's reproach and recognizing that the servant is no greater than his master. If they persecuted and rejected him, we have no reason to expect them to treat us any better.

The doubts of our detractors are well founded when there are so many Gentiles in messianic congregations. How can a congregation that is primarily Gentile be considered Jewish? What can we do to remedy this—reject the Gentiles? Of course not! We cherish unity with all who worship God in Messiah and rejoice in the fellowship such unity affords. If the Messianic Movement had the courage to opt for such an option, it would collapse for lack of financial support and would be seen to be what it really is: a fringe group of engaging individuals united around a quaint teaching. It is unlikely that our vague, not-quite-honest stand will persuade anyone of our integrity. How can someone bear the title rabbi without being ordained to the rabbinate, and how can he speak of the holiness of God and of duty to truth when he claims to be what he is not? These practices do not carry the hallmark of sincerity, let alone of holiness. They alienate rather than attract observant Jews because they are recognized for what they are—a farce.

HAS THE MESSIANIC MOVEMENT FOUND NATIONAL ACCEPTANCE?

It has not, nor will it ever so long as it insists upon faith in Jesus as Lord and Savior. Judaism is a religion of rejection. It has been formulated over the last 2000 years in conscious, determined reaction to the gospel, however poorly that gospel was represented. The contours of what is now Judaism have been defined in express conflict with the message of Messiah. Jews can believe or deny almost anything without having their Jewishness questioned. They can believe that a deceased rabbi is the Messiah, and that his illness and death were redemptive. They can believe that that rabbi is with his people by his spirit. They can believe that he will return to redeem the nation. But they must not attribute such characteristics to Jesus. Even if Messianic Jews no longer acknowledged Jesus as God, if we viewed him to be merely human, gifted by God and devoted to the Torah, we would not be accepted by Orthodox Judaism because rabbinicism refuses to view Jesus as anything but, at best, a peripheral, idiosyncratic rabbi.

The only ones who seem to have been swayed by the Messianic Movement are church leaders. Messianics are far from finding acceptance among fellow Jews. Shoshanah Feher quotes rabbis, whose response to Messianic Jews is typical. Rabbi Geller, a prominent member of the American Jewish Congress, informs us, "The community of Israel includes everybody. . . . Among that group of people are gays and lesbians . . . all of the categories of Jews you know." But "the [Messianics] are not Jews. They are people who are trying to convert Jews. . . . I don't think they're really [our] relatives. I think they are people who are pretending to be relatives and using their pretended relative status to trick the rest of my family."[1] Feher catalogues a series of rabbinic responses to the demand that Messianic Jews be accepted by the Jewish community.[2] Some statements are unnerving. Rabbi Kravitz, for example, insists, "even *no* relationship with God is better than a Messianic relationship" (emphasis his)![3]

Perceptively, Feher explains,

> The one issue that increases group consciousness in the Jewish community is Christianity, which symbolizes an external boundary and creates a strong corporate order. Those individuals who cross or straddle boundaries are particularly dangerous because they threaten the existing classification system in a fundamental way.[4]

1. Shoshanah Feher, *Passing Over Easter: Constructing the Boundaries of Messianic Judaism* (Walnut Creek, CA: AltaMira Press, 1998), 29–30.
   2. Ibid., 30–39.
   3. Ibid., 29–30.
   4. Ibid., 30–39.

Exactly! The Jewish community will need to be converted before it accepts Jewish Christians as equals. Judaism was formulated to create a mono-lithic group-consciousness under rabbinic leadership. Crossing borders created for that purpose is a direct challenge to rabbinic authority. Either we challenge their authority, or we recognize and submit to it.

Feher summarizes:

> The Jewish community gains more comfort from defining who is *not* a member of the community than from defining who *is*. The prover-bial line in the sand is drawn at Jesus' feet. Atheists and agnostics, the so-called "fox-hole Jews" are welcome. Followers of Jesus, however, by whatever name they call themselves, Hebrew Christians, Messianic Jews or Jews for Jesus, in the eyes of the normative Jewish community are Christians all the same, "the worst of the *Goyim*."[5]

In other words, Messianic Jews gain nothing by straddling two religious identities. Instead of being winsome, they antagonize the people they hope to reach.

> This exclusionary response of the Jewish community has created prob-lems for the self-definition of Messianic Jews, yet has simultaneously helped to shape that definition.[6]

How? By driving the movement to divest itself of biblical truth, shed increasingly more of its New Covenant roots, and seek to become barely distinguishable from normative Judaism.

That is one of the dangers inherent in the movement. It is so preoccupied with being Jewish that it is in danger of becoming non-Christian. As Feher noted, "many theological issues take a backseat to maintaining an emphasis on the Jewishness of the faith. No attempt is ever made to address them."[7] The danger involved in such a process should give rise to serious thought about the viability of the Mes-sianic Movement.

In the course of my work as a pastor in Israel, I have met many who attended messianic congregations in the former USSR, were baptized

5. Ibid., 41–42.
6. Ibid., 42.
7. Ibid., 51.

and considered themselves citizens of the Kingdom of Heaven. A high percentage of these had no inkling of the gospel, no idea of their inherent sinfulness, no understanding of the atoning death of Jesus, and no knowledge of his deity. They were attracted by the evangelist, his flashy car, the emphasis on Jewishness in a country where Jewishness was persecuted, and the possibility of immigrating to Israel.

HAS THE MESSIANIC MOVEMENT BEEN EFFECTIVE?

It has not, nor could it be, because its emphasis is misplaced. Following the initial stir created at its inception, the Messianic Movement has hardly addressed the Jewish nation with the gospel. Nor is the Movement characterized by evangelistic zeal. Most Messianic organizations in the Diaspora are engaged in dialogue with the church rather than with their own people, and their Jewish membership is largely made up of individuals who were converted outside of the movement and then persuaded to join. Feher confirms, "All but six of my interviewees were already 'saved' when they came to Messianic Judaism."[8] In the footnote to this statement Feher quotes Carol A. Harris-Shapiro's 1992 PhD dissertation, submitted to the Department of Religion at Temple University, *Syncreticism or Struggle: The Case of Messianic Judaism*, "who also found that most Messianic adherents had been saved previously."[9]

Jeff Wasserman reports that, among the congregations he surveyed, a mere forty percent are Jewish, and that "most couples are (sic) mixed marriages with one Jewish and one Gentile partner."[10] He asserts, "American Messianic congregations are consistently unsuccessful in attracting Jewish converts."[11] Michael Schiffman's 1988 survey showed that forty-seven percent of messianic congregations saw themselves as only slightly effective or wholly ineffective in reaching Jewish family members. He notes that Jewish elements in worship seem to have little value in outreach. Data from the 1986–1991 Jews for Jesus Jewish Believer

8. Ibid., 52.
9. Ibid.
10. Jeffrey S. Wasserman, *Messianic Jewish Congregations: Who Sold This Business to the Gentiles?* (Lanham, MD: University Press of America, 2000), 76.
11. Ibid., 103–5.

Survey supports this observation. A random sample of 300 out of 5000 surveyed shows that only four percent of believing Jews were evangelized by messianic congregations.[12]

Schiffman's 1987 survey indicated that

> only two percent [!] of American Messianic believers had come to faith as a result of Messianic evangelism. Respondents to my own survey indicated less than 300 Jewish converts as a direct result of the evangelistic outreach of 62 congregations. Only half of these continued attending the congregations that evangelized them. Gentiles attracted to Messianic doctrine and worship style account for much of the membership growth of Messianic congregations.[13]

Later on he says,

> In my survey, 98% of the Jewish members of Messianic congregations were brought to faith by Gentile Christians.[14]

Consequently,

> Some Messianic congregations presume that their simple existence is a significant element in establishing a witness to the Jewish community. Some respondents indicated a hope that, eventually, the Jewish community would take positive notice of faith in Yeshua as a viable option for Jews, a fourth or fifth branch of Judaism. Recent expressions of anti-Messianic Jewish sentiments by leaders of the Jewish Anti-Defamation League and Jews for Judaism make this recognition unlikely.[15]

There is an exceptionally high turnover of congregants in messianic congregations. There are also a growing number of mixed marriages between Jewish and Gentile believers. This raises questions as to the movement's ability to build a significant body of Messianic Jews and be able to address the nation with integrity on the grounds of a Jewish identity.

12. Michael Schiffman, *Communicating Yeshua to the Jewish People: A Study of Variable Factors Which May Influence Growth in Messianic Jewish Congregations*, ONS, M. Div Thesis, Ashland Theological Seminary, 1988.

13. Ibid.

14. Ibid., 106.

15. Ibid., 104.

Messianic Jews pick and choose aspects of Judaism to which they will adhere. Few avoid travel or the use of electric power on the Sabbath. Few avoid the wearing of mixed fibers. Most do not regularly wear fringes or kippot, all prerequisites for Orthodox Jews. Few maintain a kosher kitchen. If they keep kosher, most keep what they describe as a "biblical kashrut," which is far removed from rabbinic standards. In what sense can such practices be construed traditional Judaism? Feher is right when she says, "They keep kosher in order to identify with Judaism, and yet, because they choose to keep biblical *kashrut* they end up by not belonging. Messianics' attempts to achieve balance create a contradiction: In seeking to offend no one, they potentially offend everyone."[16]

HAS THE MESSIANIC MOVEMENT PROVIDED A SPIRITUAL HAVEN FOR JEWISH BELIEVERS?

As we have seen, an overwhelming majority of those who belong to messianic congregations are Gentiles, while most Jewish Christians are not part of the movement. Efforts by Messianic Jews to impose Christian meanings onto Jewish traditions are an offense to Orthodox Jews, and rightly so. Such an imposition does not convey a sense of honest loyalty to the traditions or respect for them. Often, Jewish customs adopted in messianic congregations are affectations rather than the substance of hearty, informed Jewishness. Many messianic congregations meet on Friday night—the eve of the Jewish Sabbath—to light Sabbath candles and worship together. Anyone who knows Jewish custom can see through the facade: Sabbath candles are lit at home, not in the synagogue. The mother of the house lights them, not a man, and women never officiate in traditional public worship.

True, Reformed Jewish synagogues follow a practice similar to that maintained by some Messianic Jews. But Reformed Judaism does not represent the national consensus and can hardly claim to be traditional. However large the Reformed Jewish Movement may be in America, it represents a minority within Jewry and has no legal status in Israel. What is more, present day trends within Reformed Judaism indicate increasing subservience to traditional forms of Orthodox Judaism.

16. Feher, *Passing Over Easter*, 83.

In spite of protestations to the contrary, the largest number of Jewish Christians now in the Messianic Movement did not join the movement because they longed to affirm their Jewish identity. Shoshanah Feher's comment is true of the majority, who "realized that they had Jewish backgrounds, or became identified with Judaism, only after they began attending services at a Messianic congregation."[17] Rather than addressing a need, the movement has labored to create one, and then strived to meet it. Messianic Judaism appeals to insecure individuals. Such insecurity may be the result of an untraditional upbringing, the fact that one parent was not Jewish, or other reasons. Messianic Judaism cannot provide the grounds for a healthy confidence because many of its leaders are themselves driven by insecurity. The confidence some might obtain by this means is certainly not biblical. Stan Telchin's introduction to this book is an excellent riposte.

Messianic Judaism provides those who have little or no knowledge of Jewish custom with the illusion that they are manifestly Jewish, but Jews who are acquainted with their national traditions are reinforced in their conviction that Messianic Jews are involved in a ploy. David Stern's words of warning here should be heeded. He spoke out against "using Jewish materials ignorantly" so as to create a "parody of synagogue procedure."[18] David goes on to ask, "What good can come of putting up a front? . . . Only the congregations whose members are seriously trying to express the Jewishness that is in fact theirs will be able to weather . . . criticism. They will weather it because they are doing something real, not acting a show."[19] A few Yiddish phrases, saying "Yeshua," wearing Jewish religious garb, and a fascination with Jewish things is not enough to make one Jewish.

How many messianic congregations are able to profess what David describes as a "Jewishness that is in fact theirs"? Feher informs us,

> Messianics dig into the past to unearth a previously unknown familial connection with Judaism. In other cases, Messianic Gentiles have long been aware of some familial connection to Judaism that eventually creates or nurtures their curiosity in the Messianic Movement. Gen-

17. Ibid., 52.
18. David H. Stern, *Messianic Jewish Manifesto* (Jerusalem: Jewish New Testament Publications, 1988), 168ff.
19. Ibid.

tile recruits recreate their historical roots in order to identify with the desired Jewish ethnicity or invent such roots in order to be fully accepted among Messianics.[20]

Hear Feher again:

Other root seekers at the congregation claim Jewish descent based on a link that is many generations old. Thomas, an older man who brings his granddaughter to the services with him, met me one Sunday and told me his story. Born and raised a Roman Catholic, he did not "discover" that he was Jewish until relatively recently, when he read that, in 1492, when the Jews were expelled from the Iberian peninsula, there was not a single family in Spain without some Jewish blood. Although his family tree indicates that in the fifteenth century his family lived in Italy, they came from a part of Italy that was primarily Spanish.

Growing up in this country, Thomas remembers that his grandmother did "Jewish things" such as following *kashrut*, or kosher ritual, when cooking. She always soaked chicken in saltwater for two or three hours before cooking it. She also boiled meat before cooking it, and butchered chickens according to rabbinic tradition, by cutting their throats rather than strangling them. Thomas' grandfather also made "those Italian biscotti which are basically *kamish*, like the Sephardic Jews." These practices, along with his grandmother's maiden name Leonbruni (which he translates as "the Lion of Judah"), indicate to Thomas that his grandmother came from a family of crypto-Jews— Jews who converted to Catholicism in Spain during the Inquisition but secretly continued to practice Judaism.

In their attempts to unearth a connection, other Gentiles also find links, however slight, to the Sephardic tradition. Liliana, in her mid-sixties, told me that some ten years earlier she had spent time in Israel because she wanted to understand her Jewish background better. She was raised in the United States as a Catholic, both of her parents were Mexican, descended from the Spanish conquistadors. Their history, coupled with her mother's name (a name "similar to Cohen"), clearly indicated to her that her ancestors were also Jews, converted to Catholicism during the Inquisition.

Even if all their ancestors are Gentiles, these respondents want to ensure that their children will be Jewish. One respondent felt strongly

20. Feher, *Passing Over Easter*, 69.

that her son (who was one and a half at the time) must marry a traditionally (matrilineally) Jewish woman so that their children in turn will be recognized as Jewish by the State of Israel and the family line will become Jewish. Likewise, another congregant wants to marry a matrilineally Jewish woman: "I feel like I want to get my name restored in Israel, because . . . I'm not Jewish, according to rabbinic laws and stuff . . . and I would like to give my children that heritage."[21]

On the other hand, most Jewish Christians (at least ninety percent by Jeff Wasserman's statistics)[22] choose not to attach themselves to messianic synagogues. This is particularly true of the few from an Orthodox Jewish background, who consider Messianic Judaism to be a distortion of rabbinic custom. None desire to come again under the yoke of rabbinic bondage, however modified.

THE MESSIANIC MOVEMENT'S ACHIEVEMENTS

The Messianic Movement has drawn the church's attention to the Jewishness of the gospel. It has also sparked new interest in the Old Testament. Although the movement has few competent scholars, it has impacted many scholars who have published works relating to the Jewishness of the gospel, the Jewish background of the New Testament, continuity and discontinuity between the Testaments, Old Testament exegesis, and related topics.

A growing number of Christians are adopting terminology framed by the Messianic Movement and are inclined to attribute to Orthodox Judaism a spirituality and a biblical integrity that are open to question. Jewish believers in Jesus are commonly described as anything but Christians. Terms such as "conversion," "church," and "Christ" are supplanted, while western-style Charismatic tunes are sung to Hebrew texts the world over.

The Messianic Movement has persuaded the church that faith in Jesus does not constitute a rejection of one's Jewishness. Large and growing sections of the church have now accepted this true yet novel view of things. The people of Israel have yet to be convinced. For 2000 years, Jews

---

21. Ibid., 72.
22. Wasserman, *Messianic Jewish Congregations*.

who believed in Jesus were taught to think of themselves as no longer Jewish and were lost to the Jewish nation. The church's insistence that Jewish Christians distance themselves from anything Jewish undermined the claim that the gospel is the fulfillment of Old Testament promise. Meanwhile, Judaism crystallized around its rejection of Jesus. It will take something far more persuasive than the Messianic Movement to turn the tide of history. It will take an act of God.

In a nutshell, the Messianic Movement has forced the church to consider important issues. In view of the fact that much of Messianic effort has not been orchestrated, that it has failed to secure meaningful unity between its various factions, and that its resources are relatively limited, these are remarkable achievements.

THE NEGATIVE IMPACT OF THE MESSIANIC MOVEMENT

The Messianic Movement has been more successful in raising the right questions than in providing biblical answers. The reason for this is that the movement has confused cultural mores with religious duties, insisted upon maintaining the Jewishness of its adherents by degrees of obedience to rabbinic religious dictum, and accorded the rabbis a legitimacy to which they have no right. Attributing to the rabbis the authority to determine what constitutes Jewishness, Messianics have undermined their own position because the rabbis have determined that faith in Jesus exceeds the boundaries of Jewishness. They have replaced God's authority over conscience with human ingenuity—so that some in the Movement (Dan Juster and David Stern, for example) have called for the creation of a distinctly Messianic Halacha, nothing less than religious legislation.

Such a call embroils the movement in impossibilities. For example, while discussing problems associated with the creation of Halacha, David writes, "whether the Spirit wants us to obey the rule or break it will be decided within a communal congregational framework in which our respected leaders and colleagues help us to determine the mind of the Messiah."[23] To call for the creation of Messianic Halacha is to call for the undoing of one of the most important accomplishments of the Reformation: an acknowledgment of the right of every man to study the Bible

23. Stern, *Messianic Jewish Manifesto*, 54.

and understand it for himself. Boaz Michael, founder and director of First Fruits of Zion, a Messianic ministry approved by the UMJC, writes that "we teach and obey Torah, the God-ordained thing to do as His redeemed people."[24]

By focusing on the centrality of the Torah, Jewishness, and Jewish custom, the Messianic Movement has minimized the person and work of Messiah. Spiritual advantage is no longer considered a gift of grace in Christ but the consequence of race or human effort. There is, therefore, a tendency among Messianic Jews to think of themselves as a higher class of believers by virtue of their Jewishness and their adherence to Jewish custom. The centrality that Jesus was accorded in the life of the apostolic church has been redirected—toward Jewish custom. Feher observes, "Messianic believers themselves create a hierarchy in which Messianic Jews are higher than Messianic Gentiles, and this often results in a search for Jewish *Roots* on the part of many Messianic Gentiles."[25]

Needless to say, this is not the intention. Messianic believers sincerely believe the body of Messiah is one and all its members are equal. But their emphasis on advantages derived from Jewish tradition inevitably foments such an error. Note the struggle of one Jewish Christian who joined a messianic congregation, to whom Feher accords the pseudonym Sara.[26] Sara was married to a Gentile Feher calls Gabe, who persuaded Sara to join a messianic congregation. Having done so, she became frustrated with the emphasis on Jewishness. "Her focus was on her walk with the Lord, with her spirituality and not with her ethnicity."[27] Now, after "years of worshipping with Adat HaRuach"[28] she has been able to settle in and feel comfortable. How so? By replacing her former focus with a focus on ethnicity. Dare we call that progress?

Dr. Rich Nichol, leader of a messianic synagogue in Boston, writes of a customary ritual in his congregation.

> We (the men) pray in unison Hebrew and English prayers appropriate to the donning of the tallit. And then the sound of a "swoosh" fills the room as we almost in unison enwrap ourselves in the tallitot. We

24. "Readers' Views and Comments," *Bikurei Tziyon* 64 (May/June 2000), 3.
25. Feher, *Passing Over Easter*, 61.
26. Ibid., 64.
27. Ibid.
28. Ibid.

then put our arms around one another's shoulders and pray that God would bless our service, one another, the women and children. We then file into the sanctuary, take our places and the service begins. The five-minute ceremony has its transcendent power. It embodies multiplied male energy directed to a holy purpose . . . the traditional male garment of prayer with its tactile and visual reality is an essential element in the ritual.[29]

He concludes,

Gathering for prayer without our tallitot would just not work![30]

Such statements indicate tendencies toward Judaistic legalism and an inability to distinguish between divine law and human inventions. It smacks of a ritualism that is far removed from worship in spirit and in truth.

Semantics adopted by Messianic Jews have created more than a hairline breech in the unity of the church. This breech threatens to widen to the point of cleavage. Messianic Jews frequently insist, "I am not a Christian." This goes far beyond what is permitted in Scripture. Why are Gentiles "converted" and Messianic Jews "completed"? A disconcerting illustration of this tendency is to be found in the fact that, in spite of the Messianics' professed unity with the wider evangelical Christian church (a unity often disavowed when speaking to Jews), second generation Messianic Jews have been cut off from the body of Messiah universal. Eve Fischer, the daughter of a Messianic rabbi, who left her hometown in order to study, writes the following:

I'm expecting to spend the next few years of my life without a Messianic synagogue to call home. And I'm faced with the challenge of finding a surrogate home. . . . I feel less tolerant of most Christian environments. Despite early exposure and an open mind—sometimes too open—I have problems with any spiritual environment different from my own Messianic Jewish Roots. . . . I find myself uncomfortable in Christian settings.[31]

29. Richard C. Nichol, "Ask the Rabbi," *Messianic Jewish Life* 72, no. 3 (July–Sept. 1999), 27–28.
30. Ibid.
31. Eve Fischer, "Youth Perspective," *Messianic Jewish Life* 73, no. 3 (July–Sept. 2000), 18–19.

Fischer goes on to say,

> Even simple terminology turns me off. The name Jesus Christ strikes
> a discordant note in my ear: His name is Yeshua, and He's my Messiah.
> My father is not a pastor; he's a rabbi, and he leads a synagogue, not a
> church. I am not a Christian—and I'm certainly not converted—I'm a
> Believer. And I am a Jew.[32]

Fischer's solution is, perhaps, inevitable:

> What will I do when I find myself in Kalispell, Montana? I've been
> thinking and praying about this question over the last year or so. And
> I think I've found an answer: traditional Judaism. . . . Given the choice
> between a conservative synagogue and a small Bible church, I think
> I'd prefer to wake up early on Saturday mornings, not Sundays. . . .
> My relationship with Yeshua is one of the most personal elements
> of my faith, I don't need anyone else to maintain that relationship.
> But the Judaic elements of my Faith—the traditions, the holidays, the
> prayers—depend on a community. . . . It's a lot easier to lose track of
> Judaism in a church than it is to lose track of Yeshua in a synagogue.[33]

In spite of its best intentions, the Messianic Movement has divided
the body of Messiah. Most Messianic Jews act according to their convictions by disavowing "Gentile" church history, creedal achievements,
hymnody, and theologizing. By so doing they rob second generation
Messianic Jews of the spiritual insight, wisdom, and experience that God
granted his church through the centuries. This has greatly impoverished
the movement. Many in the movement have never heard of John Bunyan,
John Newton, Isaac Watts, Jonathan Edwards, or William Carey.

Fellowship is a wide, wonderful, glorious thing! It is never the paltry
imitation that most Messianic Jews profess to enjoy with their Gentile
fellow believers so long as Jewish traditions are followed. An elitism that
encourages Gentiles to convert to Judaism and become Jewish Christians
is all too evident. Anything supposedly Jewish is considered superior
to anything "Gentile." As a result, the Messianic Movement has been
tolerant of deviant views. The effort to maintain a Jewish identity has

32. Ibid.
33. Ibid.

tended to obscure important issues, exposing Messianics to a barrage of questionable teachings concerning the nature of the Godhead, the deity of Messiah, the necessity of Jesus' atoning death, the perfection of his accomplishments, the unity of the church, the place of the law in sanctification, and the nature of spirituality.

Some Messianics have gone to the length of denying that faith in the atoning work of Messiah is necessary to salvation. Rich Nichol writes "in our synagogues, Messiah Yeshua takes his rightful place as the jewel in the gold setting of our Jewishness."[34] Note, not as the center because of his deity, or redeeming work, but as the jewel of our Jewishness. Mark Kinzer's recent book gives further rise to concern in this area because he calls upon the church to bring an end to its evangelistic efforts among the Jews.

In November 2001, *Israel Today* published the results of a survey among several Messianic Jews in Israel. Some of the answers give an indication of Messianic trends. One respondent, Nehemiah Fund Director Uri Marcus, says "Yeshua is God's plan, but not God Himself. . . . God is more than Yeshua."[35] Former Israel Secretary of the International Messianic Alliance, Menachem Ben Chaim, states,

> Yeshua is more than a messenger and Messiah; He is part of the Godhead. We too, as human beings, were created in the image of the Godhead. But we too, as human beings, were created in the image and in the form of God. . . . I see in Yeshua a wonderful man, pure and complete up to his death. And by means of his resurrection Yeshua has reconciled us to God.[36]

Menachem's convictions were better than his expressions of faith; the above statement leaves much to be desired.

David (Victor) Bar David from Jerusalem says, "Yeshua said of himself that he is not God, but rather his messenger. . . . Christianity has distorted Yeshua and his word, which is why the Jewish people no longer recognize their Messiah."[37] David Tel Tsur from Ma'ale Adumim, leader of a former messianic congregation, states,

34. Nichol, *Messianic Jewish Life* 73, 25.
35. *Israel Today* (November 2001).
36. Ibid.
37. Ibid.

Yeshua Ha'Mashiach is not God, he is the Son of God and the Redeemer. . . . The Trinity is completely pagan. On the cross Yeshua cried out, "Eli, Eli [My God], why have you forsaken me?" Does God turn his back to God? Can one nail God to a cross? Millions of people were murdered because they were accused of killing God, and what were their last words? "Hear O Israel, the Lord our God, the Lord is one."[38]

Tsvi Sadan decries the doctrine of the trinity as a non-Jewish theory and has devoted many pages of his Hebrew periodical, *Kivun*, to dispel convictions concerning the divinity of Messiah.

Joseph Shulam, congregation leader in Jerusalem, in response to a purported misquote of his statement in the above article, stated the following:

I have never . . . held or taught that Yeshua is not divine. . . . The Tanach teaches that Messiah is divine and is called "El Elyon" and "Aviad" and "JHWH, our Righteousness." The big question is the equality and hierarchy of this relationship and I believe that we need to use Jewish sources to understand this relationship rather than Christian creeds written by people who hated us and hated the Torah of God.[39]

Joseph's words imply more than he intended. To experienced readers of theology they must be understood as stating that the Son is God but not equally so with the Father because, speaking of Messiah's divine essence, he explains that essence by referring to a hierarchy. Whether or not Joseph intended to say that a hierarchy of essence exists, his words imply that it does. Such a hierarchy means that one divine person partakes of more of the divine essence than does another. Each is divine, but there is a quantitative difference between them. One has more divinity than the other. In Joseph's terminology, this hierarchy of deity is what distinguishes the Father from the Son and the two from the Spirit. As a result, we have a high God, one who is lesser in terms of the divine essence, and a third who is still lesser. The Jewish sources to which Joseph referred his readers all attribute to Messiah an angelic nature, a kind of lesser divinity. They would never accord him full deity, such as is attributed to Jehovah, the Lord of Heaven and Earth.

38. Ibid.
39. Ibid.

Joe has taken me to task over the above paragraphs, and I would be delighted to withdraw them. But, so long as he allows his statements to stand, their import is beyond question. I cannot but understand him to say what he insists he does not intend to say. Is this confusion the result of his Church of Christ background? I cannot tell. At the very least, his terminology is liable to grievously faulty views. He should retract it and leave no room for misunderstanding. Until he does, my criticism of his statements stands.

The Messianic Movement tends to accord eschatology an inordinate and unbiblical role. There are in Messianic literature more references to eschatology than to the Trinity, the glory of Messiah, or the regenerating work of the Holy Spirit. This inordinance indicates a lack of appreciation for the relative importance of the truths of biblical revelation. It constitutes a deviation that could become dangerous. There is also a tendency among Messianic Jews to wed their eschatology to a particular political platform, and that to a test of spirituality. Doing so relegates those who disagree (among whom are most Arab Christians) to the level of the unenlightened. It reduces the prophetic message to a projection of end-time events, flattening thinking with regard to Israel and robbing the prophecies of their depth, vigor, and moral value by transforming the prophetic message into a Christian version of fortune telling.

The main burden of the prophetic message was spiritual and moral. Israel and Judah were called to conduct their lives in the fear of God. They were warned that, if they did not, God would exile them. Dealing with the prophets should strike fear in our hearts more than exhilaration or a sense of control. It should drive us to call people to repentance, rather than to write yet another book about the identity of anti-Christ.

Zionism may be a legitimate political platform (I believe it is). But we must never frame our political views in a way that disenfranchises those who think otherwise. Our political opponents are not inevitably less spiritual than we. We must distinguish between political aspirations and the promises of God.

THE FUTURE OF THE MESSIANIC MOVEMENT

The Messianic Movement seems to have outlived its usefulness. It is likely that, as the number of Gentile Christians in messianic congregations grows, Jewish believers will face the same problems they face in churches. On the other hand, as churches learn to accommodate Jewish Christians and allow them their national, cultural distinctives while sharing a common spirituality, the appeal of messianic congregations will fade. The purpose such congregations presently serve would be better served by inter-congregational fellowships.

A major obstacle to the demise of the Messianic Movement is the conglomerate of personal and organizational interests created over the years by those in the forefront of the movement. These will, most probably, peter out in the course of time. Organizations and movements that are void of a message do not tend to last long.

Another obstacle to the early demise of the Messianic Movement is its new impetus in Israel. American-born activists have worked hard to strengthen Messianic Jewish consciousness in the country. Years are likely to pass before the movement in Israel loses its initial vigor, the weakness of its positions are discovered, and its inability to address the issues facing Israeli believers in Israel becomes evident. Meanwhile, overseas leaders of the movement will draw strength from this temporary rejuvenation.

The Messianic Movement will ultimately collapse under the weight of reality. By then, much damage will have been done to individuals and to the cause of the gospel. Messianic Judaism will never gain acceptance in Israeli society.

THE WAY AHEAD FOR THE CHURCH

The church should review its assumptions with regard to Jewish evangelism. It has much to benefit from a growing Jewish presence within the body of Messiah. The church should reconsider its denial of the legitimacy of a continued Jewish existence within the body of Messiah.

The church will never be able to appeal to Jewish people until it regains its confidence in the gospel. When the church learns to act with the courage of its biblical convictions, when it renews its commitment to declare the holiness of God to a hedonistic, opportunist, and sensual society in which morals are relative, it will have an impact. The church should regain its prophetic role and preach the gospel in the fear and power of God.

The church should not adopt Messianic Jewish terminology, nor identify modern Judaism with the religion of the Bible. It should challenge both with a gracious courage that dares proclaim the word of God.

The church should cleanse itself of incipient anti-Semitism. It should welcome Jewish believers and help them feel at home while maintaining their national and cultural identity.

The church should engage the Messianic Movement in respectful dialogue that will benefit both. The church should muster the courage to question and, when necessary, criticize Jewish believers, rather than accept everything that claims to be Jewish. The church should deal with Messianic Jewish idiosyncrasies with loving patience that is void of compromise. It should respond in a spirit of gentle meekness to the pains, concerns, and fears that gave rise to the movement. The church must admit its mistakes and work to correct them.

THE WAY AHEAD FOR THE MESSIANIC MOVEMENT

The Messianic Movement should renew its commitment to Jesus as Lord and Savior. The Messianic Movement should reject any doubt concerning its faith in the Trinity, the deity of Messiah, and the necessity and perfection of his atoning work.

Neither national nor cultural identity should be allowed to supplant the Messiah in our personal or congregational life. The movement should worshipfully accord him that primary place and reject any tendency to obscure the gospel of his grace.

The Messianic Movement should rid itself of the tendency to cultural pride. It should learn to walk humbly before God and man. It should have the courage to distinguish between divine law and human traditions, and to carry that distinction into practical effect. It should recognize and seek to maintain that freedom from the Torah Messiah purchased for us, and learn to distinguish between religious obligation and cultural mores.

The Messianic Movement should recognize the glory of the unity that all the faithful in Messiah enjoy. In consequence, it should dissolve into the church by becoming a halfway house overseen, instructed, and encouraged by the church for the purpose of primary contact with Jewish unbelievers and for fellowship among Jewish Christians. It should begin to rethink its theology, correct its methodology, and learn to distinguish between evangelistic outreach and congregational life.

The Messianic Movement should renew its acknowledgment that salvation is the Lord's doing. Our goal is not to win people over to our position, nor impact our nation. Our goal is to glorify God and enjoy him forever. Such glorification and enjoyment are contingent upon God's gracious blessing on our obedience. We need to seek God's face, pray and fast and cry out from the depths of our hearts for God to fulfill his promise and glorify himself through the salvation of Israel.

May we have the grace to be obedient, and may our blessed, glorious Lord have all the glory in this world, in the world to come and forever, worlds without end. Amen.

Afterword

THERE, I'VE SAID IT. It has been sheer joy to contemplate the wonders of our Savior and the fullness of the salvation he has accomplished. It has been a sorrow to disagree with brethren. You, dear readers, will judge the validity of my arguments. We may disagree, but we share the desire to glorify God by loving obedience. In this holy, never ending ambition we are united.

I long for a move of God's Spirit among our people, thousands of conversions, and the emergence of a body of godly Jewish Christians calling our nation back to him who is our only legitimate hope. May it please God to use this book to that end.

If I have misrepresented the Messianic Movement or any who belong to that movement, I apologize and welcome corrections. It is my sincere desire to present confirmable facts in an irenic manner so as to promote thought and discussion. I welcome criticism. My desire is not to win an argument but, with all my readers, to glorify God. I have touched on sensitive issues and have been encouraged by responses to the first edition of this book, including those from many within the Messianic Movement. I kindly ask you, dear reader, to consider what I have said in spite of the consternation that I might have caused. I implore you by the tender mercies of God to weigh my arguments by the Bible: check and see if my interpretations of the texts are valid. If I am wrong, don't write me off; challenge me. If I am right, join me in seeking to correct whatever requires correction. In any case, seek God's kingdom and his righteousness with me.

Some, who disagree with the thesis of this book, have resorted to name-calling and nit-picking, apparently because they have no reasoned response to my arguments; at least none has been offered yet. So, dear reader, think and pray through the issues, and may it please the Lord to bless us in spite of our failings.

Since the publication of the first edition, a group of us have formed the International Jewish Evangelical Fellowship (IJEF—www.IJEF.org). Our goals are as follows:

- To promote biblical convictions and biblical spirituality among Jewish and Gentile Christians
- To raise a voice for biblical Christianity among the Jews by creating a spiritually motivated and biblically informed voice for the gospel among Jews who profess faith in Jesus, interested Gentiles, and the Jewish nation
- To declare the supremacy of Jesus, Israel's promised Messiah and the Savior of the world
- To promote the unity of the body of Messiah
- To encourage Jewish believers in Jesus in their fellowship as members of the church and to encourage the church to help Jewish believers in Jesus to find within its framework a spiritual home
- To affirm and promote continued Jewish identity among Jewish believers in Jesus
- To enter gracious dialogue with the Messianic Movement
- To serve as a voice for Jewish Christians to both their nation and their churches

Appendix A
A Letter from a Gentile

—————————————

FOLLOWING IS AN unedited letter written by Michael DeHaven, who joined the Messianic Movement.

First, I must confess: I am a Gentile. I was brought up in the Assemblies of G-d and have attended churches from several Christian denominations. It has only been a year since I started to actively study the true Roots of Christianity, and this last Rosh Hashanah I began to actively practice those Roots. In this short time, G-d has put a burden on my heart concerning the identity of Messianic Judaism, and especially of the Gentile believer in our Messianic Jewish congregations.

It has become apparent to me that mainline Christianity tends to view us as little more than Christians who gather together to do Jewish things. The reasons commonly attributed to our Jewish behavior are either to learn about the Jewish Roots of our religion or to provide a Jewish-friendly way to win Jews to Yeshua. For whatever reason people believe we "act Jewish," Messianic Judaism is not viewed as being truly Jewish. This implies an insincerity in our Judaism. Although being Messianic does make us, by definition, Christian, our lives, worship and identity need to be Jewish if we are going to call our Faith Messianic Judaism.

Many of us practicing Messianic Judaism or at least attending Messianic services are Gentiles who have little understanding of what it means to be Jewish. Although it is our spiritual heritage, it is not and can never be our physical heritage. This means we don't have the upbringing necessary to understand Jewish culture or to understand or appreciate Jewish worship. Our lack of Jewish heritage also makes it difficult for us to understand the pain associated with such vital issues as the Holocaust or anti-Semitism in our culture.

Many Gentiles who attach themselves to messianic congregations are content to attend just to learn about the Jewish roots of Christianity, and those who do so should be encouraged in their efforts. I sincerely believe learning about Christianity's Jewish roots is good and is something the church needs to grab hold of.

This is an important ministry if we want to rid the body of Messiah of anti-Semitism or to help the Christian fully comprehend his or her faith. But as important as this is, it is not as important as Messianic Judaism's mission to reach out to the Jewish people with the good news of their Messiah.

In order to be totally effective in this ministry, we need to be certain of our identity. Those of us Gentiles who attach ourselves to a messianic ministry, who desire to be active in the ministry and not just learn about our spiritual heritage, need to remember we are part of a Messianic Jewish ministry.

As a Jewish ministry, it is important that we learn to fully identify with and understand Judaism and what it means to be Jewish. Consequently, we need to learn to think, live, worship and pray as a Jew and to take our Judaism seriously; to take on the identity of a Jew and be as a Jew to the Jews. It is vital to the overall identity of Messianic Judaism for the active Gentiles to fully and sincerely identify with Judaism. If we Gentiles don't willingly take on that identity, our congregations will never be truly Messianic Jewish congregations.

A major step in this direction is to willingly take on the yoke of Torah, which is the heart and soul of Judaism. We need to diligently study it, love it and live a Torah-observant life-style. Many may think this is legalism or "being Rabbinical", but if we learn to live Torah with an attitude of faith, out of love for and devotion to G-d, if our mitzvot [the fulfilling of the commandments] are done as a willing act of devotion, and not out of a legalistic attitude, then we will finally delight in Torah the way the Psalmist did. I sincerely believe that being messianic shouldn't make us less observant than the traditional Jew, but the fact that we know our Messiah and that Torah is written on our hearts and minds should compel us to be more observant, Jew and Gentile alike.

There has been an inexplicable pull on my life since I first came in contact with Messianic Judaism. I feel drawn to it in a way I can only explain as the L-rd leading me in this direction. I know I am not alone in this. I have communicated with many Gentiles who are feeling drawn to it, but most of us are left wondering what our place is within this move of G-d. I urge the Gentiles who wish to be a part of

Messianic Judaism's ministry to take hold of your spiritual heritage. I also encourage the Jews around them to be supportive of those Gentiles who are sincere in their efforts and desire to learn. The change will be difficult. It is something foreign to us. It is also very likely we will be subject to ridicule and rejection for our decision, even by friends and family who don't understand the reasons for our change. In this case, we need to remember our sufferings are temporary and insignificant when compared to our goal of the salvation of the Jews. In the end, I believe we will find joy and peace in our chosen identity as we become a part of a major move of G-d to reach out to His chosen people.

Shalom b'Shem Yeshua!
Michael De Haven

Appendix B

A Short History of the Messianic Movement

—————————————

IN 1813, ENGLAND WITNESSED the first attempt to bring Jewish Christians into an alliance that would encourage them, present the gospel to the Jewish people, and assist in relations between Jewish Christians and the churches to which they belonged. The association was called "Bnei Abraham," Hebrew for "Sons of Abraham." On May 14 of 1867 Dr. C. Schwartz proposed the organization of a Hebrew Christian Alliance of Great Britain, which later initiated and assisted in establishing similar Alliances in different parts of the world.

The Hebrew Christian Prayer Union was founded in England in 1883 to unite Jewish believers in Jesus for prayer. Within less than seven years, membership rose from 147 to 600, and branches were established in Russia, Norway, Germany, Romania, Palestine, and the United States.

By the end of the 1800s it is estimated that some 250,000 Jews professed conversion to Christianity in one form or another. Among these were prominent individuals, such as the British Prime Minister Disraeli, composers Felix Mendelssohn and Gustav Mahler, and the first Anglican Bishop of Jerusalem, Michael Solomon Alexander. Bishop Alexander was appointed with the express hope of creating a Jewish Christian community in Palestine.

In the early and mid 1900s a number of leading Jewish Christians arose. Among these we could mention Rabinowitz in Kisheneff (who, in 1882, established a community called Israel of the New Covenant), Rabbi Isaac Lichtenstein (who continued to officiate as a rabbi) in Tapio-Szele, Hungary, and Daniel Tsion in Bulgaria (who served as chief rabbi of

Bulgaria in the 1930s and 1940s and was instrumental in saving many of the Jewish community from the Nazis).

Adat Hatikvah was founded in Chicago in the 1930s. The first Hebrew Christian Church in Buenos Aires was formed in 1936. The goal was to create a Jewish Christian entity within the nation of Israel—an important distinction in comparison with that of the Messianic Movement which, following its failure to find acceptance in the Jewish community, has become a Judaized entity within the body of Christ.

Mission societies dedicated to Jewish evangelism played a significant role in forming what is now the modern Messianic Movement. In 1898 the Mildmay Mission to the Jews founded a Jewish Christian congregation in London, now claimed by the Messianic Movement as one of its early harbingers. The congregation had few Jewish trappings and was overtly a Christian congregation among the Jews.

On May 22, 1901, Mark Levy, a Jewish Christian from Britain, convened the Boston Conference of the Messianic Council. He proposed to create a formal means of association for all Jewish believers in North America. The participants agreed to organize another conference, designed to create the Hebrew Christian Alliance of America (HCAA). On July 28 to 30, 1930, the Alliance was formed with the primary goal of promoting the gospel among the Jewish people. Louis Meyer, who helped edit the famous Fundamentals of the Christian Faith, served as corresponding secretary.

In 1913, another meeting was held in Pittsburgh, with Maurice Rubens, a businessman, and Sabbati Rohold, a Jewish Christian from Palestine who later led the work of Christian Witness to Israel (under its previous name, The International Society for the Evangelization of the Jewish People). These men founded the Hebrew Christian Alliance of America (the HCAA) in 1915 and Rohold served as its first president. The Alliance was to provide fellowship to Jewish believers who worshiped in various Christian churches. Heated discussions as to the wisdom, biblical grounds, and feasibility of establishing distinctly Hebrew Christian congregations were held. The idea was firmly rejected.

In 1917, the HCAA published in English the first issue of the HCA Quarterly, with a Yiddish supplement. Dr. Emmanuel Greenbaum was called to be the Alliance's first missionary. In 1932, new missionaries were called. At the instigation of the HCA, Moody Bible Institute established in 1923 a Chair of Jewish Studies. The title was first held by Solomon Birnbaum, who left Moody for Israel in 1936. Birnbaum was followed by Max Reich, who taught until his death in 1945, and then by Nathan Stone two years later. Stone was followed by Dr. Louis Goldberg in 1965. At Dr. Goldberg's instigation, a full-fledged academic program was inaugurated. In 1995, Dr. Goldberg passed away and his chair was occupied by Dr. Michael Rydelnik.

Hebrew Christians were eager to play an active role in the Zionist movement because they sincerely believed in the political goals of the movement. HCCA support was welcomed, but not active participation. Nevertheless, the Alliance and individual Hebrew Christians took part in various endeavors to settle the land in Sinai, near the Dead Sea, in Gaza, and elsewhere in the country.

In 1925, the Hebrew Christian Alliance was broadened to form the International Hebrew Christian Alliance (the IHCA), with its main offices in London. Within a decade it had established affiliated alliances in North and South America, Europe, Australia, New Zealand, and South Africa.

In 1927, Sir Leon Levinson, first president of the IHCA, claimed in the official organ of the Alliance, that there were some 147,000 Jewish believers in the world: 17,000 in Austria, 35,000 in Poland, 60,000 in Russia, 30,000 in America and Canada, and 5,000 in Great Britain. These all held to an evangelical faith.

Since the 1920s, the HCAA had played an active role in the struggle against rising anti-Semitism in the USA and Europe. The Alliance spoke out forcefully against Henry Ford's distribution of the *Protocols of the Learned Elders of Zion*, an infamous anti-Semitic document that purported to describe international Jewish machinations. Upon its founding, the IHCA protested the treatment of Jews by Nazi Germany. During the war it ransomed and repatriated Jews from Germany to the British Isles, where they were granted asylum.

The European Alliances largely disappeared during the Second World War. Their members were persecuted by the Nazis for being Jewish and disowned by the Jewish community for being Christian. The American HCA helped some Jewish Christians relocate and, after the war, assisted in founding a mission to the Jews in Hungary.

Following the war and in response to lingering anti-Semitic attitudes, efforts were made to establish separate Jewish Christian congregations. One attempt was by David Bronstein in Chicago in 1934. This congregation became an independent messianic congregation in the early 1970s under the leadership of Daniel Juster, and its name was changed to Adat HaTikva.

The American HCA established the "Haven of Grace," a home for elderly Jewish Christians, which functioned between the years 1953 and 1966. In the 1960s, a new generation began to make its presence felt. Impacted by the anti-Establishmentarian views of those years, they had little allegiance to the church and a strong desire to distinguish themselves. They began to call for the adoption of Jewish traditions and a more aggressive assertion of Jewish identity. The American branch evolved from what was originally known as "Hebrew Christianity" into today's "Messianic Jewish Movement."

This process was hotly contested by American Hebrew Christians who immigrated from Europe, most of whom died by the middle of the twentieth century. It was also opposed by the British Hebrew Christians until 1975. The old guard were largely fundamentalist Christians of Jewish origin who were conscious of their Jewishness, avidly supported the Zionist Movement, active in their opposition to anti-Semitism, and eager to promote the gospel among their people. But most saw no room for what is now the Messianic Movement.

In June 1973, a motion was made to change the name of the HCAA to the Messianic Jewish Alliance of America (MJAA). The motion was supported by a small minority of Alliance members, yet it failed. Another attempt two years later, in June 1975, resulted in the proposed name change. The Young Hebrew Christian Alliance (established in 1966 as the Young Hebrew Christian Youth Organization) changed its name to the Young Messianic Jewish Alliance.

Martin Chernoff became the president of what was the HCAA in 1971, spearheading a stronger move in the alliance toward rabbinic tradition. He served until 1975 and was later followed by his two sons, Joel (who served as president between 1979 and 1983) and David (who served for the years 1983 to 1987). During this time a new terminology was forged: Jews were no longer to be converted; they were to be "completed." Jesus became "Yeshua," the law became the "Torah," the church was "the congregation" or even "the synagogue," biblical names were to be pronounced in their supposed original Hebrew form, and so on.

The late Manny Brotman (1939–1999) and his wife-to-be, Sandra Sheshkin, founded a messianic congregation in Washington, DC, in 1974. He established the Messianic Jewish Movement International (MJMI) and laid the groundwork for The Union of Messianic Jewish Congregations, founded in 1979.

Another prominent leader was Joe Finkelstein who, with his wife Debbie, was active in Philadelphia from the late 1960s. Unlike the majority of messianic leaders, Joe came from a Conservative Jewish background and Debbie was Orthodox. They attracted many Jewish and Gentile young people, some of whom professed conversion and joined for worship at the Finkelstein's home. Joe repeatedly insisted that there is no contradiction between being Jewish and believing in Jesus. He and his wife maintained a Jewish traditional lifestyle, which was adopted by many young adherents.

Among the associations incorporating Messianic Jewish congregations and individuals are the Union of Messianic Jewish Congregations, the International Alliance of Messianic Congregations and Synagogues, the Fellowship of Messianic Jewish Congregations, the Canadian Fellowship of Messianic Congregations and Ministries, and the Southern Baptist Messianic Fellowship.

The Messianic Jewish Alliance of America is affiliated with alliances in fifteen countries, including Israel. The International Messianic Jewish Alliance (IMJA) is the worldwide alliance that seeks to represent the common interests of Jewish believers throughout the world, whether they belong to the Messianic Movement or to traditional evangelical churches. It carries out ministries through its affiliated national alliances, which unite their efforts to fulfill the aims of the international body. The professed purpose of the International Alliance is to care for the spiritual and material welfare of all Jewish believers and to maintain within the Jewish people a witness to Yeshua the Messiah.

The alliance is involved worldwide in bringing relief to Jewish believers and groups ostracized because of their faith in Jesus, educating churches to understand Jewish people, and establishing alliances among communities of Jewish Christians. The IMJA also acts as a unifying body for organizations involved in evangelism among Jewish people. In

Israel, the IMJA shares in running the Ebenezer Home for elderly Jewish Christians, near Haifa.

The Union of Messianic Jewish Congregations was founded in 1979 and today has about seventy members in North and South America and around the world. This movement sponsors the Messianic Yeshiva, which provides messianic theological education. The UMJC Agency distributes financial aid to Jewish believers in Israel as well as to new immigrants. The UMJC has also established a joint group of American and Israeli businessmen to help both foreign investors and Israelis establish businesses in Israel.

An example of one of the more extreme forms of Messianic Judaism is OMJRA—the Observant Messianic Jewish Rabbinical Association, an association of messianic rabbis who assert that Jewish Christians must adhere to rabbinical law. One of the goals of the association, as described in the OMJRA booklet, is "to promote the validity and necessity of Torah observance amongst the leadership of the Messianic Movement in general." The association was founded in 1995 by Rabbi Yehoshua M. Othniel, who had "become disillusioned with the lack of Torah within the congregations where he studied and worshipped," and "felt the need to promote the richness of a Torah-observant lifestyle among his fellow believing Jews." Othniel was convinced that the modern Messianic Jewish Movement suffered from "a chronic identity crisis. . . . Othniel believed that a strong foundation of Torah along with Jewish culture, customs and traditions would transform the Movement, giving it a solid identity upon which to build for the future."

According to Jeff Wasserman, there are now about three hundred messianic congregations worldwide.[1] Most of these are in the United States, with two in England, one in Holland, two in Germany, and a growing number in the former USSR and its satellite countries. The so-called messianic congregations in Israel are largely made up of Jews who profess a saving faith in Jesus, most of whom do not adhere to rabbinic traditions in their congregational and private lifestyles, although the traditional Jewish holidays are celebrated as a matter of national culture. The greater majority of the messianic congregations in Israel, the USA, and elsewhere are charismatic.

1. Jeffrey S.Wasserman, *Messianic Jewish Congregations: Who Sold This Business to the Gentiles?* (Lanham, MD: University Press of America, 2000), 3.

Appendix C

Messianic Judaism or Judaizing Christianity

David Baron

————————————

THE CALL FOR MESSIANIC JUDAISM is not exclusively contemporary. At the turn of the twentieth century, David Baron and others faced a similar challenge. I discovered the text that follows after writing the first edition of this book. Baron's arguments are so lucid that they ought to be brought to the attention of my readers. I have chosen to present it as an appendix rather than incorporate it into my own material because Baron's arguments are so concise. The material is brought in its entirety, with two exceptions: I have omitted material not essential to the argument, and some material that is dated due to the progress of history. Baron's lengthy sentences have been retained. The article is taken from *The Scattered Nation*, the organ of the Hebrew Christian Testimony to Israel, published October 1911.

INTRODUCTORY

It has been a principle with us, as far as ever possible, to keep the pages of THE SCATTERED NATION clear of all controversial subjects, and to devote all its space either to the unfolding of the Word of God or to records of His work, and the spread of truthful information about the condition of the Jewish people in the different lands of their dispersion. There are, however, rare occasions when we must make exceptions to our rule, and, without entering into controversy, at least define our own position in relation to such controversial subjects which very vitally affect the cause of Christ among Israel and the spiritual welfare of those of our Jewish people whose eyes have been opened to recognise in Jesus of Nazareth the true Messiah and Son of God.

From different directions questions have been addressed to us as to our views and attitude in relation to the "Jewish Messianic Movement," which rather grand-sounding designation does not describe any movement of Jews in the direction of recognising our Lord Jesus Christ as the Messiah, but an agitation on the part of some Hebrew Christian brethren, who have evidently yet much to learn as to the true character of their high calling of God in Christ Jesus, supported by a few no doubt well-meaning excellent Gentile Christian friends, who either do not understand the real tendency of this "movement," or betray a sad lack of insight into the plainly-revealed plan and purpose of God in this present dispensation.

THE MOVEMENT DEFINED

What these brethren preach and agitate for is, that it is incumbent on Hebrew Christians, in order to keep up their "national continuity," not only to identify themselves with their unbelieving Jewish brethren, in their national aspirations—as expressed, for instance, in Zionism and other movements which aim at creating and fostering "the national idea" and regaining possession of Palestine—but to observe the "national" rites and customs of the Jews, such as the keeping of the Sabbath, circumcision, and other observances, some of which have not even their origin in the law of Moses, but are part of that unbearable yoke which was laid on the neck of our people by the Rabbis.

The following are a few utterances of the champions of this movement. One of them, writing rather grandly on a proposed "World-wide Hebrew Christian Congress," with a view to the establishment of a "Hebrew Church," and "to formulate a definite plan as to which form of church government or ritual the Hebrew Church is to assume," proceeds:

> "Whatever is likely to be adopted by Congress as a basis for the formation of such a Church, it is bound to include the retention of Circumcision,

the Festivals—such as the Passover, Pentecost, Tabernacles, Purim, Chanucah—as well as part of the Synagogue liturgy in a modified form."

And again:—

"It will be readily seen how a Hebrew Christian movement which will hold fast to the Passover, Pentecost, Tabernacles, Chanucah, and Purim; which will include in its liturgy a good deal of the traditional Synagogue prayer; which will be favourably rather than unfavourably disposed towards every ceremony that has entwined itself in the Hebrew consciousness; . . . which insists on circumcision; which attaches itself to the Hebrew consciousness and holds by the historical and Biblical continuity of Israel's Mission—can never be labelled by the Hebrew nation as a proselytising society organised by Gentile Christians, whose object is to absorb and to denationalise the Jewish people."[1]

And another[2] concludes an article on "Jewish Christianity" as follows:

"In conclusion, allow me to say that I fully endorse what may be termed the 'Minimum programme,' as suggested by our much-honoured and widely-known Brother Ch. Th. Lucky, namely: That Hebrew Christians should observe Circumcision, the Sabbath, the Jewish Festivals, and that every effort should be made to revive the Hebrew language.

"Finally, I take the liberty of bringing before the notice of Hebrew Christians the following suggestions as a possible platform for Hebrew Christian activities:

"1. Hebrew Christians should seek to develop a close attachment to Zionism, and if the Zionists refuse to accept our co-operation we then should put forth Zionistic efforts on our own lines.

"2. We should retain, as far as possible, Jewish modes of worship, and a sympathetic appreciation of the Jewish national consciousness, even when manifested in a way that does not appeal to our modern ideas.

1. Philip Cohen, in No. 1 of *The Messianic Jew.*
2. Dr. A. Waldman, in No. 1 of *The Messianic Jew.*

"3. We should encourage a hearty fraternal relationship with all Gentile Christian denominations, but on the basis of complete independence.

"4. We should put forth every effort to regain all assimilated Christians of Jewish descent.

"5. We should not permit any intolerant dogmatic principles to constitute the basis for fellowship; every Jew that is not against Jesus should be considered one of us.

"6. We should show to our unconverted brethren that we are not 'Meshumadim' (renegades), but, on the contrary, genuine, patriotic Jews, true sons and daughters of Israel."

This is the "Minimum programme." The "Maximum" includes joining in *all* the forms and ceremonies of the Christ-rejecting synagogue, to wear phylacteries and the *talith* (or prayer-shawl), to use the Jewish liturgy, just as the other Jews do, only to smuggle in now and then the Name of Jesus into those prayers!

THE MOVEMENT PARTLY A REACTION

Now let me say, before proceeding to define our own position and to point out a few of the fallacies and dangers of this movement, that it is partly a reaction and protest against certain wrong methods of Jewish missions and missionaries, and wrong views in the churches in reference to Israel.

(1) Societies and missions have not been content with merely evangelising the Jews, and bringing those whose hearts were inclined toward the Gospel into living contact with Christ, but have sought to absorb them into the particular sect and party to which they themselves belonged, and more or less to *Gentilise* as well as "Christianise" them.

(2) Christianity has for the most part been presented to the Jews as an *alien system* in a Gentile garb, and instead of presenting Christ

to them as their "very own"—the Divine King of their people, the sum and substance of their Scriptures, the Fulfiller of their Law and their Prophets, the embodiment of all the promises and covenants which God made with their fathers; and the New Testament as the continuation and completion of the self-revelation of God to Moses and the Prophets—the Gentile Churches have invited the Jews to "change their religion," and Jewish converts have been designated "proselytes."

(3) As to the nation of Israel, these "proselytes" were taught for the most part that it is dead and done for; that the names "Israel," "Zion," "Jerusalem," in the great prophecies and promises which are manifestly yet unfulfilled, are no longer to be taken literally, but apply to "the Church," excepting when those names and terms occur in connection with curses and threatenings—then, of course, they do still apply to the "Jews." In short, that the most which is to be expected in reference to the future of the Jewish people is the absorption of a certain number within the Church.

This being so, any special sympathy and interest on the part of Jewish converts for their own nation was looked down upon almost with suspicion, and any hopes for a future national restoration of their people was regarded "as Jewish," if not carnal. In short, the "proselyte" must make himself as "un-Jewish" as possible, even to the changing of his old Jewish name for a Gentile one.

OUR OWN POSITION AND VIEWS

Now, I need not explain to any reader of THE SCATTERED NATION that the Hebrew Christian Testimony to Israel holds different views, and works upon quite different principles. We are full of hope for the future of our nation, and most firmly believe with the Apostle Paul that the gifts and the calling of God in relation to Israel are "without repentance" or a change of mind on His part. We believe that Israel is still God's nation; that Zion will yet again be the centre of God's kingdom upon earth, and that not through the Churches, which are becoming more and more apostate and worldly, but through restored and converted Israel shall all the nations of the earth be led to a knowledge of Christ, and all the earth be filled with the knowledge of Jehovah, even as the waters cover the sea.

Nor is the aim of our "Testimony" to "proselytise" a few Jews for this or that particular sect or party in Christendom, but to spread abroad, and as widely as possible, the knowledge of Israel's true Messiah and Saviour among the scattered people.

We repudiate and resent the term, "proselyte" as applied to a Jewish believer, for by faith in the Redeemer promised to our fathers he has become a true "Israelite," who has entered into his own promised heritage of covenanted blessing—"a Jew" not only "outwardly," like his unbelieving brethren, but also "*inwardly*, in spirit and in truth," whose praise is not of men but of God.

But, holding these views and cherishing these hopes, and with hearts full of yearning love for our nation, we do not overlook nor forget the great though temporary *break in Israel's national history* occasioned by national apostasy and sin, nor the solemn consequences both to Israel himself and the world of this break in God's national dealings with our people, *and the special character of the dispensation which was inaugurated by the advent of the long-promised Redeemer, and the preaching of His Gospel. . . .*

. . . Christ being rejected by Israel, and despised by the world in general, those who profess allegiance to Him, and become members of the body of which He is the Head, must be ready to take up the cross and follow Him. And one very heavy part of the cross is the separation which it often involves to disciples, even from among Gentiles, and almost invariably to Jewish believers, from those near and dear to them. To the Jew and to the Gentile who would follow Christ and exchange the friendship of the world for friendship with God—though perhaps in a more literal sense to the Jew—the same call and the same holy requirements are addressed as to our father Abraham: "Get thee out from thy country, and from thy kindred, and from thy father's house, into a land which I will show thee."

Oh! it is hard to bear suffering and reproach; to be misunderstood and misjudged; to be called "Meshumed"; to be regarded as an "outlaw" by one's own kindred; and to suffer, it may be, the loss of all things for His dear Name's sake; but the conditions of discipleship are not different now than they ever were. "He that taketh not his cross and followeth after Me, is not worthy of Me. He that loveth his life shall lose it and he that hateth his life in this world shall keep it unto life eternal. If any man serve Me let him follow Me; and where I am there shall also My servant be."

As far as the Jewish believer is concerned, and his relationship to the nation, the present condition of things may be likened to that which existed after the great sin of Israel in the matter of the golden calf, when "Moses took the Tabernacle and pitched it without the camp, and called it the Tabernacle of the congregation (or 'the tent of meeting,' *i.e.*, between God and man). And it came to pass that every one which sought the Lord went out unto the tent of meeting which was without the camp" (Ex. 33:7). So also during this much longer period of national apostasy God's Tabernacle is removed from the camp of corporate official Judaism, and every one from among Israel who in truth seeks the Lord must be prepared "to go forth unto Him without the camp, bearing His reproach" (Heb. 13:13). Or, to use the figure of John 10, during the period of Israel's national rejection of Christ when the "sheepfold" is given over to "thieves and robbers, the Good Shepherd calleth His own sheep by name, and *leadeth them out*" so that together with those "other sheep" of His from among the Gentiles, who were "not of this fold," they may form "one flock," even as He is their one Shepherd.

. . . If there is one truth more emphasised than another in the New Testament it is the unity, inter-relation, and interdependence of Jews and Gentiles in the one true Church of Christ, in which "there is neither Jew nor Greek, there is neither bond nor free, there is neither male nor female," but all are one in Christ Jesus. To use only two or three of the figures in the New Testament, they are parts of one *Building*, built upon the foundation of the Apostles and Prophets, Jesus Christ Himself being the chief *Corner Stone*, in whom every part, "*fitly framed together*, grow into an holy *Temple* in the Lord"; they are members of one *Household*, in which all are equally "children" in relation to their heavenly Father , and "brethren" in relation to one another; they are members of one *Living Body*, the Head of which is Christ, "from whom all the body fitly framed and knit together through that which every joint supplieth, according to the working in due measure of each several part, maketh the increase of the body unto the building-up of itself in love" (Eph. 4:16, R.V.).

Now, to say that in the One Church of Christ one set of rules, one attitude in relation to certain rites and observances enjoined in the law, and certain earthly or "national" hopes and expectations befit and are incumbent on its Jewish members, which do not befit and are not incumbent on its Gentile members, is nothing less than to try to raise up again the middle wall of partition which Christ by His death hath broken down, and to introduce confusion into the one "House of the Living God." It is very kind of one of the Gentile champions of these Judaising views to issue a manifesto to Hebrew Christians to assure them that "this is the liberty in the Gospel of Christ that the Gentile need not take upon him the law, and the Jew need not forsake the law"; and again, "the Jew in Christ is as free to retain all that is possible for him to retain of the law, as the Gentile in Christ is free to keep aloof from all that savours of laws and ordinances,"[3] but the New Testament nowhere tells "the Gentile in Christ" that he is "free" from anything from which "the Jew in Christ" is also not freed; and to quote, as this writer does, the cases of "Moses and David and Isaiah," or even of "Zacharias and Elisabeth, the parents of John the Baptist," who walked in all the commandments and ordinances of the Lord blameless—as proof "that there is a law observance which is not unto spiritual bondage"—only betrays great confusion of thought, and forgetfulness of the sad religious development of the Jews, which is, perhaps, the most tragic element in the history of Christless Israel these past nineteen centuries.

But let it suffice here to say, in reply to the above statements, that "all the law and the prophets prophecied unto John"; that the "new covenant," into the blessings of which we have now been brought by the grace of Christ, is "not according to the covenant which God made with our fathers in the day when He took them by the hand to bring them out of Egypt"; and that since the advent of our Redeemer, Who by the rending of His flesh on Calvary's cross "abolished the enmity, even the law of commandments, contained in ordinances, that He might create in Himself of the twain (*i.e.*, of Jew and Gentile) one new man, so making peace"—we live in a different dispensation, when those who are children of God are put in a different position and relation to the law than "Moses and David and Isaiah," or even than "Zacharias and Elisabeth."

3. Professor Stroeter, in No. 1 of *The Messianic Jew.*

It was most certainly primarily to the Jewish believers in the churches of Galatia that the Apostle addressed himself in Galatians 4 and 5, in order to instruct them in this very thing. *"But I say that so long as the heir is a child he differeth nothing from a bondservant, though he is lord of all; but is under guardians and stewards until the term appointed of the father. So we also, when we were children, were held in bondage under the rudiments of the world; but when the fullness of the time came God sent forth His son, born of a woman, born under the law, that He might redeem them which were under the law, that we might receive the adoption of sons. . . . But now that ye have come to know God, or rather to be known of God, how turn ye back again to the weak and beggarly rudiments (or 'elements') whereunto ye desire to be in bondage over again? Ye observe days, and months, and seasons, and years; I am afraid of you, lest by any means I have bestowed labour upon you in vain. . . . With (or 'for') freedom did Christ set us free; stand fast, therefore, and be not entangled again in a yoke of bondage."*

Not that either the Jewish or the Gentile believer is lawless, "but under law to Christ" (1 Cor. 9:21); and since the moral law of God is written on our hearts, and put in our inward parts, the righteousness and purity which the law aimed at, but which could never be attained by mere "observances," is fulfilled in us, who walk not after the flesh, but after the Spirit.

JEWISH NATIONALITY UNLIKE ANY OTHER

"But," say these brethren, "why expect the Jew to denationalise himself when he comes to believe in Christ by giving up his Jewish 'national' observances and ceremonies, when the Christian Englishman, or German, or Frenchman, etc., still remains—as far as his earthly relationships are concerned—English, French, or German, as the case may be, and shares in the national aspirations and observances of the various nations to which they belong?"

To this my answer is: Jewish history is peculiar and unique—unlike that of any other nation, and the so-called Jewish "national" observances are altogether unlike the customs of any other nation. The peculiarity of the Jewish people consists in the fact that God called and chose it to be the medium of His self-revelation on the earth.

"For ask now of the days that are past, which were before thee, since the day that God created man upon the earth, and from the one end of heaven unto the other, whether there hath been any such thing as this great thing is, or hath been heard like it? Did ever people hear the voice of God speaking out of the midst of the fire, as thou hast heard, and live? Or hath God essayed to go and take Him a nation from the midst of another nation, by temptations, by signs, and by wonders, and by war, and by a mighty hand, and by a stretched-out arm, and by great terrors, according to all that the Lord your God did for you in Egypt before your eyes? Unto thee it was showed that thou mightest know that the Lord He is God; there is none else beside Him. Out of heaven He made thee to hear His voice, that He might instruct thee: and upon earth He made thee to see His great fire; and thou heardest His words out of the midst of the fire." (Deut. 4:32–36, R.V.)

In brief, Israel was called to be a theocracy—a people whose king and lawgiver is Jehovah; not *a kingdom* merely, but the centre of *God's kingdom* upon the earth. And the holy law with its ceremonial observances were not the natural product and development of the history of the people, or the expression of its "national" character and spirit, as is the case with the secular laws and customs of the nations, but were *divinely revealed* to Israel.

That the law and its "observances" were not the national product of Israel is attested by the continual apostasy of the people from this very law, and disregard alike of its moral and ceremonial observances, of which the prophets and psalmists are the witnesses.

Then apart from the ethical character of the law, its divinely appointed rites and ceremonies were so many types and symbols setting forth great spiritual realities, which were to find their fulfillment in the Messiah and in the "new covenant" which would be established by Him; which, as already shown, is "not according to the covenant which God made with our fathers when He took them by the hand to lead them out of the land of Egypt" (Heb. 8:9). There is, therefore, no parallel in this respect between the Christian Englishman or Frenchman and the Jew in Christ.

Their customs and "observances," in as far as they are "national," have nothing to do with religion, and as far as they are "religious" (whether or not they are right and justifiable from a Biblical point of view) are not peculiarly national, but are the common observances of all the peoples which constitute "Christendom." The Jewish observances, on the other hand, have their chief significance in their *religious* character, and their practice by a Hebrew Christian, who professes to be a son of the new covenant, is nothing else than the attempt to build up again that which is "done away in Christ." . . .

Of course we are told again and again that it is not intended that Jewish Christians should attach any *merit* to these observances, but it is none the less a *fact* that the Jews *who confound national custom with religion, and whose religion now consists in these very observances, can never dissociate the idea of merit from them*; and in spite of all disclaimers and explanations, their thought about any Jewish or Gentile Christian who observes any of their characteristically "national" or Jewish "rites" or customs, is that he is, after all, not fully satisfied with his Christianity, and is therefore *coming back to Judaism*. . . .

THE PRACTICE OF JEWISH OBSERVANCES BY THE FIRST BELIEVERS

These modern Judaising teachers never tire of pointing to the fact that the first Jewish believers "remained in unbroken continuity with the Hebrew nation," and that they attended the temple and synagogue worship, and kept the Sabbath, the Jewish festivals, etc.; in proof of which they appeal to the book "in which the historical records of Hebrew Christianity have been kept—the Acts of the Apostles."[4]

Now it is quite true that the Acts of the Apostles, especially the first twelve chapters, may from one point of view be regarded as a record of "Hebrew Christianity," but as the record unfolds we can trace already the divergent principles which would make the continuance of the "unbroken continuity" between church and synagogue an *impossibility*. And that it was the *synagogue* which always took the initiative in breaking the "continuity," by driving from its midst, and persecuting even unto death, those of their number who took upon themselves the Name of Jesus, we also see from that book. But what these brethren overlook is, that in relation to this and other matters the Acts of the Apostles introduces us to a *transition period* and describes conditions which most evidently were not intended of God to be permanent.

4. "The Hebrew Christian and His National Continuity." By Philip Cohen.

As to the adherence of the first Jewish disciples to the national customs and traditions, and the observance even by the Apostle Paul of certain rites and ceremonies, we have to remember the peculiar circumstances and conditions. But whatever doubt and perplexity a Hebrew Christian might have found himself in as to what his attitude to the "national" observances should be, so long as the Temple with its original divinely appointed ritual and ceremonies still remained, *things were altogether changed in this respect* when the forty years' probationary period of God's long-suffering after the Crucifixion of Christ, during which the Temple ritual, with its national worship and ceremonial, was allowed to drag on, came at last to an end.

When this additional time of grace, given by God to Israel nationally in the hope that through their *now empty ceremonies* they might yet perchance recognise in Jesus the true Redeemer, and repent of the great national crime of having handed over their own Messiah to the Gentiles to be crucified, was allowed by them to pass, and the heart of the nation only hardened itself against Christ, and hastened to fill up the cup of its iniquity by adding to the apostasy from the Father and the Son resistance to the Holy Ghost, by attempting to hinder the spread of the Gospel among the Gentiles—then the long-threatened judgement of God at last came. The Temple which was not only the symbol of fellowship with God but of the national unity of the people, was destroyed, the land laid waste, and the people scattered; the observance of the ritual and "national" customs, including the observance of the Passover and all the other festivals, according to their divine appointment, *made impossible*; and Jewish nationality suspended until the times of the Gentiles should be fulfilled, and the Lord shall once again arise and have mercy upon Zion.

With the breaking up of the Jewish national polity there emerged the Church of Christ—at first, indeed, regarded by Jew, Greek, and Roman as a mere Jewish "sect" (Acts 26:22), but becoming more and more clearly and distinctly defined as the "Israel of God" of the present dispensation, not dependent upon any building or land for its centre of unity, and whose worship does not consist in "observances," but in spiritual sacrifices and service which are acceptable to God through Christ Jesus. Then also, just before the Temple was destroyed, primarily for the comfort and instruction of the Jewish believers who sorrowed and were perplexed because they were excluded by their unbelieving brethren from partaking in these "national observances," the Epistle to the Hebrews was given to the Church, in which the spiritual significance of the Mosaic ritual and covenant is unfolded, and Christ is shown to be its substance and "better than" all.

IS ANYTHING TO BE GAINED BY COMPROMISE?

One point more and I am finished. These brethren seem to think that by observing the Jewish ceremonies and customs, and thus demonstrating their "national continuity," Jewish opposition to Christ will be disarmed, and a way made to the heart of Israel for the Gospel. But history and experience prove that they are mistaken. The first disciples did try to keep up their "national continuity," and conformed to the customs of their nation; but that did not open the heart of the nation for Christ, or prevent their being hated and persecuted. Some twenty or twenty-five years ago, after the death of Franz Delitzsch, a small company of young German pastors who had been his students at the *Institutum Judaicum* in Leipzig came under the influence of Theodore Lucky (who is the real father of this modern Judaistic movement), and went out to Galicia and other parts of South-Eastern Europe to convert the Jewish nation on these lines. They told Jewish inquirers to remain in the synagogue, to conform to Rabbinic Judaism, and to wait till a national Hebrew Christian Church should be formed. But nothing came of it all, except it be some mischief.

For many . . . these brethren go in for the "Maximum programme," and conform to the "national customs" of their people to such an extent that there is nothing to distinguish them in their manner of life from the strictest Talmudical Jews: have *they* in any perceptible degree disarmed Jewish opposition to Christ, or brought the Jews any nearer to the Gospel?

By all means let us follow the example and methods of the great Apostle who said, "To the Jew I became a Jew" (1 Cor. 9:20); let us adapt ourselves to the peculiar condition and needs of our people; let us show them that faith in Christ has not the effect of alienating love and sympathy in our hearts from "those which are our flesh," and that we are ready, if needs be, to sacrifice ourselves for their good; but, in the words of my friend and colleague in the Hebrew Christian Testimony to

Israel, C. A. Schönberger, "However much we may stoop to the concep-
tion of our unbelieving brethren, taking into account all their peculiar
prejudices, one thing we cannot and *will* not do—we will not lower
the standard of Christ, nor smooth over the offence of the Cross." We
will not preach another Christ than the One who is the end of the law
for righteousness to all who believe, nor preach another Gospel than
that of Christ crucified for our sins, and raised again for our justification; and by God's grace we will show to our Jewish brethren that not
"observances" make a true Jew, but a character moulded after the pat-
tern of Him who was the only true Israelite, though at the same time
God over all blessed forever!

But in truth, to quote in conclusion some pertinent words from an
able article by our fellow-worker, Naphtali Rudnitzky, in his little German quarterly, *Der Oelberg*:

> "It is neither our freedom from the law which separates us from our
> brethren, nor is it faithfulness to the law which unites us. One name
> divides us; at one hill is the parting of the ways. Jesus is the Name;
> Golgotha and the cross the point of divergence.
>
> "This was the experience of the first disciples of Jesus, although
> under the conditions of their time they held on to the synagogue a
> ground of contact with their people. 'Let us threaten them that they
> speak henceforth to no man in this name; and they called them and
> charged them not to speak at all, nor teach in the name of Jesus'
> (Acts 4:17, 18).
>
> "This has been the position of the Jewish people since its rejection
> of the offer of salvation in Jesus of Nazareth. The cross of Golgotha
> was to the self-righteous people, boasting of the works of the law, an
> offence, and has continued to be so to the present day. However we
> might slavishly humble ourselves under the yoke of the law, it would
> be but to hear again in the synagogue the cry, 'Away with such fellows
> from the earth, for it is not fit that they should live!' so soon as we
> proclaimed Jesus the Crucified as 'Prince and Saviour,' to give to Israel
> repentance and the remission of sins.
>
> "The Judaising opponents of the Gospel who preached a strict
> observance of law were aware of this, and therefore they did not
> come with the teaching of the cross, or with the full Christ. They
> degraded the Lord, representing Him as a servant of Judaism, and
> His first elected witnesses as train-bearers of the Pharisees. With

one voice the whole company of these Spirit-filled witnesses opposed such misrepresentation.

"The success which the disciples had to record among their people was not the consequence of their strict observance of the law, but of their bold testimony to Him who was crucified and risen. Individual souls in Israel who thirsted for the truth and yearned for redemption from sin received their testimony; the others either took offence at it or scoffed (Acts 3:11–13; 2:12, 13). And the same is the case also to-day. . . .

"Now, as concerns the orthodox Jews—*to them these observances are the mark not only of their peculiar national character, but of their religion*; to them it is the practice of these observances which constitutes the Jew. He who would win *them* for Christ must first of all show them that their view of religion is a false one; that they have enveloped the heart—the kernel of the religion of Israel—in a shell.

"This law-observing Judaism will not be contented were we to observe its national religious customs and yet believe in Jesus: if we would have its recognition we must deny Christ. This is the price required by the synagogue for our approach to it. Alas! some have paid this price who began by seemingly harmless 'observances.'

"But if, in truth, we, as Jewish Christians, are to claim unity with our people, then there is a much more excellent way open to us (1 Cor. 12:31)— unfeigned devotion to Jesus, and untiring wooing of the heart of our brethren through His Gospel."

Appendix D
Justification in Judaism[1]

Blessed is he
    whose transgressions are forgiven,
    whose sins are covered.
Blessed is the man
    whose sin the Lord does not count against him
    and in whose spirit is no deceit.

When I kept silent,
    my bones wasted away
    through my groaning all day long.
For day and night
    your hand was heavy upon me;
my strength was sapped
    as in the heat of summer.   *Selah*
Then I acknowledged my sin to you
    and did not cover up my iniquity.
I said, "I will confess
    my transgressions to the Lord"—
and you forgave
    the guilt of my sin.   *Selah*

Therefore let everyone who is godly pray to you
    while you may be found;
surely when the mighty waters rise,
    they will not reach him. (Ps. 32:1–6 NIV)

1. The substance of an address given at the 2006 General Assembly of the Association of Reformed Baptist Churches in America held in Atlanta, Georgia, © 2006 by Baruch Maoz.

How wonderful it is to have such an assurance of forgiveness, such a confidence that, in spite of our many and awful sins, we have been justified, have been sanctified in the name of the Lord Jesus, and by the Spirit of our God (1 Cor. 6:11)!

This is the glory of the Christian faith. It is also one of its special and most endearing distinctives. There are really only two religions in the world: the religion of God's grace in Christ, and all the rest. In spite of their protestations to the contrary, all other religions teach that man must find acceptance with God by his own efforts, on the strength of his own merits, through the virtue of his achievements.

There is hardly a truth Satan hates more than the truth of God's grace. It makes men grateful. It drives them to love God and serve him with all they have. No longer dependent on their achievements, they are driven to higher and still higher achievements for him who loved them and gave himself for them. No longer in need of hanging on to God by their efforts, they invest all the more effort in serving him than when they thought that they must somehow earn favor with God and thereby be their own justifiers.

This is true of the religion of my people. Of course, there are as many Judaisms as there are purported versions of the Christian faith, but all versions of Judaism agree on this point. The New Testament witnesses to such a view: "I am not like other people. . . . *I fast* twice a week, *I pay* tithes of all I get" (Luke 18:11–12). "Good teacher, what shall *I do* to inherit eternal life?" (Luke 18:18). Note that the assumption which underlies the young man's question is that it is up to *him* to do something to inherit eternal life. "For they being ignorant of God's righteousness, [went] about to establish their own" (Rom. 10:3).

For many long, dark years, the glorious truth of justification by faith was lost in the morass of traditionalism, ritualism and popish clericalism. Then the light shone once again. Luther tells us:

> Though I lived as a monk without reproach, I felt that I was a sinner before God with an extremely disturbed conscience. I could not believe that he was placated by my efforts to satisfy him. I did not love, yes, I hated the righteous God who punishes sinners. . . . At last, by the mercy of God . . . I gave heed to the context of the words . . . "In it the righteousness of God is revealed, as it is written, 'He who through faith is righteous shall live.'"

I began to understand that the righteousness of God is that by which the righteous lives by a gift of God, namely by faith.... I had been altogether born again and entered paradise itself through open gates! ...

A totally other face of the entire Scripture showed itself to me! ... I also found ... that ... what God does in us (is) the power of God with which he makes us wise; the strength of God, the salvation of God, the glory of God, and I extolled my sweetest words with a love as great as the hatred with which I had before hated the words "righteousness of God." ... That place in Paul was for me truly the gate to paradise.[2]

We live in an age when this heart-rejoicing truth is once again denied. Theological liberalism has raised it head to insist that man can be good enough for God. Similar mistaken claims have been made recently in a somewhat different form by those who promote what is known as the New Perspective on Paul. According to N. T. Wright, one of the best-known propagators of the New Perspective, Luther and Calvin misunderstood the teaching of Paul on justification. Justification is not to be perceived in the terms that became the clarion call of the Reformation, but as God's declaration that someone is in the covenant.[3] According to N. T. Wright, Paul taught that man "gets in by grace but stays in by works." That is to say, by grace he is justified in potential and made a member of the covenant people, but he remains in covenant and ultimately obtains justification only as the fruit of his ongoing covenant faithfulness.

Seeking support for these views, the New Perspective insists that we have not only misunderstood the apostles, but that our view of Judaism is mistaken. Adherents to the New Perspective insist that Judaism does not teach salvation by works. Rather, they insist, it is a religion of grace. The works Judaism requires are the natural response to grace. They are and should be. But Judaism does not teach what it should. Judaism teaches that works are in order to grace, not the other way around.

We are told that we "get in" by grace and "stay in" by works just as Israel was called out of Egypt and brought into covenant by grace, but then was called upon to work. Disobedience to the covenant led to excommunication from the covenant community and therefore from blessings

2. Martin Luther, *Luther's Works: Career of the Reformer IV*, Vol. 34 (St. Louis: Concordia Publishing House, 1960), 336–37.
3. N. T. Wright, *What Saint Paul Really Said: Was Paul of Tarsus the Real Founder of Christianity?* (Grand Rapids: Wm. B. Eerdmans, 1997), 115.

that the covenant bestowed. This view mistakenly conflates individual and national fates. It further ignores the difference between the Testaments, misunderstands the process of revelation, and therefore treats the Old Testament as if it were a New Testament revelation. Hebrew 1:1 describes the revelation God has given in his Son in terms of a climax, not just as the last stage in an extended process.

Paul teaches that we stay in by the same grace that brings us in: "Having been justified [past tense, aorist—a deed accomplished in the past and not needing to be repeated] we have [present tense, ongoing] peace with God. . . . We have obtained [past tense] our introduction by faith into this grace in which we stand [present tense, ongoing]" (Rom. 5:1–2). Paul insists in Galatians 5:4 that any effort to be justified by the law is nothing less than to fall from grace.

"Ah," we are told with a note of triumph. "You do not understand. Our deeds are not meritorious!" I reply, "You're absolutely right. I do not understand. In my dictionary, 'unmeritorious' means 'without merit,' 'without value,' valueless." Precisely because the best of our deeds are unmeritorious, they can never justify. Only grace can do that. Salvation is from the Lord—from beginning to end!

A somewhat identical mistake is made by those who are closer to home—at least to *my* home—by many modern adherents of the Messianic Movement. Philip Ryken got it wrong when he said of the Galatian heretics that "they taught a Gentile had to become a Jew *before* he could become a Christian."[4] What they actually taught was what some are saying today, that a Gentile must become a Jew *because* he had become a Christian (note the emphasis)! They claim that a Jewish lifestyle is necessary to sanctification—thereby implying that the justification provided by Christ does not include sanctification.

Paul's words to the Galatians on this matter are very clear:

I live by faith in the Son of God, who loved me and gave Himself up for me. (Gal. 2:20)

Did you receive the Spirit by observing the law, or by believing what you heard? Are you so foolish? After beginning with the Spirit, are you now trying to attain your goal by human effort? (Gal. 3:2–3 NIV)

4. Philip Graham Ryken, *Galatians* (Phillipsburg, NJ: P&R Publishing, 2005), 9 (emphasis added).

The law was put in charge to lead us to Christ that we might be justified by faith. Now that faith has come, we are no longer under the supervision of the law. You are all sons of God through faith in Christ Jesus, for all of you who were baptized into Christ have clothed yourselves with Christ. (Gal. 3:24–27 NIV)

Paul longed to be found in Christ, "not having a righteousness of my own derived from the Law, but that which is through faith in Christ, the righteousness which comes from God on the basis of faith" (Phil. 3:9).

Jesus promised, "he who hears My word and believes in Him who sent Me *has* everlasting life and shall not come into judgment but *has* passed from death into life" (John 5:24 NKJV). "Your life *is hidden* with Christ in God" (Col. 3:3). We are a new creation, born again, from above, "old things *have* passed away; behold, all things *have become* new!" (2 Cor. 5:17 NKJV). We have died and "*have been raised* with Christ" (Col. 3:1 NIV) and are therefore, by grace, "*accepted* in the beloved" (Eph. 1:6 KJV). The New Testament is replete with the use of the past tense in describing the joys of salvation.

Justification by grace through faith is far more than a bare legal pronouncement. It is a mighty act of God, a transforming deed. God works in the innermost hearts of sinful men and women, boys and girls. Justification always involves sanctification and that, too, is an act of grace; not by human effort, although not without such effort; not through self denial and discipline, although not without self denial or discipline; not as the grounds of justification, but as its natural fruit: "How shall we who died to sin still live in it?" (Rom. 6:2). Indeed, Paul teaches in Galatians that self-discipline is an aspect of the fruit of the Spirit, not a means to obtaining the Spirit.

Not understanding this, many adherents of the Messianic Movement draw the logical conclusion of their preoccupation with the law by converting to Judaism. They do understand the relationship between justification and sanctification. Having accepted Judaism's premise, they have come to its inevitable conclusion.

That is also why some of the finest adherents of Judaism have died without the assurance of salvation. Knowing themselves to belong to the covenant people of God, they were insecure at the ultimate hour because they recognized that their best efforts had been faulty.

This is well illustrated by the famous story of one of Judaism's most influential rabbis, Rabbi Yochanan ben Zakai. Ben Zakai is reported to have wept bitterly as he died. When asked by his disciples why, he responded,

> If they would be taking me before a mortal judge, here today and gone tomorrow, whose anger toward me would be only for a short time; if he tortures or kills me it is not permanent suffering; I would nevertheless cry (in trepidation). Certainly now that they are taking me before the King of Kings, the Holy One Blessed Be He who Lives forever, whose anger is an eternal anger and if he tortures me it will be eternal torture, and if he kills me it will be eternal death—should I not cry?[5]

What a terrible religion! How can it be compared with the faith which taught David Brainard to say on his deathbed, coughing and spitting blood as he died of tuberculosis: "You have put gladness in my heart, more than in the season that their grain and wine increased!" (Ps. 4:7 NKJV)?

Brethren, do not buy into a romantic view of Judaism. Do not buy into Judaism's conviction that man, even elected man (for that is how a Jewish person sees himself) can somehow please God or achieve spiritual heights by his own efforts.

There are "Christian" versions of this error. Beware of them too; any form of legalism is mistaken, unbiblical. It is spiritually, morally, and emotionally corruptive, even if it goes by the respectable name of Christianity. It offers no hope. It represents a major departure from the joyous, confident faith of David, whose testimony we read as we began our meditation. It is far removed from the relief Isaiah knew when a seraph flew to him with a live coal from the altar and said, "See, this has touched your lips; your guilt is taken away and your sin atoned for" (Isa. 6:6 NIV).

In Psalm 32, David presents true, biblical Judaism. It is to the shame of all who would deny justification by faith that they could do so in light of the fuller revelation of God's saving grace in Christ, found in the New Testament. It is all the more to their shame when we note that David, who knew so much less, had so triumphant a confidence in his justifica-

5. *Mishnah*, Berachot, 28 B.

tion, such as is expressed in this psalm. His words were penned for our edification. His testimony in Psalm 32 was written so that, learning from him, we might have a similar confidence.

Note with me that David's testimony includes the words, "Therefore let everyone who is godly pray to you while you may be found; surely when the mighty waters rise, they will not reach him" (Ps. 32:6 NIV). Pray about what? Of which "mighty waters" is David speaking? He explains:

> When I kept silent,
>   my bones wasted away
>   through my groaning all day long.
> For day and night
>   your hand was heavy upon me;
> my strength was sapped
>   as in the heat of summer. (vv. 3–4)

The mighty waters that threatened to engulf David were the gracious, insistent proddings of God's Holy Spirit, convincing him of sin, of righteousness, and of judgment to come.

Like Yochanan ben Zakkai, David had a troubled conscience. So long as he remained silent, refusing to confess his sins and cast himself on God's mercy, "your hand was heavy upon me; my strength was sapped as in the heat of summer" (v. 4).

We are told by those who profess to know these things that a sense of guilt is one of modern man's most persistent emotional difficulties. In that sense, David was a very modern man. Like most today, he suppressed his conscience, sought to silence it, ignored its pricks, and sought peace by various means. But it was all to no avail. God the Spirit gave him no release. God's hand was heavy upon him. His emotional strength was sapped dry, just as the Israeli landscape is annually sapped as soon as the rains end and the summer heat beats upon the thirsting fields. Somehow, deep in his heart, David knew God was pursuing him, but he resisted. He believed he could resolve the problem some other way.

Finally, David tells us, he succumbed. "Then I acknowledged my sin to you and did not cover up my iniquity. I said, 'I will confess my transgressions to the LORD'" (v. 5 NIV). When David came to his senses, he invested no further effort in resolving his difficulty. He offered no compensation. He merely confessed and in this way put himself at the mercy of God. What a good place to be: at the mercy of God! Our God delights in mercy.

Anger is a strange work to him. He is merciful to a thousand generations! Evidence? Well, what was God's response to David's confession? "You forgave the guilt of my sin" (v. 5 NIV)! What more could David have hoped for? Unlike ben Zakkai, but like Luther, David had found the gate to paradise, and it had been thrown wide open before him. Relief! Peace! Freedom from a troubled conscience was at hand at last. Little wonder that David penned this wonderful psalm, his heart overflowing with joy and gratitude!

Strange as it may seem to many today, it is not by denial that we find relief. The nagging, persistent thorns of memory will not let go. However many mattresses of good works and of determined suppression we may seek to pile on the pea of our troubled mind, like the princess in the story, it will permit us no rest.

This is not a coincidence. It is a loving work of God, geared to our salvation. It is through grace we are saved and through the work of Christ on the cross that we may be justified, not through efforts of our own.

There is another important lesson, relevant to the discussion on justification now raging in theological circles, and which is to be found in David's words. When did David confess his sin? When did he receive forgiveness? Was David speaking here of his conversion? I think not. This seems to have been one of David's prayers "when the prophet Nathan came to him after David had committed adultery with Bathsheba" (Psalm 51—subtitle in NIV).

I believe this is clear from what David says in verse 6 of Psalm 32: "Therefore let everyone who is godly pray to you while you may be found; surely when the mighty waters rise, they will not reach him" (NIV). Why should the godly pray as David has described? Why should they fear the rising of what David calls "the mighty waters"? Because David was speaking as a man who has known God for some time and yet failed, as one who was, to use his own term, "godly," although he had not always acted in a godly manner.

In other words, David was not only initially justified by the gospel; he lived by the gospel. He "got in" by grace and he "stayed in" by that same grace. David had, at the very least, an intuitive understanding of the relationship between justification and sanctification. He understood what Paul meant when the apostle rebuked the Galatians for having begun in the Spirit and then turned to seek completion through the flesh. He understood that salvation is of the Lord—all of it, from beginning to end!

> Blessed is he
>> whose transgressions are forgiven,
>> whose sins are covered.
> Blessed is the man
>> whose sin the Lord does not count against him
>> and in whose spirit is no deceit. (vv. 1–2 NIV)

This blessedness is not attributed to him who has no transgressions, who is responsible for no sins, but to him whose transgressions God has chosen to forgive, whose sins he has mercifully covered. Christianity is for sinners, not for the righteous. The Christian life is for sinners. Justification is the rendering just of those who do not deserve such kindness. Under no circumstances may it be perceived as the product of human endeavor.

Rabbinical Judaism has no such knowledge. Liberalism cannot offer it. Messianic Judaism knows increasingly less of it. The New Perspective has lost sight of it. Yet it is here, enshrined in God's word for our comfort, exhortation and active faith. Justification is by grace, and by grace alone. Synergism is unbiblical, be it a synergistic view of the initial experience of salvation or of its ongoing reality.

I cannot leave the matter here. How about us? Do we know grace? Do we *truly* know grace? Do we *live* by the grace through which we have been justified?

Some of us are inclined to live as if we too thought that we get in by grace but stay in by works. Some of us behave as if justification is by grace but sanctification is the fruit of our self-denial, self-discipline, theological rightness, spiritual experiences, and determined sacrifice. We then become harsh, doctrinaire, judgmental, almost fundamentalist toward all who cannot dot our *I*s and cross our *T*s. Does grace characterize the way we relate to others, even when we differ from them?

No less important: do we live by the grace that justified us, or do we drive ourselves remorselessly, as if everything depended on us? Can we accept failure in a truly Christian manner, trusting in grace and finding in Christ all we need for forgiveness, restoration, and renewed vigor?

Equally important, how much does a recognition of God's grace drive us to live for him? Paul said that Christ died "that those who live should no longer live for themselves but for him who died for them and was raised again" (2 Cor. 5:15 NIV). He understood the doctrine of justification to teach him to trust in grace throughout his life and to give himself without reservation to the God of grace: "through the law I died to the law so that I might live for God" (Gal. 2:19 NIV). That is what he meant when he said, "I have been crucified with Christ and I no longer live, but Christ lives in me. The life I live in the body, I live by faith in the Son of God, who loved me and gave himself for me" (Gal. 2:20 NIV).

Paul was a Christian in his everyday life as well as in his theological convictions—are we? He was a man driven by an awareness of the amazing grace of God, so that everything else was equal in his eyes to dung. Are we so driven by the grace we have received? Are we perceived by those who know us to be devoted to God, his gospel, his glory, and his will? What is the primary motive behind all our Christian action, the education we give our children, the way we conduct our business, relate to our spouses, and handle our possessions? Are we, like Paul, Christian?

None but Christ can satisfy the perfect justice of God, and he has achieved that satisfaction by his death on the cross for all who put their trust in him. None but Christ can satisfy the spiritually enlightened human conscience, but, it is important to note, Jesus *can* indeed satisfy that conscience when it is enlightened by the Spirit and guided by the word of God. We need not add anything to Christ for we are complete in him. Salvation—from beginning to end—is to be found in none but Christ, the Lamb of God who takes away the sin of the world. How thankful we should be for him and for those who followed him before us and showed us the way to him!

Faith in him provides us with a holy yet humble and confident joy, with comfort and a hope that will never disappoint. It motivates us to declare the wonderful news from the rooftops of our cities: Jesus saves!

Are you saved? Have you been justified? Are your sins forgiven? If not, turn to God. Knock and he will answer. Call and he will respond. Whoever calls on the name of the Lord will be saved.

Are you saved? Have you been justified? Are your sins forgiven? Live it out. Live like one who knows the sweet, overpowering tang of grace. Relate by the same grace to others, and give God thanks: let the heavens fall tonight—I don't care because I am forgiven! I am justified by the blood of God's Son, raised by the power of his resurrection! Because he lives, I too live! Because I need not do anything to be justified, I am free to do all things for the Son of God who loved me and gave himself for me.

What, then, shall we say in response to this? If God is for us, who can be against us? He who did not spare his own Son, but gave him up for us all—how will he not also, along with him, graciously give us all things? Who will bring any charge against those whom God has chosen? It is God who justifies. Who is he that condemns? Christ Jesus, who died—more than that, who was raised to life—is at the right hand of God and is also interceding for us. Who shall separate us from the love of Christ? Shall trouble or hardship or persecution or famine or nakedness or danger or sword? As it is written:

"For your sake we face death all day long;
    we are considered as sheep to be slaughtered."

No, in all these things we are more than conquerors through him who loved us. For I am convinced that neither death nor life, neither angels nor demons, neither the present nor the future, nor any powers, neither height nor depth, nor anything else in all creation, will be able to separate us from the love of God that is in Christ Jesus our Lord. (Rom. 8:31–39 NIV)

Hallelujah!

Bibliography

Assemani, Stefano. *Acta Sanctorum Martyrum Orientalium at Occidentalium*, vol. 1. Rome, 1748.

Aviad, Janet. *Return to Judaism: Religious Renewal in Israel*. Chicago: University of Chicago Press, 1983.

Baeck, Leo. *Judaism and Christianity: Essays by Leo Baeck*. New York: The Jewish Publication Society of America, 1958.

Bagatti, Bellarmino. *The Church from the Circumcision*. Translated by Eugene Hoade. Rome, 1970.

Bauer, Walter. *A Greek-English Lexicon of the New Testament and Other Early Christian Literature*. Translated by William F. Arndt and F. Wilber Gingrich. Chicago: University of Chicago Press, 1957.

Ben Chaim, Menachem. *King of Kings News* 98 (January 1998).

Berkowitz, Ariel and Devorah. *Torah Rediscovered*. Littleton, CO: First Fruits of Zion, 1996.

Calvin, John. *Sermons on Galatians*. Edinburgh: The Banner of Truth Trust, 1997.

Christians and Jews: A Report of the Conference on the Christian Approach to the Jews, Atlantic City, New Jersey, May 12–15, 1931. New York: International Committee on the Christian Approach to the Jews, International Missionary Council, 1931.

Colquhoun, John. *A Treatise on the Law and the Gospel*. Morgan, PA: Soli Deo Gloria Publications, 1999.

Danielou, Jean. *The Theology of Jewish Christianity: A History of Early Christian Doctrine Before the Council of Nicaea*, vol. 1. Philadelphia: The Westminster Press, 1964.

Dauerman, Stuart. "It Seems to Me." *Boundaries* (March/April 1999).

Elgvin, Torleif. *Israel and Yeshua*. Jerusalem: Caspari Center for Biblical and Jewish Studies, 1993.

Feher, Shoshanah. *Passing Over Easter: Constructing the Boundaries of Messianic Judaism*. Walnut Creek, CA: AltaMira Press, 1998.

Fischer, Eve. "Youth Perspective." *Messianic Jewish Life* 73, no. 3 (July-Sept 2000).

Fischer, Patrice. "Tradition: Keeping the Faith." *Messianic Jewish Life* 72, no. 3 (July–Sept. 1999).

Flannery, Edward F. *The Anguish of the Jews: Twenty-Three Centuries of Anti-semitism*, rev. ed. Mahwah, NJ: Paulist Press, 1985.

Fruchtenbaum, Arnold G. *Hebrew Christianity: Its Theology, History, and Philosophy.* Washington, DC: Canon, 1974.

Gartenhaus, Jacob. *Famous Hebrew Christians.* Hixton, TN: International Board of Jewish Missions, Inc., 1979.

Goble, Philip E. *Everything You Need to Know to Grow a Messianic Yeshiva.* South Pasadena, CA: William Carey Library, 1974.

Gordon, Sheri Ross. "Inside Jews for Jesus." *Reform Judaism* 22 (Winter 1993): 22–27, 32.

Gruen, Erich S. *Heritage and Hellenism: The Reinvention of Jewish Tradition.* California: University of California Press, 1998.

Hagner, Donald A. *The Jewish Reclamation of Jesus: An Analysis and Critique of the Modern Jewish Study of Jesus.* Grand Rapids: Zondervan, 1984.

Hengel, Martin, and C. K. Barrett. *Conflicts and Challenges in Early Christianity.* Edited by Donald Hagner. Harrisburg, PA: Trinity Press International, 1999.

Horbury, William. *Jews and Christians: In Contact and Controversy.* Edinburgh: T & T Clark, 1998.

Hort, Fenton John Anthony. *Judaistic Christianity.* Grand Rapids: Baker Book House, 1980.

"Jews for Jesus." *Mishpochah Message* (Fall 1993).

Jocz, Jakob. *The Jewish People and Jesus Christ: A Study in the Controversy between Church and Synagogue.* London: S.P.C.K., 1962.

Juster, Daniel C. *Growing to Maturity: A Messianic Jewish Guide.* Denver: Union of Messianic Jewish Congregations Press, 1996.

———. *Jewishness and Jesus.* Downers Grove, IL: IVP, 1977.

———. *Jewish Roots: A Foundation of Biblical Theology for Messianic Judaism.* Rockville, MD: Davar Publishing, 1992.

Kinzer, Mark S. *Post-missionary Messianic Judaism: Redefining Christian Engagement with the Jewish People.* Grand Rapids: Brazos Press, 2005.

Kjaer-Hansen, Kai. *Jewish Identity and Faith in Jesus.* Jerusalem: Caspari Center, 1996.

———. *Joseph Rabinowitz and the Messianic Movement.* Edinburgh: Handsel Press, 1995.

Leupold, Herbert C. *Exposition of Isaiah.* Grand Rapids: Baker Books, 1978.

Levison, N. *The Jewish Background of Christianity: A Manual of the Political, Religious, Social and Literary Life of the Jews from 586 B.C. to A.D. 1.* Edinburgh: T & T Clark, 1932.

Levitz, Baruch Vos. "Israel, Unique Amongst the Nations." *Bikurei Tziyon* 68, 2001.

Liberman, Paul. *The Fig Tree Blossoms: Messianic Judaism Emerges.* Harrison, AR: Fountain Press, 1977.

Lipson, Juliene G. *Jews for Jesus: An Anthropological Study.* New York: AMS Press, 1990.

Longenecker, Richard N. *The Christology of Early Jewish Christianity.* Grand Rapids: Baker, 1970.

———. *Paul, Apostle of Liberty: The Origin and Nature of Paul's Christianity.* Grand Rapids: Baker, 1976.

Marks, Michael W. *The New Testament and the Law: A New Testament Study on the Validity of Jewish Law.* Pueblo, CO: Shammash Ariel Messianic Congregation.

Mass, Eliezer. *Stand Firm: A Survival Guide for the New Jewish Believer.* Lansing, IL: American Messianic Fellowship, 1990.

Metro Voice 10, no. 9 (Sept. 1999).

Montefiore, Claude G. *Liberal Judaism and Hellenism.* London: MacMillan and Co., 1918.

Morrison, Moshe. "Rejoice Sukkot." *First Fruits of Zion* 57 (Sept.–Oct. 1998).

Moshe, Michael. "Whatever He Says, Parashat Mishpatim." *Bikurei Tziyon* 68, 2001.

Nichol, Richard C. "Messianic Judaism—So What Exactly Is It?" *Messianic Jewish Life* 72, no. 3 (July–Sept. 1999).

Parkes, James. *The Conflict of the Church and the Synagogue.* Philadelphia: The Jewish Publication Society of America, 1964.

Prestige, G. L. *Fathers and Heretics.* London: S.P.C.K., 1940.

Rausch, David A. *Messianic Judaism: Its History, Theology, and Polity.* Lewiston, NY: The Edwin Mellen Press, 1982.

"Readers' Views and Comments," *Bikurei Tziyon* 64 (May/June 2000).

Resnik, Russell L. "Torah for Today, the Festival of Exile." *Boundaries* (March–April 1999).

Rich, Lawrence J. "Jewish Practices and Identity in the Book of Acts." *Messianic Jewish Life* 72, no. 3 (July–Sept. 1999).

Riner, R. *The Calling: The History of the Messianic Jewish Alliance of America.* Wynnewood, PA: MJAA, 1990.

Rosen, Moishe, and William Proctor. *Jews for Jesus.* Old Tappan, NJ: Revell, 1974.

Saal, Paul L. "Let's Reason." *Boundaries* (March–April 1999).

Saperstein, Mark, ed. *Essential Papers on Messianic Movements and Personalities in Jewish History.* New York: New York University Press, 1992.

Schoeps, Hans Joachim. *The Jewish-Christian Argument: A History of Theologies in Conflict.* London: Faber and Faber, 1963.

Smolkin, Melinda. "Creativity and the Soul." *Boundaries* (March–April 1999).

"So Ask the Rabbi." *Messianic Jewish Life* 73, no. 2 (April–June 2000).

Stendahl, Krister. *Paul Among Jews and Gentiles.* Philadelphia: Fortress Press, 1976.

Stern, David H. *Messianic Jewish Manifesto.* Jerusalem: Jewish New Testament Publications, 1988.

Strickland, Wayne G. *Five Views on Law and Gospel.* Grand Rapids: Zondervan, 1996.

"To the Editor." *Messianic Jewish Life* 73, no. 2 (April–June 2000).

Wasserman, Jeffrey S. *Messianic Jewish Congregations: Who Sold This Business to the Gentiles?* Lanham, MD: University Press of America, 2000.

Whittaker, Molly. *Jews & Christians: Graeco-Roman Views.* Cambridge: Cambridge University Press, 1984.

Wilken, Robert L. *Judaism and the Early Christian Mind: A Study of Cyril of Alexandria's Exegesis and Theology.* New York: Yale University Press, 1971.

Wilson, Marvin R. *Our Father Abraham: Jewish Roots of the Christian Faith.* Grand Rapids: Wm. B. Eerdmans Publishing Company, 1989.

Young, Edward J. *The Book of Isaiah*, vol. 2. Grand Rapids: Wm. B. Eerdmans, 1969; repr. 2001.

———. *The Book of Isaiah*, vol. 3. Grand Rapids: Wm. B. Eerdmans, 1972; repr. 2001.

Index of Scripture

Index of Subjects and Names